In memory of my father,
Leland Elsworth Omans,
who loved nature

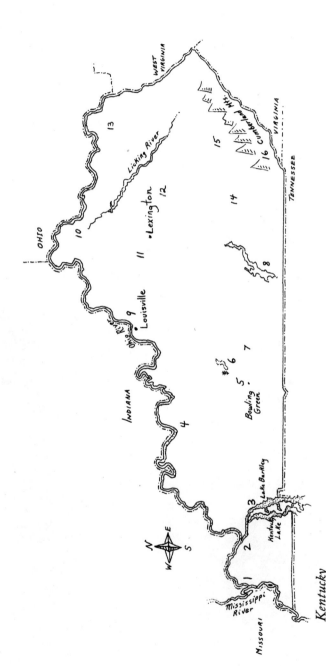

Kentucky

(Figures correspond with chapter numbers.)

Contents

16 Pine Mountain to The Breaks 331

Acknowledgments

I thank these individuals for their input and assistance in providing valuable information for this book:

Natalie Andrews, Judy Austin, Hannah Baird, Helen Barnett, Brucie Beard, Joyce Bender, Carol E. Borneman, Lisa Bray, Betty Brewer, Connie Bruther, Kim Burchett, Steve Capps, Mary Lou Carey, Bob Cetera, Sue Clark, Soc Clay, Jennifer Covington, Sherry Crose, Larrie Curry, Gus Daeuble, Randy Denfip, Diana DeVaughn, Sandy Doane, Karen Doolin, Howard Duncan, Barb Dykstra, Mary Dee Ellis, Lynn Evens, Don F. Fig, Joseph M. Ford, Roger and Carrie Fortney, David G. Foster, Wilson Francis, Nore J. Ghibaudy, Steve Goodwin, John Gorham, Bobbie Gothard, Matt Graham, Bill Hainsworth, Clara G. Hall, Gordon Hall, Mary Hammond, Charlie Hanion, Ed Hay, Paul Hayes, Dean M. Henson, Shirley Howard, Josh Huffman, Bobby Lee Hurt, Jim and Juanita Ingram, Robert Jackson, Betty Jacob, Marc A. Johnson, Morgan O. Jones, Norma Jones, Nancy Kiernan, Angie King, Robert King, Gerald Kiser, Deloris Knight, Ann E. Kraft, Laura Lang, Karla Launius-Hagen, Marianne Lesher, Charlie Logsdon, Michael Lorton, Frank and Alison Lyne, Mike Lynn, Sarah Mace, Jimmy Mann, Lee Ellen Martin, Richard Matthews, Bob Maxwell, Bernita McCloud, Beverly McKinley, Rae Jean McKinney, Gertrude McMahan, Joyce McNelly, Scott and Rhonda Mello, Sharon Messamore, Anna Miller, Christi Miller, Shannon Millikan, Janice Miracle, Louella Moore, Evelyn Morgan, Bill Morris, "Ro" Morse, Meg Nowack, Mary McGee O'Neill, Roger Paige, Mike Paley, Dawn Parrish, Jim Parrish, Josh and Jamie Parrish,

Betty Payne, Burley Phelan, Sam Plummer, David Polk, Eric Reid, Laurie Risch, Emma Rogers, John Rufli, Darrin Samborski, Ophelia Scott, Steve Scott, Nancy Shreve, Tony Sills, Stephen Smith, Marchetta Sparrow, Debby Spencer, Steve Spencer, Tyler and Beau Spencer, Roy Stephens, Carlie Thompson, John Tierney, Mary Ann Tobin, Harry O. Todd, Tom Trousdale, Danny Troxell, Scott Turner, Ron Vanover, Robert Watts, Evelyn Welch, Kit Wesler, Gary P. West, Jack West, Gene Wilkerson, and Tim Williams. A heartfelt "thank you" also to Liza Fosburgh for her editing, encouragement, radar vision, and helpful suggestions.

Introduction

Kentucky's embayments and plateaus, escarpments and knobs, caverns, rivers, sweeping vistas, waterfalls, and peaceful wooded coves provide backdrops of unlimited variety to delight nature enthusiasts. Whether your preference is for quietude or high adventure (or something in between), this state offers abundant opportunities. You'll find water sports, mountain trails, underground caverns, dinosaur bones, prairie ecosystems, and some features found nowhere else in the Western Hemisphere.

The landscape we see and appreciate now began millions of years ago. From an isolated peninsula at the Mississippi River across from New Madrid, Missouri, eastward to the great walls of massive Pine Mountain and Cumberland Mountain at Kentucky's southeastern border, an exciting topography was slowly taking place as, over geologic time, the earth groaned, mountains were thrust upward, rivers churned relentlessly against yielding rocks, and ice age glaciers scalloped the shape of the great Ohio River, touching Kentucky at Louisville and around Covington. If Kentucky has a recurring theme through all this, it is a duel of opposites: mountains and waters.

Ultimately, waters win out, forming complex river systems above ground and below. Among Kentucky's many rivers are those that border the state: the Big Sandy, the Ohio, and the Mississippi. Of the three, it is the Ohio that counts most, since Kentucky "owns" the river to the high-water mark on the far bank. That's a lot of water!

The mountains had better success against man, staving off exploration and settlement for decades, until the discovery of the Cumberland Gap. Surmounting such a formidable barrier says something about the character of Kentucky's people, a hardy and persistent lot.

It is refreshing that the character of both remains—a people and a land somehow in sync, even in this technological age. Rural landscapes predominate, which is what nature enthusiasts appreciate, yet Kentucky has its share of exciting metropolitan museums and research facilities, too.

As this guide introduces you to widespread locations— some famous and others worthy of discovery—I hope you will find it to be a valuable resource. I've included some of my experiences, but of course yours will be different and unique.

On the other hand, if you fall in the mud and become a "swamp thing" as I did, maybe you, too, will enjoy recalling the event and watching it grow funnier with time.

1

Great River Road Country

The "Great River Road" is a designation of highways that are never far from the Mississippi River. They are marked with a distinctive square green-on-white sign showing an outline of a ship's wheel and, inside it, the silhouette of a river boat. In Kentucky, as in other states, the route follows flyways of migrating waterfowl and songbirds along the sometimes steamy delta bottom lands of sloughs and swamps and periodically flooded fields.

Whenever I am in the area, I think of my dad, Leland (Lee) Omans. On his many trips from northern Minnesota to my home in Nashville, Tennessee, the miles along the Mississippi flyway were the ones he enjoyed the most and on which he lingered the longest.

Snoopy, his dog of dubious extraction and gentle disposition, always rode in the cab of his pickup truck. At the sight of birds or other wildlife, my dad would say in a surprised tone, "Well, well, well!" This was Snoopy's cue to lean out the window, nose whiffing the air, and make her own tail-wagging observations.

Geologically, the western region of Kentucky includes the Mississippi Embayment west of Land Between the Lakes

(LBL), plus a part of the Mississippian Plateau and Dripping Springs Escarpment east and northeast of LBL, and the Western Kentucky Coal Field found in a circular area west of Owensboro.

Earthquake tremors are still felt in the area of Reelfoot Lake, which lies partly in Kentucky but mostly in Tennessee. The lake was formed during a series of violent quakes in 1811 and 1812. The story is told in *Natural Wonders of Tennessee*, also published by Country Roads Press.

Wickliffe Mounds Research Center

Wickliffe Mounds, Kentucky's first designated archaeological landmark, sits almost in a world of its own along a well-traveled route that enters Kentucky from Cairo, Illinois, across the Ohio River or alternately from Missouri across the Mississippi River. It is one of the few significant prehistoric town sites left in western Kentucky, dating roughly from A.D. 800 to 1300. Its location, well above the river but with easily accessible water and fertile bottom lands for growing crops, provided an ideal setting for the needs of a community.

The Wickliffe Mounds Research Center, a facility of Murray State University (MSU), is easy to find on U.S. Routes 51/62 in Wickliffe. Visitors arriving at the museum are shown a short orientation video that explains the standard layout of Mississippian Period towns. All had a central plaza used for town meetings, sports events, and ceremonies. Public buildings sat on flat-topped, four-sided earthen mounds that flanked the plaza. Other dwellings nearby were homes for high-ranking tribal members.

Around the mound complex among some large trees are three buildings and a ceremonial mound. Research center director Dr. Kit Wesler suggests visiting the Lifeways Building first. It is a shed built over a large plot of bare soil that has fenced areas in which artifacts have been revealed by digging. Boardwalks are provided for foot traffic. Vertical displays hang from the ceiling. One is a drawing of a man playing a Native American stickball game which French explorers called lacrosse. Another shows how women worked in agriculture. There are many more.

Since this is an actual dig site, each individual location is numbered. Strings are laid out, mapping the dirt surface in blocks to identify location and depth. "F" means feature, so F18 is Feature Eighteen, which has ceramics and a hearth. Small rectangular slabs mark the location of infant burials. No human remains are displayed in any part of the mound community.

In this society, women gathered firewood, ground corn, tended fields, cooked, cured skins, made pottery and baskets, and gathered wild plants. Men were concerned with politics and ceremonies, but women were allowed to speak in the council gatherings.

As we go through the Lifeways Building, we learn the meaning of terms like "site" and "artifact." We gain an understanding of archaeology, its methods, what archaeologists look for, and how they tabulate and catalog their findings. Among the exhibits are game stones, chipped-stone and ground-stone tools, and pottery examples.

From archaeological research, we learn not only the culture and practices of ancient communities but also what types of animals and vegetation existed in earlier times. We note some changes but are quite surprised to learn how little the natural world has really changed.

The animal species that were here during this period include white-tailed deer, raccoon, river otter, swamp rabbit,

gray squirrel, red fox, black bear, spotted
skunk, woodchuck, eastern chipmunk,
muskrat, mink, opossum, beaver, eastern
cottontail, fox squirrel, gray fox, dog,
striped skunk, bobcat, coyote,
mountain lion, and rice rat,
plus many amphibians, rep-
tiles, and species of fish. Among the bird species were the
sandhill crane, whistling swan, peregrine falcon, greater prairie chicken, and several dozen others that are common to this
area today.

A grassy path leads to our next stop, the ceremonial mound.
Symmetrical hills found in otherwise flat country near the
Mississippi River or other rivers are often Indian mounds.
The history of this mound shows an early village, an addition
built on top of the early mound, and then a late mound—each
new layer adding to the height. Archaeologists find these layers by excavating into the side of the mound. On top of the
mound is a pattern of postholes that clearly indicates the horizontal dimensions of the building that stood there. This is
because the postholes that were dug in the ground left a stain
still visible centuries later.

Paved walkways connect the Lifeways Building to two
others. The Cemetery Building explains burial practices of
Native Americans, including their insistence that the sanctity
of burial plots be respected. Their belief about the afterlife is
that a person's spirit continues on and journeys to the "great
mystery" and that to disturb the burial place would be disre-
spectful and inhibit this spirit journey.

Archaeologists, on the other hand, defend the practice of
using bone chemistry to learn about the environment, diet,
life span, and way of life of ancient people. The controversy
over this issue is an international one.

In the Architecture Building, the walls have been painted to show the major construction layers of a public building that once existed here. One small glass case explains a method called "wattle and daub." Posts were set in the ground, then woven with branches and vines to make the wattle framework. Next, a solid wall was made by daubing clay on the wattle. To complete the building, thatched roofs were made of bundles of grass tied together. Just outside the Cemetery Building is a reconstructed house made in the same manner.

At the office again on my way out, I couldn't resist buying a replica of a small "fish" bowl. Other items for sale are videos, T-shirts, books, drawings, and maps.

Wickliffe Mounds holds special events on weekends in April, May, June, August, and September. Woods Walk and Medicinal Workshop, led by a Native American herbalist, identifies useful wild plants found in the area. River Explorers Encampment focuses on a particular time period demonstrated by historical interpreters. Archaeology Weekend features an active archaeological dig and demonstrations of flint knapping, pottery making, finger weaving, shell and bone tool making, hide tanning, and primitive weapons. The First Nation Dancers weekend offers performances of music, dance, and storytelling by Native Americans in authentic costumes. Flint Knappers Weekend is a show and sale of stone arrowheads, knives, and implements and demonstrations of how they are made.

Where: Entrance is on U.S. Routes 51/62 in Wickliffe.
When: Daily, March through November, 9:00 A.M. to 4:30 P.M.
Admission: Very moderate fee for adults, seniors, and children 6 to 11; under 6 free. Tours and group rates available by advance arrangement.

Amenities: Picnic area, museum, gift shop, mound sites, nature trail. Barrier-free access.
Activities: Individual and group tours.
Special events: Woods Walk and Medicinal Workshop (April), River Explorers Encampment (May), Archaeology Weekend (June), First Nation Dancers (August), Flint Knappers Weekend (September).
For more information: Wickliffe Mounds Research Center, PO Box 155, Wickliffe, KY 42087, 502-335-3681.

Swan Lake and Ballard WMAS

It is possible to attract wildlife to almost any location by creating habitat that provides food, water, shelter, and a place to raise young. Providing for migrating waterfowl in the hundreds of thousands requires these elements on a grand scale and something more: the right location. Large acreages of bottomlands along the Ohio River and the Mississippi flyway are Wildlife Management Areas (WMAS), managed for both resident and migrating species by the Kentucky Department of Fish and Wildlife Resources. Because of this, they are premier places for viewing wildlife. WMAS also allow hunting and fishing, camping, and hiking.

The kind of terrain you will encounter in these WMAS includes sloughs, marshes, open water, fields, and wooded plots. Roads of dirt or gravel are often built up above the surrounding lowlands, though not always.

Both WMAS have plentiful waterfowl, white-tailed deer, squirrels, turkeys, rabbits, coyotes, beavers, muskrats, minks, red and gray foxes, quail and doves, as well as songbirds, frogs, and turtles. Among threatened or endangered birds on the state list that you might see are the bald eagle, bank swallow, double-crested cormorant, great blue heron, great egret, hooded merganser, interior least tern, least bittern, and Mississippi kite. Other animals on the state list that are likely to be found here are the bird-voiced tree frog, green tree frog, river otter, swamp rabbit, and western ribbon snake.

Both Swan Lake and Ballard are closed October 15 through March 15 (except at designated observation areas) and during periods of high water. The high water is hard to predict. A heavy rain might flood the low areas for a day or more, and springtime flooding is common. Hunting is governed by statewide regulations, with some local restrictions. Nonhunters should be aware of hunting seasons and boundaries and at the very least should wear blaze orange during those times.

The entrance to the 2,536-acre Swan Lake WMA is a gravel road 2⁷⁄₁₀ miles west of Wickliffe on the northeast side of U.S. Routes 51/60, marked by a sign. It descends immediately into the river bottom and goes past fields of corn and other food crops. In a grove of trees at the edge of Swan Lake, the largest of 11 lakes on this property, is a place to park or to launch a small fishing boat. The lake was named by the renowned naturalist, John James Audubon, for the trumpeter swans he saw here on a visit in 1810. A small observation tower at the lake's edge overlooks an idyllic setting of lake and cypress trees.

Pick a good (dry) day and enjoy exploring the six miles of gravel roads. Be familiar with the dos and don'ts. Boating is allowed, but motors are limited to 10 horsepower on Swan Lake and trolling motors only on the other 10 lakes. Tent camping, the only kind allowed, is restricted to designated sites. Activities that are *not* allowed are: dog training, waterfowl hunting (on Swan Lake), turkey hunting, or hunting frogs with firearms.

Ballard WMA, legendary as a wintering area for waterfowl, is a huge 8,373-acre bottomland tract containing sloughs, agricultural food plots, oxbow lakes, and stands of hardwood. It is on the Ohio River (north from Wickliffe, west from Paducah, northwest from La Center, and west of the little town of Bandana).

A drive through this peaceful countryside has the remarkable effect of taking an eraser to any furrows in your brow. A nice pond on the right, a little bridge over a canal, fields full of tall yellow flowers; the eraser is at work.

The headquarters building is open Monday through Friday from 7:00 A.M. to 3:30 P.M., but it is not necessarily staffed at all times. A little wandering, though, will reveal a human at work somewhere who will be happy to answer a visitor's questions.

My question (for the human on a tractor) was how to find Shelby Lake, which has an elevated walkway for viewing wildlife. As you approach the headquarters building (it will be on your right), just continue straight on a dirt road for a short distance. Shelby Lake is a beautiful lake with cypress trees standing in the water. Splashes of sound and color are provided by jumping fish and flitting cardinals.

At Ballard, a pair of nesting eagles created a sensation in 1986 and again when they returned the following year. It was the first time in 40 years that this had happened in Kentucky. The comeback of the eagle population is now an established fact, of course, but it was a shaky situation for several years.

Though WMAs have long been known as primarily hunters' paradises, deer hunting is not allowed at Ballard—probably because the deer herd here is used to stock other areas of the state. Also, waterfowl hunting is by application only, with a September 30 deadline. Fishing is permitted on the 11 lakes, though boats may be fitted with electric motors only. No dogs are permitted except as retrievers during hunting seasons.

Camping is free on the four available primitive sites, which do not have water or electrical hookups. Stays are limited to 14 consecutive days.

Where: Swan Lake WMA: 2⁷⁄₁₀ miles west of Wickliffe on U.S. Routes 51/60 (watch for entrance sign). Ballard WMA from Wickliffe: north on U.S. Route 60 to Barlow, then north on State 1105 through Oscar and left on State 473. From Paducah: west on U.S. Route 60 to La Center, north on State 356 to Bandana, west on State 1105 for 3²⁄₁₀ miles, then west on State 473 for 2³⁄₁₀ miles, and left on Wildlife Lodge Road to the WMA headquarters.

When: March 16 through October 14, but both locations have viewing platforms accessible year-round.

Admission: Free.

Amenities: Both locations have fishing lakes, primitive camp sites, viewing platforms, interpretive display. Barrier-free access at Ballard on Shelby Lake pier (seasonal, as access road can be muddy). During periods of high water, Swan Lake is closed to boat access and Ballard is closed entirely.

Activities: Fishing, hunting, wildlife viewing, photography, primitive camping, hiking.

For more information: Kentucky Department of Fish and Wildlife Resources, #1 Game Farm Road, Frankfort, KY 40601, 502-224-2244 or 502-564-3400.

Westvaco-Columbus Bottoms WMA

Just south of Wickliffe along U.S. Routes 51/62 is the Fine Papers Division Mill of Westvaco Corporation, a longtime industry leader in environmental management for air and water quality and wildlife protection. If you're on your way to the 3,200-acre Westvaco-Columbus Bottoms WMA south of

Berkley, I suggest stopping at Westvaco's corporate office for a free copy of the drive-through tour brochure. It has a map of the property and describes areas of special interest. Incidentally, the town is "Burkley" on the city-limits sign, and it is also sometimes spelled "Berkly" on maps. Take your pick.

Unlike other WMAs managed by the Kentucky Department of Fish and Wildlife Resources, this one is on private land. It demonstrates how forestry practices can actually improve habitat for wildlife. In addition to the features that say "wetlands"—cypress groves, sloughs, and little oxbow lakes—are food-and-cover plots of corn, soybeans, and other seeds and grains. Tree farms on the property grow genetically superior cottonwoods and sycamores that are fast growing and oaks that are coddled into becoming acorn producers in record time.

We access the Westvaco WMA from State 123. The auto tour is numbered from the southern entrance, located just north of Columbus. From 123, go west on State 1313, also called Drew Road. The main road within the WMA, Fish Lake Road, basically winds through the bottoms in a north/south direction. (To start from the northern entrance, go west on State 1217 in Berkley and follow the signs.)

Along the auto tour are nine marked stops. The first provides parking for the Town Creek Interpretive Trail, where a boardwalk and observation tower overlook a moist-soil unit encircled by the trail. Display boards tell about early explorations and the first white settlement in 1804. Binoculars will aid your viewing, but you won't need a hearing aid to listen to bullfrogs.

Down the road, we observe how managing the fragile moist-soil areas provides habitat for wild creatures. The sloughs would naturally dry out during summer and fall, but special water-control structures employ removable "stop-logs" to keep water levels at a 12-inch depth. Maintaining the water level is critical to waterfowl and other wetland plants and animals.

Agroforestry is a system of planting crops in specified zones among rows of trees. In the demonstration plot here, we see where milo, millet, and buckwheat were planted among cottonwoods to provide food and cover.

The waterfowl and migrating songbirds come in spring and are present until fall. In summer, sandbars are favorite places for shore birds. Year-round inhabitants include deer, wild turkeys, quail, bobcats, gray foxes, squirrels, rabbits, raccoons—and of course, snakes and frogs.

June through October are normally the best months to visit, since flooding often occurs in winter and spring (but also the WMA is closed from November 1 through March 15). Animals are most active in early morning and late evening. The richness of light at these times of day can lend a surreal quality to the scene.

We appreciate nature for many reasons, including just the beauty of it. Sometimes the simple elements are what we remember: a white-tailed deer in a buckwheat patch, backlit by shafts of deep golden light pushing long shadows toward us as they paint shimmering outlines on objects of forest and field.

Where: West of State 123 between Berkley and Columbus. To follow numbered sites, turn west on State 1313 (Drew Road) just north of Columbus. Or turn west on State 1217 in Berkley and travel a reverse route.

When: Open March 16 through October 31.

Admission: Free.

Amenities: Interpretive trail, observation areas, self-guided auto tour, parking at trailhead or roadside.

Activities: Wildlife viewing, photography, hiking, hunting. Slide show and video shown by advance request.

Other: No rest rooms.

For more information: Westvaco Corporation, Timberlands Division, PO Box 458, Wickliffe, KY 42087, 502-335-3151 or 502-335-3156.

Columbus-Belmont State Park

This 156-acre park high on a bluff overlooking the Mississippi River is named for two towns on opposite banks: Columbus, Kentucky, and Belmont, Missouri. Columbus was fortified so heavily during the Civil War that it became known as the "Gibraltar of the West." Belmont was a partner, a secondary rebel camp that aided in the scheme to prevent Union gunboats from going downriver past this point.

Little has been published about a great mile-long chain that was stretched across the river and held in place on the Columbus side by a six-ton anchor to stop unwanted river traffic. It was somewhat of a fiasco: not long after it was put into operation, the chain broke. Visitors can see the anchor and several feet of the chain on display here and can visit the park museum to learn much more about the local Civil War action.

At Columbus-Belmont, history and nature combine in a very pleasant way. The site is on attractive hilly grounds with immaculate landscaping and blacktop walkways for foot travel. Well-defined depressions in the landscape mark the trenches of so long ago where 140 heavy cannons were once placed and which now form a 2½-mile self-guided hiking trail.

The bluff above the picnic area gives a sense of how an army commanding this position would have had a strategic advantage. From the lookout pavilion on a rainy April day, I could clearly see a barge sitting at the bank across the river. The day was brightened by flashes of red as a cardinal flew by and a redheaded woodpecker, unfazed by drizzle and mist, inspected a nearby tree trunk.

Large display boards at the main parking area tell about the town of Columbus, how it was destroyed by a flood in 1927 and how the whole town was relocated on top of the cliff, about the development of Columbus-Belmont Park, details of local Civil War history, and fascinating accounts of the New Madrid earthquakes of 1811 and 1812.

The campground is open year-round and is available on a first-come, first-served basis. Its 38 sites have utility hookups and grills, and a central laundry building provides rest rooms and showers. The extraordinary setting has made it very popular with tourists from Germany, Switzerland, Spain, Australia, New Zealand, South Africa, Canada, and all over the United States.

The museum is a neat, white clapboard structure that has Civil War relics and Native American Indian artifacts on display and a video about the Battle of Belmont. Books can be purchased here, including *Columbus, Kentucky as the Nation's Capital: Legend or Near Reality?* by Allen Anthony.

It is hard to imagine this remote and quiet place as the nation's capital. It is still a place of vision, though. The grandest dream of park superintendent J. Richard Gaw has been to see a bridge built across the Mississippi to connect Columbus and Belmont. I've been told that he requisitions a budget for it every year (unsuccessfully, so far).

Columbus, Capital of the U.S.A.?

A persistent local tradition claims that the little town of Columbus was once seriously considered as the site for the nation's capital. Allen Anthony's book, *Columbus, Kentucky as the Nation's Capital: Legend or Near Reality?*, relates the historical basis for this claim.

Naysayers point out that when the U.S. Congress squabbled about the placement of the capital in 1789 and again in 1812, the town of Columbus didn't exist (and when the question came up again later, no mention of Columbus was entered into the Congressional record).

The little town did encompass an unusually large area—4,000 acres—indicating "someone" might have had expansion in mind.

The speculation continues, but if the town had become our nation's capital, at least one element would certainly have changed; and J. Richard Gaw wouldn't be just hoping for Columbus-Belmont's Mississippi River bridge!

Where: On the Mississippi River at Columbus via State 60 west of Mayfield, State 58 northwest of Clinton, or State 123 south of Bardwell.

When: Park and campground open year-round. Museum open seven days a week, May 1 through September 30, from 9:00 A.M. to 5:00 P.M. and weekends only April and October. Snack bar, gift shop, and miniature golf open seven days a week from May 1 through Labor Day and weekends the rest of September.

Admission: Free except moderate fees for camping, miniature golf, and museum. Picnic shelters may be reserved up to one year in advance (fee charged).

Amenities: Campground, Civil War artifacts, museum, gift shop, snack bar, miniature golf, activities building, picnic sites, playground, volleyball court, horseshoes area.

Activities: Camping, picnicking, self-guided hiking trail, wildlife viewing, photography, volleyball, horseshoes, Civil War research.

Other: Barrier-free access. Bicycle riding prohibited in picnic areas.

For more information: Columbus-Belmont State Park, PO Box 8, Columbus, KY 42032-0008, 502-677-2327.

2

Paducah Area

Discovering Paducah, a small city hugged by the Ohio and Tennessee Rivers, can be exciting for people who love old historic districts with reminders of bygone days and hospitality expressed everywhere. Those are just two of the reasons so many riverboats stop here while their passengers sample local cuisine and shop for antiques, art objects, and gift items. (I was excited to find Rick Cain's wildlife sculptures at Bernard Lewis & Company on Broadway at Third.)

For overnight stays, consider the magnificent two-story Fox Briar Farm Inn, a bed-and-breakfast on a 100-acre farm where nine guest rooms look out from arched windows toward Belted Galloway cattle grazing in a fenced field, wild turkey gobblers emerging from the woods, or wild ducks paddling in the lake. It is just 15 minutes from the center of town and only 3½ miles from Interstate 24 at the U.S. Route 45 exit.

At Fox Briar Farm, the pastoral scenes can be fully appreciated from a large wraparound veranda. The hosts provide amenities far beyond the ordinary (even a grand piano!). All rooms are decorated with visually exciting wildlife sculptures, paintings, and authentic objects that follow outdoor or traditional themes. As you would suspect, a full breakfast is freshly prepared each morning and served in a spacious dining area perfect for viewing visiting wildlife.

For additional nature enjoyment and outdoor activity, preserves, parks, and wildlife management areas are easily accessible from this "home base."

April, when the weather is cool and pleasant, is an active month in Paducah. Two major events are the National Quilt Show and the Paducah Dogwood Trail Celebration that includes bus tours and a bicycle tour. City tours and candlelight home tours are given on special dates, a bird walk is sponsored by the Jackson Purchase Audubon Society, and "A Day in the Woods," sponsored by Paducah Parks & Leisure Services, provides fun for children. This April extravaganza also features art, music and theatrical productions, and dining events.

Paducah residents gather outdoors again in June for a summer festival featuring marine industry exhibits, a cross-river swim, hot-air balloons, sky divers, and other entertainment.

For more information: Paducah/McCracken County Convention & Visitors Bureau, 128 Broadway, PO Box 90, Paducah, KY 42002-0090, 800-359-4775 or 502-443-8783.

Bernard Lewis & Company, 313 Broadway, Paducah, KY 42002, 800-455-6789.

Fox Briar Farm Inn, 515 Schmidt Road, PO Box 3129, Paducah, KY 42002, 502-554-1774.

Museum of the American Quilter's Society

Featuring a quilters' museum in a nature book may seem a bit of a stretch, but consider the popularity of wildlife art and sculpture. Quilts are another art form, often incorporating nature motifs in creative and exciting ways, providing a perpetual reminder of the outdoors. The idea of viewing outstanding examples of quilts in a museum, then, begins to seem quite, well—natural.

Paducah has been known as "Quilt City U.S.A." since 1984 when the American Quilter's Society was formed there. In 1991, the society opened its 30,000-square-foot museum known as MAQS—Museum of the American Quilter's Society. The museum shows contemporary, historical, thematic, and regional collections on a rotating basis in three galleries. Other rooms are used for workshops, and a gift shop has an extensive collection of books and other appropriate items, many handcrafted.

The museum features more than 400 quilts and quilted wall hangings, changing the examples from its permanent collection every few weeks and mounting special exhibits so repeat visitors always have something fresh to see.

Assistant curator Eric Reid accompanied me around the museum, pointing out quilts with nature or western motifs. Some of them used photographs as a starting point.

"This quilt by Nancy S. Brown is called *Mt. Pleasant Miners*. It traces a family history from a photograph taken in the 1870s," Reid said. "Another, *Wild Rose*, by Fay Pritts, uses a pattern, Whig Rose, that is about 200 years old. Yet it is a contemporary quilt inspired by a photograph taken around the time of the Chicago fire."

Another had a bald eagle on it and a beautiful large tree.

"It is by Dawn Amos, whose husband is a Native American," Reid said. "I especially like the way she uses quilting stitches to define the designs of clouds in the background and mountains."

Toujours Nouveau (Always New) by Suzanne Marshall, won the Gingher Handworkmanship Award in 1993. The artist's love of flowers and plants shows in her impeccably rendered treatment of vines.

Dawn Splendor (a flower garden) by Nancy Ann Sobel won Best of Show in 1991, perhaps helped by an accident. As the artist was dyeing the cloth, some unwanted spots resulted. Her solution was to stitch bugs and spiders in strategic places to make it look like a garden in the morning.

Many of the quilts on display focused on plants and animals: a border of willow trees around a little schoolhouse; rosebuds (gathered, of course); barnyard hens; butterflies; geese flying; snakes; leaves; and *Gaia*, the Greek goddess of the earth.

"We took a group of children one time 'on safari' around the museum to find animals," said Reid. "Animals and flowers are recurring in quilts from all time periods, from 200 years ago up until yesterday."

One of my favorites was *Under the Log Cabin Sky*. The rendering, done in the traditional Log Cabin pattern, was very naturalistic, with fish swimming in water and roses blooming on the bank.

Another striking quilt was titled *Revelations*. Waiting to be revealed by close inspection were 22 kinds of wild animal tracks done entirely of stitching, hidden in the quilting.

Marine Mammal Quilt was the work of a group of volunteers in Homer, Alaska, a town known for arts, fishing, and support for the environment. These quilters produce a quilt each year for the Pratt Museum/Homer Society of Natural History, and this one depicted 15 sea mammal species done mostly in purple, blue, and green.

The quilts from the MAQS permanent collection are owned by the museum and are not for sale. To see them, just head for Paducah.

Where: From Interstate 24, take exit 4 and follow the Interstate 24 loop to downtown Paducah, turn left on Broadway, then left on 3rd Street (next block). Museum is on the right, past the corner of Jefferson.

When: Year-round. 10:00 A.M. to 5:00 P.M. Tuesday through Saturday and 1:00 to 5:00 P.M. on Sunday (extended hours during National Quilt Show). Closed Sundays November through March. Closed New Year's Day, Easter, Thanksgiving, and Christmas.

Admission: Moderate fee; adult and student prices. Group rates available.

Amenities: Galleries, reference library, book and gift shop, conference room, classrooms.

Activities: Write for a current schedule of activities.

Special events: National Quilt Show & Contest (April).

Other: Barrier-free access.

For more information: Museum of the American Quilter's Society, 215 Jefferson Street, Paducah, KY 42001, 502-442-8856.

Metropolis Lake State Nature Preserve

It was at Metropolis Lake, a little 50-acre oxbow lake next to the Ohio River a few miles west of Paducah, that I fell in the mud. But I'm getting ahead of the story.

This nature preserve, 123 acres including the lake, is one of those places that are hard to find unless you happen to live in the area. Fortunately, I had directions from Joyce Bender, who is stewardship coordinator for the Kentucky State Nature Preserves Commission.

Go west from Paducah on U.S. Route 60 to Future City, then north on State 996 (the intersection has a traffic light). Three and a half miles north, 996 intersects with State 358 going west; but continue north on 996 exactly 2²/₁₀ miles farther and then turn right on a small unmarked paved road.

This road curves left almost immediately, passing in front of a farmhouse and into the woods ahead. At the entrance to the woods, a sign announces the preserve.

When I arrived, the trees were alive with the sound of music. It was the singing of birds. Joyce was beaming. "This place is a paradise," she announced. "I've been listening to pro-thonotary warblers and white-throated sparrows and watching the mist rising from the lake."

Sure enough, the sparrow's song pierced the morning air: ta-dee-dee-dee.

Besides being a favorite stopping place for migrating warblers and a home for wild turkeys, beavers, muskrats, raccoons, deer, and river otters, Metropolis Lake has some aquatic species that are endangered or threatened in Kentucky: a species of crayfish, the cypress minnow, the taillight shiner, a little "silverside fish," and the spotted sunfish. Periodically, new ones come in from the Ohio River when it spills over its banks. A candidate for federal listing that has been seen here is a northern copper-bellied water snake.

The lake's surface was a near-perfect mirror reflecting cypress and tupelo trees and birds flying overhead. A few fishing boats moved quietly, powered by trolling motors. Nothing spoiled the serenity of the moment.

"It's really pleasant to come here early, before the fishermen arrive," said Joyce. "I like to sit on the shore and watch the herons come in to fish and the kingfishers swoop down and get their breakfast. From 7:00 to 8:00 A.M. would be a good time to show up."

The nature trail starts off to the left from the parking lot. For two days it had rained, so the trail was pretty muddy at the start before it led to higher ground. I was looking up at a dead tree, trying to spot some cavity nesters when Joyce said, "Oh, gosh!"

There I was, off balance and falling on my back into the slick mud, but in control to a degree (that is, holding my tape recorder and binoculars safely aloft). It only took a second for the cold wetness to get through my clothes, and I knew I'd be "swamp thing" for the rest of the morning. For a few minutes, the only sounds we heard were laughter and slogging-through-the-muck noises.

We soon came to a trail display that pointed out some young pawpaw trees, which had just finished blooming. These trees are ready to spring up whenever larger trees fall and cause openings in the forest canopy. In this environment, the pawpaws are seen in several places.

The trail has a sort of lasso configuration. After a short distance, you can fork to the left or right. Taking the left fork leads into uplands and then returns by the lake, which is the sequence we chose.

Bird sounds filled the air. Another white-throated sparrow, and then another. Dueling warblers—how nice.

We went up a bank, successfully crossed a trickle of a stream, watched for copperheads, and did not fall. Shagbark hickory, said another marker. The nut is favored by turkeys. Since hunting is not allowed in the preserve, the wild turkeys have two good reasons to hang out here.

On top of the ridge, we are close to where there used to be barracks for workers who were building the nearby Shawnee Steam Plant. It is hard to believe, looking at the natural environment all around, that a few decades ago this place was very commercial. It had a ball diamond, cabins, a bait shop, boat rentals, and cattle grazing in fields. The woods are still quite young now, but little remains to suggest what went on before.

Going down from the ridge toward the lake, deer tracks are on the trail. Other animals to look for at the lake are beavers, belted kingfishers, and turtles (usually sitting on logs). Near the water, we can also find crayfish holes with their telltale chimneys. In the lake are soft-shelled and red-eared turtles, while land-loving box turtles are sometimes found in shallow puddles.

Even though this preserve is wetter in spring, that is probably the best time of year for bird-watching and wildflowers. Yellow and purple violets, trout lilies, and purple phlox are just a few of the many flowers here that carpet the ground lavishly or provide "flags" of accent color.

This is definitely a premier place to study and enjoy plants and animals, no matter what the season. It's not overused, so the animals are relatively undisturbed.

"I've been lucky enough to see turkeys running through the woods and the nest cavity of the bright yellow prothonotary warbler right along the trail," said Joyce.

That's worth quite a lot.

The Morning the Ice Chimed

Something extraordinary happened at Metropolis Lake once, as Joyce Bender related:

"My boss and I were here one cold morning very early after a freeze had caused a thin skim of ice to form around the edges of the lake. The wind came up, creating waves on the lake. They in turn started breaking up the ice into tiny fragments.

"The ice layer being so thin, as it was broken by the waves it made sounds I had never heard before, sort of a sh-sh-sh-sh of fragments crashing into each other, but with a musical tingling timbre to them. All the pieces were chiming together in notes that related to their size and the intensity of the wave action, almost like wind chimes in that respect.

"It was a singular moment that may never be duplicated, a most lovely tinkling that carried through the air for quite a distance. I was overcome: it was so beautiful."

Ice chimes on Metropolis Lake, a 1,000-year sound: wouldn't we all love to have been there?

Where: West of Paducah off U.S. Route 60, then north on State 996 at Future City. Continue north 2²/₁₀ miles past where State 338 turns west, then turn right on unmarked paved road. *When:* Year-round, sunrise to sunset. Fishing allowed February 15 to October 15. Gate closed October 15 to February 15, but preserve open to foot traffic. Spring excellent for birdwatching; beavers active in winter.
Admission: Free.
Amenities: Fishing lake, self-guided nature trail, boat-launching area.
Activities: Hiking, birding, wildlife viewing, fishing.
Other: Electric motors only allowed; no gill nets, jugs, or trotlines; camping and picnicking not permitted; hunting and trapping prohibited.
For more information: Kentucky State Nature Preserves Commission, 801 Schenkel Lane, Frankfort, KY 40601-1403, 502-573-2886.

West Kentucky WMA

The 7,000-acre West Kentucky Wildlife Management Area, with its proximity to Paducah, is one of the most-visited WMAs in Kentucky. It is about five miles from Metropolis

Lake, so an outing to both places in one day is easy to accomplish. The WMA is northwest of Future City. Follow State 996 north for 3½ miles, then go west (left) on State 358 for 2½ miles to WMA headquarters.

Several agencies are involved. Both TVA and the U.S. Department of Energy own part of the WMA's land. They license its use to the Kentucky Department of Fish and Wildlife Resources.

Fifty thousand to 100,000 people come each year to participate in fishing and hunting, dog training and field trials, auto touring, wildlife viewing, and special events. Managing for habitat preservation, conducting scientific research, and allowing heavy recreational use on a single piece of property can be a real challenge. Additionally, a portion of the WMA, the Bayou Creek Ridge Natural Area next to the Ohio River, is managed for environmental protection.

WMA supervisor Charlie Logsdon took me on a tour that began in a field where prairie plants were starting to reappear. From the 2½ million acres of prairie originally in Kentucky, only about 700 acres remain. "We have some of the largest tracts of native tallgrass prairie remaining in the state, due to our extensive controlled burning program," Charlie explained.

Controlled burning is a science that works because even though seeds and root systems may have been dormant for decades, they are ready to come to life under the proper circumstances. It is truly a renewal technique, and one that Native Americans used skillfully to attract game, drive game, or clear the ground for agriculture. The lush green vegetation that appears almost immediately after burning is irresistible to deer.

In a field that had been burned the year before, we saw little bluestem, broom sedge, big bluestem, and Indian grass— all typical tallgrass prairie species. The Indian grass reaches a height of six to eight feet by September. We also spotted prairie false indigo, *Baptisia leucantha*, a bushy plant with cream-colored, pea-like blossoms that was not found here before the burning.

Walking through a field reveals what cannot be seen while driving by. "Most people think nothing is in here," Charlie said, pointing out a woodcock nest, two hen turkeys, insect hatchings, wood sorrel, and compass plants (considered endangered in Kentucky).

A handicapped-accessible fishing pond and picnicking spot was opened in 1995. Six chutes allow wheelchairs to roll right up to the lake where people can fish for bass, bluegill, and catfish. Water primroses bloom in spring, with little yellow flowers, around an island that attracts wood ducks and geese. For more wildlife viewing pleasure, a hawk nest is in a power-line structure nearby.

Surprises happen, as when a white ibis appeared in the WMA in 1995, far from its Gulf Coast home. How did it get here?

"Just following the great blue herons and the egrets," said Charlie. "As DDT is disappearing or being removed from the food chain, heron rookeries are showing up everywhere, and some of these other birds tag along."

The WMA also has a 15-mile self-guided auto tour and a pamphlet that contains a map and a brief description of each stop. Pick it up at a kiosk next to the headquarters building.

The first stop shows an old ammunition-storage igloo built during World War II when this was part of the Kentucky Ordnance Works. It was designed so that in case of an explosion the debris would be blown out the top to cause the least damage.

Each stop is an opportunity to learn about something different.

A beaver pond, complete with beaver lodge, is an excellent place to look for beavers, otters, waterfowl, and turtles. Charlie spent 15 months studying otters and appreciates their efficiency. During that time he was amazed to see one otter go into a beaver lodge and run the beavers out.

Outside the Chief Paduke Gun Club near a large information board is an Eagle Scout project. Specimens of prairie grasses and other plants grow in a bed, identified by markers.

Crop rotation and the changes in plant succession are explained at a food plot frequented by quail and smaller birds; and at a ground water monitoring well, the why and how of checking for contaminants is discussed.

A moist-soil unit has water-control structures for manipulation of water levels to stimulate vegetation for waterfowl use, as ponds are drained and refilled periodically.

Close to the Ohio River is a tupelo swamp, a haven for reptiles and amphibians. The trees stand in several feet of water for much of the year, but the ground dries out during late summer and early fall. Charlie said that when the leaves fall, they form a golden carpet underneath. The tupelo trees with their natural nesting cavities make this a perfect motel for wood ducks.

The Bayou Creek Ridge Natural Area is on rugged ground that supports 26 species of trees. One cottonwood is nearly 20 feet in circumference, and several pecan trees are 4 feet or more in diameter. Cherry-bark oaks and white oaks thrive on the higher elevations. Eagles come through in winter, and wild turkeys congregate in the area. Seven species of bats have been identified in the bottomland hardwood area near the river where they live in the trees.

The 500 acres of woods provide unlimited places to look for wildflowers. Expect to find trillium and trout lilies in early spring and, later, Indian pink, spiderwort, phlox . . . and the list goes on.

Where: West from Paducah on U.S. Route 60 to Future City, then north on State 996 for 3½ and west on State 338 for 2½ miles.
When: Year-round.
Admission: Free.
Amenities: Thirty-one miles of roads, kennels and stalls (during field trials), ponds (one barrier free with special fishing piers for wheelchairs), skeet range.
Activities: Fishing, hunting, primitive camping, picnicking, wildlife viewing, birding, photography, self-guided tours.
Special events: Earth Day activities (April), Quail Championship Field Trial (Saturday after Thanksgiving).
Other: Barrier-free access. Parking along roadways limited. Caution: nonhunters, be aware of hunting seasons.
For more information: West Kentucky Wildlife Management Area, 10535 Ogden Landing Road, Kevil, KY 42053, 502-488-3233.

Kentucky Department of Fish and Wildlife Resources, #1 Game Farm Road, Frankfort, KY 40601, 502-564-3400.

3

LBL and Vicinity

TVA's massive Land Between the Lakes Recreation Area
or "LBL," as it is commonly called, lies on a 40-mile long
inland peninsula between Kentucky and Barkley Lakes in
Kentucky and Tennessee. Before the lakes were impounded,
this was a remote and sparsely populated area referred to
locally as "the land between the rivers." Kentucky Dam on
the Tennessee River was built first, then Barkley Dam on the
Cumberland. Since the dams were close together, the two
navigable rivers were joined by a canal instead of having separate lock systems.

In the meantime, TVA acquired 170,000 acres of the rolling
fields and woodlands between them and began work on what
was to be one of the nation's largest public playgrounds. No
one who has visited the area can deny that TVA succeeded
magnificently. LBL has also gained world attention: in 1991 it
was declared a biosphere reserve under the UNESCO Man and
the Biosphere Program, giving it international recognition as
a laboratory for environmental problem solving.

This book focuses on the roughly two-thirds of LBL territory in Kentucky and the nearby parks and other places of
interest to nature enthusiasts. For a discussion of the Tennessee portion, see *Natural Wonders of Tennessee.*

For more information: Free vacation guide, *Kentucky's Western Waterlands*, a region including Land Between the Lakes, 800-448-1069.

Tva's Land Between the Lakes

Visitors to LBL will find activities for all outdoor interests and an enormous diversity of animals and birds that live here or migrate through this 270-square-mile area. It has the largest publicly owned buffalo herd in the Eastern United States and has a population of nesting bald eagles. The visitors center, the welcome stations, and The Nature Station all have information about the eagle's current status.

The visitors center and planetarium is on The Trace at the junction with U.S. Route 68 between Cadiz and Aurora. The Trace is LBL's main north-south highway that goes through a tranquil countryside of cedars, mixed hardwoods, and fields. I saw the wisdom of the 50-mph speed limit as I rounded a curve and two sleek white-tailed does beside the road jumped, bounded across, and disappeared into the woods.

Outside the visitors center is the original "Golden Pond" for which a pioneer community was named. Inside the center are all the desired amenities, including a well-stocked gift shop. Planetarium shows are offered two to four times a day, depending on the season. The planetarium's 40-foot dome re-creates realistic images of planets and galaxies, and each show ends with an exact representation of the night sky for the current date.

Illustrated display boards in a large room at the center tell the history of whiskey making, including the "moonshine years" at Golden Pond. The process had its beginnings in 3500 B.C. in Mesopotamia and saw many refinements over time. The making of "corn likker" officially ended in LBL in 1967.

Hiking, Biking, OHVs

Mountain bikers (the sport was popularized during the 1996 Summer Olympics) can park at the visitors center when they ride the intermediate/advanced portion of the 12-mile Jenny Ridge Mountain Bike Trail. Another parking place is the hunter checkstation. Beginning bikers should park at the Jenny Ridge Picnic Area and get on the trail at Road 141. The beginner's portion has both paved and dirt roads and some stream crossings, while the advanced section on the North-South Trail is more rugged and scenic.

Another trail designated for this use is the 18-mile Energy Lake Mountain Bike Trail, which loops around the lake through ridges, meadows, forests, and creeks. It has parking lots at Energy Lake Dam and at the Hematite picnic area.

All in all, LBL has 60 miles of trails open to mountain bikes. Portions of these trails are closed during deer- and turkey-quota gun hunts.

OHVs have their designated place, too. Turkey Bay is a 2,500-acre tract for off-highway vehicle riding and camping. It is west of The Trace about two miles south of the visitors center and adjacent to Kentucky Lake. Its camping facilities allow informal and tent trailer camping with chemical toilets and picnic tables but no drinking water or electricity.

Challenge races are scheduled most months. A Hare Scramble (a race over a closed-circuit course) for off-highway motorcycles is held in March. For mountain bikes, the Bald Eagle Challenge in April, a Cross-Country Challenge in June, and an Off-Road Triathlon in September are annual events (but check current events schedules for changes).

For hikers, the 65-mile North-South Trail goes from one end of LBL to the other on the Kentucky Lake side. It sometimes follows old logging roads or meanders through valleys, beside streams, and along the lakeshore. That's just part of the story: LBL has 200 miles of trails, with some designed for both hiking and biking. Bicyclists can also take advantage of little-traveled roads.

Camping Opportunities

Those wishing to stay awhile in LBL have several camping choices, from primitive tent camping to developed campgrounds that offer RV sites and full amenities. The Hillman Ferry family campground, open March 1 through November, is easy to access from the North Welcome Station, while a year-round horse camp, Wranglers Campground, is about six miles southeast of the visitors center. For groups, the Energy Lake Campground and Day Use Area are logical choices.

Hillman Ferry has 380 sites from nonelectric to fully furnished with electricity, water, and sewer. The area can handle sizes from tent trailers to large motor homes. Practically everything is here to make your stay enjoyable: cabins, dumping station, fishing pier, two boat-launching ramps, archery range, ball field, shelters, picnic tables and grills, playgrounds, bike rentals, bike trails, bike skills court, campfire theater, hiking trails, equipment checkout station, large swimming beach, camp supplies, ice and firewood sales, washers and dryers, barrier-free access in several areas, and public telephones.

Wranglers Campground is open year-round on a first-come, first-served basis. It provides electrical and nonelectrical tent and trailer sites, informal camping, flush and chemical toilets, drinking water, bathhouse (the showers are closed in winter), activities court, picnic tables and grills, washers and dryers, food concession, soft drink machine, hitching/tethering posts, watering troughs, stables, stall and horse rentals, tack and farrier services, horse trails, and barrier-free access.

For more austere camping but with some amenities, fee campsites are available at the Birmingham Ferry, Smith Bay, Redd Hollow, Sugar Bay, and Twin Lakes access areas on

Kentucky Lake and at Bacon Creek, Cravens Bay, Devil's Elbow, Nickell Branch, and Taylor Bay access areas on Lake Barkley. Most of these locations have picnic tables, grills, drinking water, chemical toilets, nonelectric campsites, and launch ramps. Some have courtesy docks, flush toilets, and ice and firewood supplies in addition to the other features.

If you seek truly primitive conditions and solitude, take advantage of LBL's open camping policy that allows free camping anywhere except in posted areas. If, on the other hand, you prefer more luxurious accommodations, you will find them in the three state parks surrounding LBL and in other nearby resorts.

Recreation Galore

Fishermen and boaters have access to both Kentucky and Barkley Lakes at launching ramps scattered around the 300 miles of undeveloped shoreline. In Kentucky, the nonfee lake-access areas are Pisgah Point on Kentucky Lake and at Demumbers Bay, Eddyville Ferry, and Kuttawa Landing on Lake Barkley. These have no facilities other than launching ramps.

Throughout Kentucky, fishing is allowed even without a license during Kentucky Free Fishing Days, a designated weekend usually in June.

For hunters, LBL offers open seasons on waterfowl and over a dozen other animal species including white-tailed deer and wild turkey. It is a good idea for anyone who plans to explore off the main road to know the hunting seasons and wear blaze orange for protection.

The Nature Station

Nature enthusiasts will surely want to visit The Nature Station on Honker Bay of Lake Barkley, a few miles north and east of the LBL visitors center. It is an outstanding location, one of those places so full of opportunity that you hardly know which way to look or whether to listen to the honkers, the warblers, or the croakers.

That turned out to be my dilemma. I was at a pavilion with wetlands, fields, trees, and a finger of the lake spread before me. Two Canadas flew by, one honking pretty desperately, but suddenly hundreds of per-chick-a-ree voices took over. The ground was covered with goldfinches, flashing yellow and black as they darted from spot to spot, getting in a shallow puddle and bathing with a vigorous flutter of wings. These beautiful birds look like yellow butterflies when they are on the ground. Forget listening for frogs! I thought.

The Nature Station offers, as their literature says, "encounters with nature." Inside are exhibits, a children's activities corner, a theater, and a gift shop. Displays emphasize how beavers build their dams, how animals are hurt by things humans carelessly discard outdoors, and how to build bluebird houses, feed hummingbirds, and recognize trees by their bark.

Outside, large fenced environments keep live animals in natural habitats. A curious melange of sounds greeted me there. Coyotes were yelping, and some people were trying to imitate wolf sounds, while the red wolves simply ignored the commotion.

Several theme areas added interest. A natural pond had iris and tall cattails. A children's wildlife garden had a "crawl-through" space under muscadine vines.

A hummingbird-and-butterfly garden featured trumpet honeysuckle, geraniums, butterfly weed, monarda (bee balm) and petunias (all with red blossoms), and hummingbird feeders. Another, cypress vine, is a native plant with tiny trumpet-shaped flowers of brilliant red, the size of a dime and irresistible to hummingbirds. It was planted in a barrel.

Two large fenced areas held white-tailed and fallow deer. A

golden eagle, black vulture, red-tailed hawk, barn owl, screech owl, and a barred owl were some of the birds on display.

I asked Darrin Samborski, a program aide, about the electronic security fence around the red wolf habitat.

"There aren't many of these animals in existence. Back in the early 1970s and into the '80s, biologists rounded up the remaining 14 pure-strain red wolves, and due to captive breeding programs like ours, their numbers have increased to around 200 worldwide," said Samborski. "We keep these wolves for educational purposes and to dispel a lot of wolf myths that keep circulating."

Education, said Samborski, is the heart and soul of this facility.

"We take folks out in the fields and woods every day," he continued. "We offer wildlife viewing excursions and pond explorations. And we give programs about endangered species or reptiles and amphibians or birds, tailoring them to a specific part of the ecosystem."

Nancy Kiernan, who develops the educational programs, said that in summer the facility has programs most days. Every morning and late afternoon, visitors can watch the animals being fed and see a parade of raptors. Naturalists also guide woodland walks each morning.

The special activities throughout the season include sunset canoe excursions, moonlight hikes, pond-life prowls (looking for salamanders and insect larvae), van tours for wildlife observation, wildflower walks, jig-tying workshops, gardening tips for attracting wildlife, and a day-long Earth Day celebration.

Though The Nature Station is closed in winter, it sponsors three eagle weekends in January and February in conjunction with nearby state parks. People can get on a mailing list and be notified when reservations are being taken for these events (call 502-924-5602).

If you wish to explore some of the trails here, ask for the trail and wildlife observation maps.

Drive (or walk) a few hundred yards to the Hematite Lake and picnic area, an excellent waterfowl and wildflower viewing spot, to spend an hour and a half walking the 2²⁄₁₀-mile nature trail around the lake. Along the way are two observation stations, a photography blind, and a section of boardwalk over a low-lying area. If you have time for a three-hour walk, try the Honker Trail. It will take you on a meandering route around the south shore of Honker Lake, over Honker Dam, and through woods and fields for an up-close look at deer, osprey, bald eagles, and Canada geese (who will also provide a serenade). The quarter-mile Long Creek Trail is perfect for people who want an easy short walk or a handicapped-accessible one and views of some interesting plants. A favorite mile-long trail is Woodland Walk, which circles The Nature Station in a shady forest overlooking the lake and provides excellent wildlife-viewing potential from its three observation stations. It goes close to an electrical tower that has an active osprey nest about two-thirds of the way up. You can also find a carpet of Virginia bluebells on this trail in the right season.

And, there's Center Furnace. The ruins only suggest its heyday. Walk the three-tenths-mile trail that loops around behind the furnace to see relics of a centuries-old mining community.

Center Iron Furnace, "The Granddaddy of Them All"

You can't miss it on the way to The Nature Station. The legendary Center Furnace is a reminder of the glory days of iron ore production in Kentucky when the hills were rich in ore, timber was plentiful, and a burgeoning industrialized nation needed iron. Even richer deposits would be found up north and new methods invented of extracting the ore; but for a time, the never-ending fires of Center Furnace lit the night sky.

The furnace was built in the 1840s, operated nonstop until after the Civil War, then resumed operation for two brief periods in the late 1800s and early 1900s.

The whole process of producing the "pigs" (pig iron) that were floated downriver to market is explained here. The traditional cold-blast method of extracting the ore required charcoal to heat the furnace (and therefore timber) and limestone to intensify the heat. In this place, the limonite and hematite iron ores were in shallow deposits where they could be extracted using picks and shovels. Oxcarts brought the ore to the furnace, which was connected to the top of a nearby hill by a bridge on which an ore box was pushed along trolley tracks. The ore was then dumped into the top of the furnace. Air was forced into the furnace through a pipe, and gravity and the fires did the rest.

Today at Honker Bay, geese fly, trees once again shade the land, and only these ruins crumbled by time whisper about an era long gone.

Another possibility a few miles away is a visit to the Silo Overlook, a tall concrete farm silo from which you can view Lake Barkley and Honker Bay.

Visiting "Yesterday"

For a different visit back in time (and a foray into Tennessee), take The Trace south to The Homeplace-1850, an interpretive center just south of the state line that shows how rural families lived in the 19th century as they worked the land, planted crops, raised livestock, made cloth, and produced nearly everything they needed for food, clothing, and shelter. Did they live well? This old recipe for bread fritters might give a clue:

> *Boil a quart of milk with cinnamon and sugar to taste. When done, stir in a tablespoon of rose water. Cut some slices of bread into a circular shape, soak them in milk until the milk is absorbed, then drain. Beat some yolks of eggs until frothy. Dip the bread slices into the yolks and fry them in butter. Serve them up dusted with powdered sugar.*

Summer programs focus on butter making, fall plowing, tobacco firing, bread making, spinning, dyeing, weaving, and oxen working. In June, the Four Rivers Folk Festival offers music, storytelling, and crafts demonstrations. In October, the Apple Festival salutes the American apple. Baking contests, demonstrations, cider making, wagon rides, storytelling, and music are all included.

One last caution about LBL: in the woods are ticks, ticks, ticks! If you didn't bring tick spray, you can buy it here. You are strongly encouraged to do so.

Where: In Kentucky, The Trace, the main north-south road through LBL, can be reached from U.S. Route 68 west of Cadiz and east of Aurora. Also, from Interstate 24 east of Paducah, take exit 31 and go south on State 453 past Lake City and Grand Rivers. From U.S. Routes 62/641 at Lake City, turn

south on State 453 to the entrance. From U.S. Route 79 in Tennessee, turn north on The Trace three miles west of Dover.
When: Year-round. Golden Pond Visitors Center is open seven days a week from 9:00 A.M. to 5:00 P.M. (closed Thanksgiving, Christmas, and New Year's Day); The Golden Pond Planetarium (at the visitors center) has scheduled show times 11:00 A.M. and 2:00 P.M. March through August, with additional shows at 1:00 P.M. and 3:00 P.M. on Saturday and Sunday in March through May and seven days a week June through August (show times vary September through December); The Nature Station and The Homeplace-1850 are open seven days a week April through October (closed Mondays and Tuesdays March and November) from 9:00 A.M. to 5:00 P.M., and closed entirely December through February.
Admission: Free. Fees to enter planetarium at Golden Pond, The Nature Station exhibit area, The Homeplace-1850, and developed campgrounds. Campgrounds offer second-night, 14-night, Golden Age and Golden Access Passport discounts. Fees for special events.
Amenities: Welcome station, visitors center/planetarium, campgrounds, hiking and biking and equestrian trails, lake-access areas, fishing piers, playgrounds, nature center, environmental education area, off-highway vehicle area, firearms range, picnic areas (in Kentucky), The Homeplace-1850 (in Tennessee near state line).
Activities: Fishing, boating, hunting, camping, backpacking, swimming, hiking, biking, horseback riding, boat rentals, wildlife viewing, scenic auto tours, photography.
Special events: Eagles Weekends in conjunction with adjacent state parks (January, February); Crappiethon U.S.A (March). Typical summer schedule includes triathlons, drag boat races, National Trails Day, Four Rivers Folk Festival, Mountain Bike Cross-Country Challenge, Paddling by Moonlight, Independence Day at The Homeplace-1850, road bike races, Wetlands

Wonderland, LBL Homecoming, Eco Challenge (multisport wilderness adventure), Sunset Canoe Excursions, and National Homecoming (horseback) Ride.

Other: Twenty-four-hour visitor-assistance number: 502-924-5602. Anyone who intends to hunt or fish should request a *Hunting and Angling Guide* (published annually and available on request or at welcome stations). Regulations apply to all use areas. Tick repellent sold at welcome stations and visitors center (recommended!).

For more information: To request a seasonal calendar of events and other general information: Recreation Services Section, TVA's Land Between the Lakes, 100 Van Morgan Drive, Golden Pond, KY 42211-9001, 502-924-5602.

Planetarium information and reservations, 800-455-5897. Weekly fishing reports, 502-924-1340.

Kentucky Free Fishing Days (statewide, on a June weekend), 502-564-4336 for details.

Kentucky Dam Village
State Resort Park

Kentucky Dam Village is one of three state resort parks that "surround" LBL. Located on U.S. Route 641 at the western shore of Kentucky Lake adjacent to Kentucky Dam, it offers a full slate of amenities and recreational opportunities, plus easy access to LBL's northern entrance, the Kentucky Dam State Nongame Wildlife Natural Area, the Barkley Dam Visitors Center with its "Steamboating on the Cumberland" exhibits, and other nearby preserves.

The park is recreation oriented. It has a marina, 18-hole golf course and pro shop, airport with a 4,000-foot paved and lighted landing strip (and its own camping area with rest rooms and showers), four lighted tennis courts, riding stables, miniature golf, swimming beach, paddleboat rentals, lakeshore stage, a 221-site campground with utility hookups and camp store, 72 cottages, and its own "village" with game room, post office, and several shops. Renovation projects at all Kentucky state parks were completed in 1996, giving dining rooms, lodge rooms, cabins and other facilities a fresh look and updated decor.

The "big three" here are fishing, boating, and golf. With Kentucky's largest state park marina on its largest lake, the fishing and boating part is not surprising. The marina offers houseboat, ski boat, pontoon boat, fishing boat, and Sea Doo rentals. Access to Lake Barkley is by the connecting canal just three miles from the marina. A courtesy dock is also provided at the park. Fishing is a year-round attraction here. Largemouth, smallmouth, Kentucky or white bass, plus bluegill, channel or blue catfish, crappie, or sauger will almost certainly go for your bait or lure.

Pick your lake overlook spot. Enjoy the view from a deck at the lodge or in the wild at other places along the shoreline. A swimming beach (where you can rent paddleboats) and adjacent sand volleyball lot have both the lake and Kentucky Dam as a backdrop for activities.

As for golf, a special package available from October through April offers three days, two nights' lodging and two meals a day for a reasonable price.

The park has accommodations to satisfy most preferences, from campsites to a lodge room overlooking the lake, to the Village Green Lodge at the golf course. It has 14 rooms that can be reserved as a unit (making it popular for family reunions). In between are one-, two-, and three-bedroom cottages of varying descriptions, all placed among trees.

The summer season, Memorial Day through Labor Day weekend, offers daily scheduled activities. The stables are open then, too, providing guided trail rides through wooded areas. Some park visitors also take part in the Crappiethon U.S.A. competition on Kentucky and Barkley Lakes from mid-March to mid-May, where catching some of the 2,500 tagged fish can bring a portion of the $50,000 in prizes.

Special events may change from year to year, but some recent ones give clues about what to expect. In January, "Becoming an Outdoorswoman" was a workshop for women, teaching survival skills, goose hunting, and fishing, and included a bald-eagle-watching tour. The park also hosted one of the LBL Eagles Weekends in January, offering both cruise boat and land tours, plus special programs at the park. A Buffalo Dinner and Native American Heritage Day in February had storytelling, weapon demonstrations, music, and crafts. Two crafts-oriented annual events are Crafts in the Village (May) and Good Ole U.S.A. Days (July).

Wildlife Area at the Dam

Even though nature trails and naturalist-led activities aren't provided at this park, just across the dam is the State Nongame Wildlife Natural Area on TVA property managed by the Kentucky Department of Fish and Wildlife Resources. From the park, drive over the dam (at 1⁶⁄₁₀ miles in length, it is the longest dam on the Tennessee River) and look for a sign pointing to the lock and powerhouse. The wildlife viewing area is on a bluff just below the dam, with additional viewing access from within the powerhouse.

I saw clouds of gulls there, three great blue herons, and many fishermen in boats and on the bank. In winter, the gulls number in the thousands. Hundreds of cliff swallows were there, too, gathering mud in their beaks and taking it to build nests on the concrete under the eaves of the dam.

The observation area has a concrete walk with benches and displays that tell about the fish and bird species that can be found. Thousands of ducks and geese winter here, coming from as far away as Hudson Bay. Enter the visitors center inside the powerhouse to learn about the history of the area and how the dam was constructed and enjoy the interactive computerized exhibits on generation of electricity and operation of reservoirs.

Barkley Dam, just a few miles away, is a good place to see Canada geese and learn about life along the Cumberland River in Kentucky and Tennessee in bygone days.

Where: From Interstate 24 east of Paducah, take exit 25 (U.S. Route 62) and go east, then south on U.S. Route 641 to the park's main entrance on the left.

When: Year-round, although village shops, swimming areas, and the miniature golf course are open seasonally.

Admission: Free. Fees charged for golf, camping, miniature golf, horseback riding, and boat rentals.

Amenities: Inn, dining room, lodge, swimming pool and swimming beach, cottages, campground with grocery store and laundry, airport and air camp, golf course, tennis courts, marina, shops, on-site post office, shuffleboard, picnic areas, playgrounds.

Activities: Fishing, boating, swimming, golf, tennis, outdoor games, planned recreation in summer, picnicking.

Special events: Becoming an Outdoorswoman (January), Gathering of Eagles (January), Buffalo Dinner and Native American Heritage Day (February), Crappiethon U.S.A (March), Crafts in the Village (May), Sand Volleyball Coed Classic (June), Good Ole U.S.A. Days (July). Kentucky State Parks special events brochure, 800-255-7275.

Other: Barrier-free access. Special golf package from October through April. Wildlife viewing across dam at Kentucky Dam State Nongame Wildlife Natural Area.

For more information: Kentucky Dam Village State Resort Park, PO Box 69, Gilbertsville, KY 42044-0069. Information, 502-362-4271. Toll-free reservations, 800-325-0146. Fax, 502-362-8747. Eagles Weekend, 502-924-5602.

Kentucky Dam State Nongame Wildlife Natural Area (owned by Tennessee Valley Authority), 502-362-4318 or 502-924-1230.

Resource Manager, Lake Barkley Corps of Engineers, PO Box 218, Grand Rivers, KY 42045, 502-924-5602.

Crappiethon U.S.A (sponsored by America Outdoors), 205-343-8447.

A Livingston County Auto Tour

Lockhart Bluff, Mantle Rock, Birdsville Island, Sanders' Archaeological Site—the names are hints that Livingston County is rich in wild places and history. If you think a tourist information office is an unlikely place to ask about unspoiled country, just talk with Bob Maxwell, director of Kentucky's Western Waterland. Bob also raises buffalo breed stock on a 235-acre farm, and his love of the land is genuine.

The information center is just off Interstate 24 at exit 31 on State 453 next to the Best Western Inn. Bob met me there and took me on a day trip around Livingston County. The southern part of the county is actually an "island" flanked on all four sides by the Cumberland, Tennessee, and Ohio Rivers and a canal that connects the first two.

Our tour took us first to the county seat, Smithland, 17 miles east of Paducah on U.S. Route 60 at the confluence of the Cumberland and Ohio Rivers. Bob pointed out a statue of famed orator Henry Clay that was carved in 1780 from a huge maple tree growing on a bank of the nearby Cumberland. At Smithland Dam just north of town, a bonanza of fishing opportunity awaits, either from a boat or from the bank. Crappie, catfish, white bass, and largemouth bass are caught in Smithland Pool, and tailwater fishing for catfish and striper is good.

"In a lot of places, the tributary creeks come under the highway and are good places to fish, and in some of them, you can go up a couple of miles or more by boat," Bob said.

U.S. Route 60 goes north, then curves eastward toward Burna. The road goes through woods beside Dyer Hill Creek, rounding a series of S-curves. At Burna, we turned right on State 1433, heading for Lockhart Bluff, the highest point in the county. It is on a 2,500-acre tract owned by Westvaco Corporation and open to the public. Hunting is allowed by permit.

"This part of the county has a good flock of wild turkeys and plentiful white-tailed deer, and of course upland game such as quail, woodcocks, squirrels, rabbits, and all kinds of nongame species like songbirds," Bob said.

We passed the old community of Cedar Grove where only a church remains now, then took the next left on an unmarked road that leads to the top of the knob. Westvaco could put a sign here, I thought. Bob's truck handily negotiated the rutted road that climbed through a young pine forest. On top, blackberries were growing in all the open spaces, but pine trees obscured some of the distant views.

"Except for the trees, you could easily see 25 or 30 miles from here," Bob said. "Looking west on a clear day across Illinois and past Paducah, you would see the smokestacks of the steam plant near Metropolis Lake."

It's a good idea to check out the hunting seasons before you visit. We knew turkey hunters would be claiming the top of the knob that day, so we drove back to another lookout point from which we could see the tipple of an old fluorite mine. From 1876 through World War II, Livingston County was one of the largest producers in the state of this mineral, also called fluorspar. Now it is more cost-effective to import the resource.

Four miles east at Salem we turned northwest on State 133 and drove beside cattle and farm ponds in fields surrounded by woods. Black locust trees were covered with cream-colored blossoms, while the dogwoods had lost most of theirs. A big rain had come in during the day and night before, bringing out bullfrogs en masse, as Bob had discovered. When the unexpected happens, you just have to be out in nature at the right time and place to experience it.

It is 10³⁄₁₀ miles from Salem to Joy, near the northern end of Livingston County and close to one of our destinations, Mantle Rock Nature Preserve. If you don't take the side trip to Lockhart Bluff, you can also get to Mantle Rock by turning north off U.S. Route 60 at Burna and following State 135. At Joy, continue another 2²⁄₁₀ miles west on 133. A marker on the south side of the road identifies access to the preserve.

Not much has been published about Mantle Rock. It was donated to The Nature Conservancy by Reynolds Metals after botanists with the Kentucky State Nature Preserves Commission identified some unusual sandstone glades and a number of rare plant species on the property. It also has historical significance, from archaeological sites to its role in the 1830s during the forced relocation of Cherokees to Oklahoma known as the Trail of Tears (which passed through Livingston County).

The arch is an impressive sandstone formation that has a 60-foot-tall "mantle" stone, a 240-foot-long natural arch, and sheer rock cliffs hundreds of feet wide. During the winter of 1838–39, the Cherokees who were being driven were allowed to camp under the arch and the limestone overhangs when ice on the Ohio River rendered a ferry inoperable. Hundreds of them died and were buried at Mantle Rock.

On top of the rock butte is a savanna ecosystem like no other in Kentucky or the surrounding states. There are large moss-covered glades, rare shrubs and grasses, prickly pear cactus, and wind-gnarled cedar trees.

Each nature preserve has its own character that humans do not tamper with. At Mantle Rock, a recent downpour will bring water bubbling from wet springs right on the trail. Prepare to slog if necessary!

A little farther west on State 133 is Mandy Falls, a triple cascade on little McGilligan Creek that would be an ideal picnic area except it is on private property. Low and wide, with the right camera it could look like Niagara.

Continuing the tour, double back from Mantle Rock on State 133 and turn right (southwest) on County Highway 1436, also called Pisgah Road. This takes you along a high bluff that offers scenic views. In early spring and late fall, when trees are not fully leafed, the long views are outstanding. The fall colors, with brilliant yellow hickories and red and yellow maples, can be spectacular.

At the end of the road, we had descended to the Ohio River and its floodplain where ahead were islands in the stream. Turning left on River Road (State 137), we saw a great blue heron standing in a backwater-flooded field. We passed Chip Lake, an oxbow lake similar to Metropolis, formed when it was cut off from the old river channel and now ringed with cypress trees.

Soon Bayou Creek, a tributary to the Ohio, was on our left. It is one of the really good fishing spots that small boats can navigate for two to three miles upstream.

"See the osprey nest on the power pole?" Bob asked.

Sure enough, it was two-thirds of the way up, and an osprey was sitting on it. The power line and osprey nest are just north of Bayou Creek Bridge where the creek empties into the Ohio River.

"This was one of the first osprey nests established when the birds were reintroduced in western Kentucky, and this is one of the fledglings that came back to raise its young," Bob said.

From the power line all the way south past Birdsville to Smithland Dam is the Ohio River Islands Wildlife Management Area, including Birdsville Island, several smaller islands, and a large marsh area. It is owned by the U.S. Army Corps of Engineers and managed by the Kentucky Department of Fish and Wildlife Resources. The WMA has a large herd of deer and an abundance of wild turkeys, raccoons, rabbits, and fox squirrels. Also, large flocks of ducks and Canada geese winter here.

From Bayou to the town of Birdsville, River Road stays close to the Ohio River under a canopy of shade trees. At Birdsville, a Corps of Engineers facility has a boat ramp, wildlife viewing area, picnic sites, rest rooms, and shelters. The best waterfowl activity can be viewed from the Ohio River shore at daybreak between October 15 and March 15 (the refuge is closed during these dates).

Planning your day trip could include being near Knoth's Bar-B-Cue restaurant on U.S. Routes 62/641 in Lake City at lunchtime. Bob called it "the best barbecue in the world." If you like all-lean meat, no gristle, cooked to perfection, and a tantalizing sweet-pungent sauce that's a house secret—well, try it and see.

At the visitors center, new nature facilities opened in 1996. Two self-guided loop nature trails on property owned by Vulcan Materials Company begin at the center. Both are two miles long. One is a footpath with a half-mile handicapped-accessible section, and the other is a paved, eight-foot-wide trail for bicycles. Both go through woods and open areas, past nesting and feeding boxes for wood ducks and bluebirds, and skirt a beaver pond complete with beaver dam. A picnic area and benches for resting are also provided.

From the trails, you can visit the Sanders' Archaeological Site owned by TVA. It preserves and interprets the lives of Native Americans of the Mississippian Period that began a thousand years ago. A short paved path leads uphill in a series of switchbacks to a place where a village compound was located. Visitors can learn about house construction of that period and burial practices of the culture. At the top, we stood surrounded by ground cover in bloom with five-lobed purple flowers one and a half inches in diameter. The site primarily is in a hackberry forest, but one spectacular oak tree was fully five feet in diameter.

Another new facility is a 70-acre nature preserve along State 453 at Interstate 24 across from the visitors center and best viewed from 453. A buffalo herd and some elk are among the first species to be placed within this area.

One end to a perfect day could include viewing the sunset and then taking your famished self and companions to Patti's 1880s Settlement in Grand Rivers. State 453 leads south to both.

A place to stop and do some bank fishing or watch the parade of fishing boats is the Canal Overlook on the north side of the canal, where you will find a large parking lot, stone benches, and steps leading down to the water's edge.

The bridge over the canal is high and arched. Just south of it, turn west onto Kentucky Lake Drive for a scenic loop. The road follows the eastern shore of the lake, rising to hug the edge of a bluff. As the sun turns red and breezes stiffen, find a place to pull off and watch the waves on the lake and all the colors of the sunset reflected there.

Patti's is a restaurant with legendary cuisine, but it's also more: a collection of log-cabin boutiques, a woodland-theme miniature golf course, an animal park and landscaped gardens, and Bill's restaurant with he-man cuisine and nightly live entertainment.

When I ate there, apologizing for the trail dust, it happened to be prom night. In came couple after couple decked in tails and cummerbunds and evening gowns with sequins and beads.

A meal to remember needs food perfectly prepared with the freshest of ingredients (as Patti's does), of course. But it doesn't hurt to have something else, too—I call it true glitz!

Where: From Interstate 24, take exit 31 (at State 453) toward Grand Rivers. Tourist information station is next to Best Western Inn.

When: Year-round for area (some activities seasonal).

Admission: Featured locations are free.

Amenities: Nature preserves have few or no amenities. Others, such as picnic areas, have expected amenities.

Activities: Fishing, boating, wildlife viewing, hiking, hunting, nature study, wildflower viewing, birding, picnicking, photography, scenic auto touring.

Other: Includes barrier-free access locations. If hiking, inquire about hunting seasons and wear appropriate clothing. Caution: water can cover highways near the Ohio River during periods of flooding.

For more information: Kentucky's Western Waterland, Attn: Bob Maxwell, Executive Director, 721 Complex Drive, Route 1, Box 28A, Grand Rivers, KY 42045, 502-928-4411 (information for all locations mentioned).

Pennyrile Forest State Resort Park

About 9 miles south of Dawson Springs, 20 miles northwest of Hopkinsville, and less than an hour east of LBL's northern entrance is Pennyrile Forest State Resort Park. Its name comes from pennyroyal (*Trichostema brachiatum* or False Pennyroyal), a small summer-flowering plant in the mint family that grows prolifically here.

Surrounded by Kentucky's largest state forest, the park offers a secluded, scenic location, newly revamped facilities, and full amenities for a wide variety of activities. For example, the cabin I stayed in was near the lodge, had views of trees with the lake peeking through, and was nicely furnished with practically everything one would have at home. Each site takes advantage of the forest's cool shade and the lake-viewing potential.

The scenery can be enjoyed everywhere: from lakeside cottages; a nine-hole, challenging golf course with many ponds, sand traps, and little hills; a recreation area on Pennyrile Lake with swimming beach, sand volleyball court, picnic shelter, and a boat dock where pedal boats, rowboats, and trolling motors are rented; another shelter (which can be reserved) on a cliff overlooking the lake; and 68 campsites in a modern campground with water and electric hookups, a new bathhouse, a camp store, and an 18-hole miniature golf course.

The park has over five miles of hiking and nature trails that are described in its visitor's guide. The most popular (for its variety and lake views) is the Lake Trail. It is rated difficult because of steep stairs but is otherwise a moderate hike that follows the lake for the most part, going atop a bluff for a time and along the lakeshore in other places. I found rock overhangs, huge boulders with crevices, a spectacular clump of crested dwarf irises right beside the trail, bluets, and many squirrels. I also witnessed a "turkey drama" when some loud gobbles inspired a hen turkey to fly down from its roost in a tree 50 yards away.

The 1¼-mile Cane Trail intersects with the Lake Trail to provide a loop to the lakeshore cottages. It changes elevation, passing through mixed hardwood on an upland forest ridge, some wild cane growing near a stream, and a stand of loblolly pine where reforestation is underway.

The three-quarter-mile Pennyroyal Trail loops off the Lake Trail on the opposite side of the lake and can be hiked as a full loop from the beach/boat dock area. It takes hikers through a variety of forest communities.

Two other trails, each a quarter mile in length, are short but rich in features. Indian Bluffs Trail leads to a natural arch called "Indian Window" and the largest rock overhang in the park. Clifty Creek Trail follows the stream, passing giant sycamores, a small waterfall, and abundant wildflowers and ferns.

For another kind of hike, try the Macedonia Trail in the state forest adjacent to the park.

The Macedonia Trail: Demonstrating Forest Management

The Macedonia Trail is a triple-loop trail in Pennyrile State Forest, part of 413 acres set aside for environmental education. It can be walked as a $1^4/10$-mile single loop, but by adding the second and third loops, the length extends to $2^8/10$ or $3^2/10$ miles. From the trailhead at Macedonia Cemetery on State 398, hikers follow trail markers indicating Loop #1 (blue), Loop #2 (orange), and Loop #3 (yellow).

The first loop leads through loblolly and white pine plantations, along a stream where ferns and mosses grow and red spotted salamanders may be seen. In the lower elevations, look for white-tailed deer, prairie warblers, indigo buntings, squirrels, and groundhogs. On higher ground along dry ridges and protected coves, look for oaks and hickories, gray and fox squirrels, and wild turkeys. Play the forester's role at one of the markers and decide which trees should stay and which should be harvested according to your management scheme. At a pond, learn about placement of water sources for wildlife management.

Loop #2 continues the demonstration of forestry practices in oak and hickory timber and teaches about destructive plants, erosion control, how animals use natural features as habitat, and how exposure to sun affects soil formation.

Loop #3 demonstrates other issues of forest management and the value of animal-friendly plants like lespedeza, bluestem, blackberry, sumac, sassafras, dogwood, and oaks.

Nearby Lake Beshear, managed by the Kentucky Department of Fish and Wildlife Resources, offers fishing and boating. It is adjacent to the west boundary of the park and only four miles from the park inn.

It rained the night before I left, and as I drove away I was aware of how it "rains twice" in the forest. Drops that land on leaves collect there awhile before falling to the ground with loud plopping sounds. Eventually, you have a dual rain shower. The delay can sometimes allow unprepared hikers to get to shelter in a race that's just part of the excitement of being in the woods on a rainy day!

Where: From the Western Kentucky Parkway, take exit 24 and go south on State 109 past Dawson Springs, then west on State 398 (the entrance road). From Hopkinsville, take State 109 north for approximately 20 miles, then west at park entrance (State 398).

When: Year-round. Campground open March 15 through October 31. Boating, April 16 through October 31. Swimming, Memorial Day through Labor Day. Playgrounds and picnic grounds open March 1 through December.

Admission: Free. Fees for boat rentals and golf.

Amenities: Lodge, restaurant, gift shop, meeting rooms, cottages, modern campground, nine-hole golf, miniature golf, pedal boat and rowboat rentals, athletic courts, picnic sites and shelters, playgrounds.

Activities: Camping, hiking, photography, wildlife viewing, fishing, boating, swimming, golf, miniature golf, tennis, picnicking, sand volleyball, daily planned recreation in summer.

Special events: Wildflower Weekend (April), Forest 5K Run (July), Folk Heritage Weekend (September), Fall Photography Weekend (October). Kentucky State Parks special events brochure, 800-255-7275.

Other: Barrier-free access. Shelter reservations available up to one year in advance. Motors not allowed on Pennyrile Lake. Marina at nearby Lake Beshear. Trails are maintained in "natural condition" and close at dusk. Pennyrile Forest has additional trails.

For more information: Pennyrile Forest State Resort Park, 20781 Pennyrile Lodge Road, Dawson Springs, KY 42408-9212. Information, 502-797-3421. Reservations, 800-325-1711. Fax, 502-797-3413.

Kenlake State Resort Park

When faced with a choice of resort parks in close proximity, as is the case near LBL, how do you make that decision? In all

4

`2

Kentucky resort parks, visitors can expect modern accommodations and a wide array of recreational offerings. The answer may come down to location, facilities, or activities that are more appealing.

Of course, there *are* differences!

Kenlake, at the western shore of Kentucky Lake just off U.S. Route 68 near the small town of Aurora, draws many of its visitors from Illinois, Ohio, Missouri, and Tennessee.

"The lake is the big draw," said park manager Bill Hainsworth. "But once visitors come here, it's our super staff that makes the difference. They're the best I've had in my career."

He gave me a guided tour of the 2,500-acre park on a cool Saturday. The park has four distinct activity areas. The Bay View Picnic Area and Tennis Center (a year-round facility) is on a shoreline peninsula. It has many picnic shelters and a large amphitheater. Across Ledbetter Bay is the marina, which has more than 200 slips and a launching ramp. Across U.S. Route 68 in a secluded spot is a camping area with 92 sites and full amenities such as utility hookups, playground, dump station, and a central service building with rest rooms, laundry facilities, and vending machines. The hotel-and-cottages complex facing another bay is a place to enjoy the beauties of nature and of professionally landscaped gardens. People who have mobility challenges will appreciate the elevators and the easy access to dining, gift shopping, and indoor activities. Swimming, golf, and tennis areas are nearby, as is a playground.

All months of the year have their own special appeal. I visited in April. For fishing, this was the height of crappie season. At the marina, Sea Doos were the hot rental item. For birders, it was prime time for watching thousands of goldfinches. Photographers had gathered for a three-day nature photography workshop. And picnickers—well, some would have to wait until after the wedding to use Lakeview Shelter, which was being readied for an afternoon ceremony.

Daffodils gaily surrounded tree trunks along the main drive. Kenlake has the distinction of having a professional horticulturist and its own greenhouse.

"Paul Murphy likes to sneak plants in wherever he can," said Bill. "The dogwoods were gorgeous this year, and later, we'll have begonias, wildflowers, daisies, impatiens, and azaleas. You just missed the tulips in the woods."

Tulips in the woods?

"We broadcast them, toss them among the trees, and they bloom there. I've wanted a guy like Paul all my career."

Two nature loop trails go through gardens and wooded areas. Cherokee Trail, a ⁷⁄₁₀-mile loop, is accessible from the hotel parking lot or from the marina access road. Chickasaw Trail begins at the Bay View area and forms a loop but also connects with the Cherokee Trail. If the two are walked in a figure eight configuration, the total is about 1½ miles. Deer and squirrels are plentiful here, and foxes, raccoons, and coyotes are sometimes seen.

It's a toss-up as to whether it's cooler in January or August at Kenlake when you consider the very "cool" Hot August Blues & Barbeque Festival, Kenlake's biggest annual event. It draws several thousand people to the park amphitheater by the lakeshore to hear the likes of Ko Ko Taylor, Gatemouth Brown, Honeyboy Edwards, and the ever-popular Unknown Blues Band.

Where: On U.S. Route 68 (west of Hopkinsville and southeast of Paducah) at the western shore of Kentucky Lake.
When: Year-round. Marina store, daily 6:00 A.M. to 7:00 P.M. Pro shop, March through November. Campground, April 1 through October 31. Indoor tennis center, October 1 through April 15. Swimming, Memorial Day through Labor Day.
Admission: Free. Fees charged for golf, camping, indoor tennis courts, and some events.

Amenities: Campground; nine-hole golf course; marina with fishing, pontoon, ski boat, and wave runner rentals; outdoor swimming pool; indoor/outdoor tennis courts; outdoor basketball courts; game room; dining room; gift shop; meeting rooms; nature trails; picnic area; pavilions.

Activities: Camping, hiking, wildlife and wildflower viewing, photography, wind surfing, boating, fishing, swimming, tennis, golf, daily planned recreation in summer.

Special events: Eagles Weekend (February), Nature Photography Workshop (April), Arts & Crafts Festival (June), Hot August Blues & Barbeque Festival (August), Aurora Country Festival (October). Kentucky State Parks special events brochure, 800-255-7275.

Other: Barrier-free access. Senior citizen discounts for 62 and over; accommodations free for 16 and under and Kentucky POWs; reservations available one year in advance.

For more information: Kenlake State Resort Park, 542 Kenlake Road, Hardin, KY 42048. Information, 502-474-2211. Reservations, 800-325-0143. Fax, 502-474-2018. Fishing Hotline and Eagles Weekend, 502-924-5602.

National Scouting Museum

Memories are sure to surface when adults visit the National Scouting Museum (NSM) in Murray. For former Scouts, it is a pleasure to recall the days of Scouting and a first camping experience. The Norman Rockwell illustrations from the *Saturday Evening Post* and Boy Scouts of America (BSA) publications depicting the goodness and patriotism of being American and of being a Scout during World War II render a different nostalgia. For the younger set, coming here is a sure way to build valuable memories for the future.

From Kenlake State Resort Park, the museum is just 15 miles away via State 94. From U.S. Route 641 in Murray, turn west on Chestnut (just south of the Murray State University stadium) and south on 16th Street, then right on Calloway to the museum parking lot on the left. The museum is on the east side of 16th Street, a very short walk. Also, a loading area at the museum entrance allows dropping off passengers.

Kids have fun here from the moment they are greeted inside by Murray the Robot, who offers to sing a funny song, do something funny, or ask a funny question. It sets the mood for interactive participation in all areas of the two-story facility where visitors learn about BSA and the organization's history.

Kiosks on the entrance level are viewing stations for videos that play programs on demand. Some of these bring history to life, as in newsreel footage of BSA service projects during World War II. Others show Boy Scout commercials from the 1950s or world-famous people who were Scouts. Still others are more interactive, posing dilemmas that we help solve or asking our opinion on important Scouting issues.

The Trading Post (gift shop) is full of Scouting merchandise and memorabilia. It has gift items with BSA or NSM logos, including mugs, T-shirts, sweatshirts, neckerchiefs, hatpins, and patches. Readers and art lovers can select books and pamphlets (including Bill Hillcourt's *Baden-Powell: The Two Lives of a Hero*, about the BSA founder) and Norman Rockwell art prints.

This level also has a large Scoutaround Theater and changing exhibits. A recent one, "Scouting Illustrator," emphasized how illustration has been a Scouting tradition since the days when the founders all personally illustrated the books they wrote. On display was the cover illustration from the first patrol leader's handbook, plus others produced over several decades.

A canteen area has snack and soda machines, and it is okay to bring a sack lunch.

Going downstairs is a trip backwards in time to the beginning of BSA on February 8, 1910. Lighted signs announce each decade as we descend. In an area called "The Beginnings," animated life-size figures of four founders carry on a lively discussion around a campfire. In another area a storyteller entertains with a Native American legend, the rollicking spoof called "Rinderceller," and other tales. The maze is very popular. Kids can go through it by following directions or using a compass, but they have to watch out for a rattlesnake and a rampaging grizzly bear.

Two interactive theaters ask the audience to control the story by deciding what the on-screen characters should do. In the Values Theater, a movie called *You Decide* places emphasis on doing the right thing, and in the Patrol Theater, the object of the movie is to help find a lost child.

Other areas exhibit Scout uniforms worn during a period of nearly 90 years, show "A World of Brothers" (the international emphasis of Scouting), and feature celebrities who endorse Scouting. Homage is paid to the early leaders, telling of their interests and the impact each made.

D. C. "Uncle Dan" Beard (1850–1940) was a particularly colorful character who was photographed around 1935 wearing a buckskin jacket and a BSA campaign hat. He wrote *The Boy Pioneers: Sons of Daniel Boone* and said: "I kept thinking of Kit Carson, Davy Crockett, Daniel Boone. I was sure every American boy would feel the same thrill if he could regard himself as part of the history of our country."

The "Spirit of America" illustration collection and the Norman Rockwell Gallery of original illustrations are impressive. This is the second-largest collection in the world, with more than 60 of Rockwell's original works. They tell the tale of

Scouting and chronicle Americana over a remarkable span of years, from 1913 to 1976.

One of the most popular areas of the museum is Gateway Park, the outdoor ropes and teams course; and it's not just for Scouts but for anyone 7 years or older (11 years for the high ropes course). Bystanders gather as the youngsters test their courage and skills by crawling on hands and knees over a rope bridge high in the air and mastering the other course challenges. A small extra fee is charged to use the course, and groups need to make reservations.

Here's another tip: if you're in Murray at dinner time, and want some good seafood, try the Seafood Express Restaurant.

Where: Murray State University campus in Murray. From U.S. Route 641, west on Chestnut, south on 16th, and west on Calloway to parking lot on left. From Interstate 24 east of Paducah, exit on Purchase Parkway to exit 41 (U.S. Route 641), then south to Murray.

When: March 1 through November 30. Tuesday through Saturday, 9:00 A.M. to 4:30 P.M.; Sunday 12:30 to 4:30 P.M. Closed Mondays, Thanksgiving Day, and Easter Sunday. Gateway Park (ropes courses) open same schedule June 1 through Labor Day and weekends only in April, May, September, and October.

Admission: Modest fees based on ages. Group rates and discounts for seniors, Scouts, and Scouters. Additional fee for Gateway Park participation.

Amenities: Museum with interactive features, Norman Rockwell Gallery of original art, gift shop, snack area, ropes courses for ages seven and up, free parking.

Activities: Active viewing/learning/puzzle-solving displays and games, storytelling, ropes challenge course.

Special events: Rockwell Country Fair (October), Jamboree-on-the-Air (October). Ask about others.

Other: Barrier-free access. Chewing gum is not allowed.
For more information: National Scouting Museum, 1 Murray Street, Murray, KY 42071-3313, 502-762-3383.

Murray Tourism Commission, 805 North 12th Street, PO Box 190, Murray, KY 42071, 502-753-5171.

Woods & Wetlands Wildlife Center at Cadiz

Once upon a time, there was a barber in Cadiz named Harold Knight who was also an accomplished woodsman. He had learned to mimic the animals of the forest and knew of their ways. This led him to start inventing and manufacturing sportsmen's game calls. Word got around, and soon he had to get a bigger mailbox to hold all the orders that were coming in. After a while, he quit barbering and built a business called Knight & Hale Game Calls. The business expanded, and Harold and his partner, David Hale, became known all over the world. In 1994, they opened a wildlife center dedicated to "conservation, education, and appreciation of our natural world."

This story almost sounds like a fairy tale, but it is real. The Woods & Wetlands Wildlife Center is evolving but is already impressive. It is professionally managed to help educate the public and school groups about the habits and needs of the region's wild creatures.

Interior displays include an aquarium and serpentarium. One tank holds stream fishes collected locally, and a 12,000-gallon aquarium has all the game-fish species native to

Barkley and Kentucky Lakes, including (when I visited) an eight-pound largemouth bass, some striped bass, bluegill, carp, crappie, drum, spoonbills, flathead catfish, blue catfish, gar, and 25 others. Even the rocks, weighing up to five tons each, are real.

The serpentarium, with its "natural-look" desert vignettes under glass, has more than 40 species of live North American reptiles and amphibians—snakes, alligators, salamanders, crocodiles, and turtles from Texas, Arizona, Arkansas, California, Florida, and other states.

Curator Steve Scott pointed to a diamondback rattlesnake. "If you were to see this snake in the wild, it would be around sand and rocks, so we have landscaped the exhibit to look like a natural habitat. The sign explains what kind of snake, the counties in which it is found, what it eats, and whether it is poisonous or not. It also gives both the scientific and the common name, which will often relate to a feature of the animal's appearance."

Snakes and Crocodiles:
Some Questions Answered

Questions are always welcome at the Center, and the staff receives many of them from the school groups. Curator Steve Scott has a special interest in reptiles. His responses to often-asked questions in this area might include these observations:

"The water snakes are popular with visitors, since they are non-venomous and are seen around here, especially around the lakes. It is easy to distinguish them from a poisonous snake like a copperhead, which they resemble.

"The eyes of nonpoisonous snakes have a round pupil. Also, the poisonous snakes in this area are pit vipers, having a pit between the nostril and the eye which is a heat sensor. The nonpoisonous snakes don't have that pit.

"We also demonstrate the difference between an American alligator and an American crocodile, which is an endangered species that lives in brackish swamps in Florida. The wild population is down to about a thousand. Our crocodile is a baby, but by comparing them you can see that the crocodile has a very narrow, long-looking mouth while the alligator's mouth is as wide as its head. Also, on the crocodile, the third tooth on the bottom jaw protrudes outside the top jaw when the mouth is closed, but this is not so with the alligator."

Hmmm. I suppose I could check this out in the wild when the mouth is closed!

Behind the Center is a 400-acre wildlife park with natural habitats provided for mammals and perching stations for birds of prey. The animals have either been injured or imprinted in some way (handled by people) and can't survive on their own in the wild. The mammals are captive-grown animals from populations in zoos; and the birds were all injured or orphaned. It is illegal to catch a wild animal and display it, thereby robbing it of its natural way of life.

"You can't go out and catch a bird just to put it in a cage," said Steve. "We're not taking these animals' lives away but are actually saving them."

Among the 20 or so birds of prey species are a great horned owl, saw-whet owl, American kestrel, sparrow hawk (actually not a hawk at all but a true falcon), red-tailed hawk, Swainson's hawk (the only bird of prey that migrates from Canada to Argentina), and goshawk (a favorite of falconers, according to Steve).

I almost missed seeing the saw-whet owl. It is very rarely seen—and no wonder, since there aren't very many and it is the smallest owl species in the world. Fully grown, it is about four inches tall.

The education aspect is very important at Woods & Wetlands.

"We show schoolchildren why animals have certain body parts. Like the snake's tongue—what does it do? And the feathers on a bird of prey are not to keep it warm but to make it silent in flight," said Steve.

Other facts might surprise us. Prairie dogs are really ground squirrels. Raccoons are unpredictable and can be very dangerous. The opossum is a marsupial, like a kangaroo. The striped skunk doesn't have stripes when it is born. The silver fox and gray fox are color phases of the red fox; and gray foxes like to climb.

"The silver fox is beautiful," I commented. "Four white feet and a white tip on his tail."

"Yes, I agree," Steve replied. "He's one of the red foxes, of course, found in Canada."

Coyotes, cougars, bobcats, white-tailed deer (including some big trophy bucks), black-phase timber wolves, black bear, and beaver are also visible here, but eagles can only be held in captivity in a government-run or nonprofit organization facility.

A picnic pavilion is provided, so why not make a day of it? We can also purchase food to feed the animals and even buy a souvenir of the day in the gift shop.

Where: U.S. Route 68 west of Cadiz and a half mile east of Lake Barkley State Resort Park. From Interstate 24, take exit 65 (west of Hopkinsville) and go west past Cadiz on U.S. Route 68.

When: Year-round. Daily, 9:00 A.M. to 6:00 P.M. April 1 through September 30. Winter hours are Tuesday through Friday, 9:00 A.M. to 3:00 P.M.; Saturday, 10:00 A.M. to 4:00 P.M.; Sunday, 1:00 to 5:00 P.M. Closed Mondays.

Admission: Modest fee for ages 6 to 12 and over 12; very inexpensive annual pass.

Amenities: Aquarium, serpentarium, birds-of-prey exhibit, wildlife park, gift shop, picnic area.

Activities: Wildlife viewing, animal feeding, photography, picnicking.

Other: Barrier-free access.

For more information: Woods & Wetlands Wildlife Center, 5732 Canton Road, Cadiz, KY 42211, 502-924-9107.

Cadiz-Trigg County Tourist Commission, PO Box 735, Cadiz, KY 42211, 502-522-3892.

Lake Barkley State Resort Park

This park may be the best known of the western Kentucky resort parks due to its national reputation. It was the only Kentucky state park to win the AAA's four-diamond award in 1992 and was named by *Money* magazine as one of the 12 best state parks in the nation.

Motorists traveling Interstate 24 through the state cannot fail to notice the signs at exit 65. In the LBL area, Lake Barkley SRP is the only state park on that lake (but technically, it is on a cove of the impounded waters of Little River, a Barkley tributary and three-quarters of a mile from the main body of the lake).

Though fully developed, Barkley has a sense of vastness and seclusion, since the activity areas are spaced widely among the park's 3,600 wooded acres that include a nature preserve.

Barkley Lodge sits on a high, rounded peninsula and is oriented to the site in a semicircular configuration so that each lodge room looks directly onto the water. In the center is the massive dining hall built of western cedar, Douglas fir, and glass. It has an excellent cuisine and a relaxing ambiance, with live music provided during dinner hours. The lodge has many game rooms and areas and, as you would expect, a gift shop well stocked with Kentucky craft items.

In front of the lodge is a floating dock where boats can tie up for two hours. The park marina is visible from here. It has rental pontoon boats, fishing boats, ski boats, paddleboats, and wave runners.

Along the shore, a wide concrete walkway encourages bank fishing. At one end is a kiddie playground and the trailhead of the seven-tenths-mile Lena Madesin Phillips Memorial Trail, a nature loop that offers scenic lake views and a swinging bridge. It also provides access to the 1²/10-mile Wilderness Trail that leads to the stables and the two-mile Cedar Grove Trail that ends at the beach area.

Fishing can be very good.

Two fishermen passed by the lodge carrying rods and bait. One was saying, "This was the biggest crappie I've ever seen. I've seen some that were 14 inches long, but this was a monster! They were jumping all over the place!"

"Monster Crappie at Barkley." It sounded like the next day's headline to me.

A convention center near the lodge seats up to 1,000 people theater style and 500 banquet style. It's also a place for special dances like the Barkley Bash and Sweetheart Weekend.

Among the premier facilities at Barkley is the Fitness Center, which is open year-round and has Nautilus equipment, free weights, stationary bikes, treadmills, tanning beds, whirlpool, steam room, sauna, a racquetball court, an open area where aerobics, exercise, and country line dance classes are taught and, outside, two lighted tennis courts.

Little River Lodge is an annex to the main lodge that accommodates groups of 20 to 25 people and is popular for family reunions. The 1⁷⁄₁₀-mile Blue Springs Trail starts from the main park drive across from Barkley Lodge, goes toward the Little River Lodge, and winds down to the bottoms near the lake across a field from the fitness center. Seasonally, the field is a solid yellow mass of blooming butterweed.

On a ridge about a quarter-mile from the main lodge are cottages that overlook Blue Spring Bay and others in a wooded area. All have two bedrooms, fully equipped kitchens, and porches, and some have wood-burning fireplaces.

Barkley is the only state park that has a trap range, according to park manager John Rufli, who said, "It's a good opportunity for people to experience using a shotgun under a very controlled and supervised situation. We're limited to shotgun only and teach the basics of safe gun operation and use, and instruct in the finer points of trap shooting as a sport. We have no age limits as long as the person can handle a shotgun in a safe manner. A range officer is on site whenever it is open, and we provide guns and sell shells. The clay targets are the only fee that is required of everyone."

Golf is one of Barkley's most consistent year-round draws. The golf package offered during winter and early spring attracts people from colder states like Michigan and Wisconsin. The 18-hole golf course is one of the best in western Kentucky. Though fairly flat, it has challenging holes with sand traps and ponds. Behind the pro shop is Blue Spring, which feeds into Blue Spring Bay. It has become an attraction due to the stocked rainbow trout in it.

Barkley's lighted airstrip, 4,800 feet long and 120 feet wide, handles small corporate-type jets and some of the larger twin-engine planes up to around 20-passenger capacity. It is open 24 hours a day. Free services include tie-down, overnight parking, and complimentary transportation within the park.

Other facilities include riding stables (open daily from Memorial Day through Labor Day and on weekends during the rest of September); a full-featured campground with 78 paved campsites; public picnic areas with pavilions, rest rooms, and large grills; and a swimming beach that is open Memorial Day through Labor Day and has lifeguards on duty, a bathhouse, a picnic area, and a sand volleyball court.

It is the wonderful natural spaces among all these facilities, though, that are most impressive to nature enthusiasts. On a drive to the airstrip, notice where beavers have impounded a little creek, making a wetlands habitat. Rows of turtles lie on logs; wood ducks and other waterfowl, muskrats, and many more creatures are drawn to this watering hole. The beavers were building a secondary dam below the existing one. John explained that the beaver dams here provide habitat for aquatic life and also form a natural filtration process for runoff water, which helps reduce pollution problems in the lakes downstream.

Early morning and late afternoon are usually the best times to see wildlife in the park. The wildlife population includes large numbers of deer, plus wild turkeys, rabbits, raccoons, opossums, skunks, foxes, and other small mammals, plus songbirds, reptiles, and amphibians. Bobcats are present, though they are elusive and rarely seen.

"We're trying to maintain a diversity of habitat and wildlife and plant life," John said. "We think one of our purposes is to have a broad spectrum of environments and habitats. We have large lakes, smaller wetlands, small streams, springs, open fields—some grown up with coarse and brushy plant life and others mowed regularly to keep them in grasslands—and the forest. It gives an opportunity to see and actually compare these different plant communities and enjoy the associated animal life that goes with them."

Getting There: Fly, Drive, or Paddle Your Canoe!

Another way to reach Lake Barkley State Resort Park (and get in a little camping on the way) is by a scenic Class I float on the Little River or in combination with its Muddy Fork Branch. (Class is an indicator of river difficulty.) From the Muddy Fork, put in at John King Road near Interstate 24 (the road loops off State 139 north of Cadiz) for a 12½-mile run or at State 139 or State 778 for a 9-mile or 7-mile float, respectively. The upper portion is runnable generally from late fall to midsummer. To float the 15½-mile Little River Canoe Trail in its entirety, begin at State 272 off State 139 south of Cadiz. The upper six miles can be run usually from November to mid-July. The portion below Cadiz is floatable year-round.

In either case, you can continue past Barkley Lodge for another mile and take out at the end of State 778 on the shore of Lake Barkley.

The canoe trail route is perhaps a little more scenic as it winds through some old-growth forest. It is also recommended as very appropriate for a family outing.

For more information: *A Canoeing and Kayaking Guide to the Streams of Kentucky*, by Bob Sehlinger, Menasha Ridge Press, 3169 Cahaba Heights Road, Birmingham, AL 35343, 1994. Paper.

Where: U.S. Route 68 west of Cadiz. From Interstate 24, take exit 65 (west of Hopkinsville) and go west past Cadiz on U.S. Route 68, then north on State 1489 (look for billboard).

When: Year-round. Restaurant serves Monday through Saturday from 7:00 to 10:30 A.M., 11:30 A.M. to 2:30 P.M., and 5:00 to 9:00 P.M. and Sunday (buffet style) from noon until 9:00 P.M. Fitness center open daily (8:00 A.M. through 9:00 P.M. Monday through Friday and until 4:30 P.M. Saturday and Sunday).

Admission: Free. Fees for camping, fitness center (ages 13 and up), golf, trap supplies, and some picnic shelters. Senior discounts (as at all Kentucky state parks).

Amenities: Lodge/swimming pool, gift shop, conference center, cottages, campground, marina, fitness center, 18-hole golf course, tennis courts, airport, trap range, hiking trails, stables, picnic shelters, playgrounds, public beach.

Activities: Fishing, hiking, camping, swimming, golf, tennis, trap shooting, riding, boating, photography, wildlife viewing, outdoor games, picnicking. Daily planned recreation in summer conducted by naturalists and recreation specialists.

Special events: Eagles Weekend (February), Spring Bike Tour (April), Fabulous 5K Run (October), many fitness-center-sponsored events. Kentucky State Parks special events brochure, 800-255-7275.

Other: Barrier-free access. For water conditions on floating the Little River call the Cadiz Police Department, 502-522-3305.

For more information: Lake Barkley State Resort Park, Box 790, Cadiz, KY 42211-0790. Information, 502-924-1131. Reservations, 800-325-1708. Eagles Weekend, 502-924-5602.

Lake Barkley Marina, PO Box 1889, Cadiz, KY 42211-1889, 502-924-9954.

Cadiz/Trigg County Tourist Commission, PO Box 735, Cadiz, KY 42211, 502-522-3892. (Ask about the Cadiz railroad trail.)

Resource Manager, Lake Barkley Corps of Engineers, PO Box 218, Grand Rivers, KY 42045, 502-924-5602. (Little River Canoe Trail information.)

4

In and Around
Owensboro

Except for some coal trucks on the highways heading for
Ohio River ports, travelers along U.S. Route 60 from
Paducah to Owensboro would hardly suspect that this part of
the state is in the Western Kentucky Coalfield. This geologic
region is shaped generally like a bowl but has a rolling-to-
hilly interior and a ring of knobs, sandstone cliffs, and rocky,
narrow valleys around the outer edge. The Ohio River is Kentucky's border to the north, though the bowl extends past it
into neighboring states. Adding to the scenic interest is Rough
Creek Fault, a trenchlike depression 1 to 5 miles wide and
sometimes 300 feet deep. It bisects the region for 80 miles or
so, from west of Morganfield to the vicinity of the Falls of
Rough (one of this book's featured locations).

The 5,400-acre Higginson-Henry WMA just southeast of
Morganfield on State 56 is an interesting place. The WMA's
Lake Mauzy (a mecca for local fishermen) is an 80-acre jewel
in the woods, formed by an earthen dam. A campground is
nearby, and the WMA has miles of roads and hiking trails to
satisfy hikers, birders, and other wildlife watchers.

Owensboro exudes a "can do" spirit that shows up in many
ways. The fresh and new coexist nicely with the revered and

traditional elements of this city, whose motto is "Life Without Limits." That feeling is expressed in quality-of-life insti-
tutions and activities.

As in so many Kentucky towns and cities, the river is a
constant presence, a flowing backdrop that draws people to it.
Like babies, rivers can steal scenes simply by being there.

I think of the Ohio River here as it appeared from a window high above. It had rained the night before, leaving misty
gray skies. Flats loaded with railroad cars were being pushed
upstream. The barges' measured pace amid a kaleidoscopic
darting of gulls and swallows was a strange juxtaposition. At
any rate, there's something hauntingly romantic about a gray
river morning viewed from a cozy room.

For more information: Owensboro Tourist Commission, 326
Saint Elizabeth, Owensboro, KY 42301, 800-489-1131 or 502-
926-1100.

Owensboro Area Museum of Science and History

This museum's new building (opened in May 1995) is a focal
point for Owensboro's look at the past. Finally—and just in
time for its 30th birthday in 1996—it had the space to show
in innovative ways the area's natural and cultural history and
developments of the industrial age.

A life-size fossil cast of a mammoth skeleton commands
the high-ceilinged museum lobby. Surrounding this reminder
of the ancient past are larger-than-life historic photos from
the 1800s and other exhibits from that era.

National touring exhibits related to history, science, and

nature are always popular attractions. They are changed periodically. Of special interest to kids is a 1926 pump engine, part of a historical firefighters collection on display. Young "firefighters" can climb up into it, sit behind the wheel, and ring the clanging bell.

In fact, this museum is very much a children's place—especially in an area called Encounter that is full of hands-on participatory science exhibits. Even the two-year-olds have fun in their very own space, the Toddler Tunnel.

I saw some of this action as a group of preschoolers came in, each holding a knot on a long rope as they crossed the street and entered the building. Excitedly, they went from place to place, to play with optical illusions, a parabola created by mirrors, air currents that keep a ball aloft, magnets, and a host of other fascinating scientific "games."

Betty Brewer, the museum's executive director, explained what the museum would ultimately hold, since it was being readied for opening when I visited. Ultimately, two stories will be fully utilized and will include a planetarium.

"Our focus is the Ohio River Valley in Western Kentucky. The subject matter ranges from natural history—broad categories such as animals that lived here and their extinction, paleontology, geology, and the environment—to all of the sciences: biological, physical, and chemical. Historically, we cover from 12,000 years ago up to today," said Betty.

This museum is a leader in incorporating live dramatic presentations in its approach. "Dramaworks" involves teenagers in the collaborative effort between the museum and the Theater Workshop of Owensboro's Youth Theater. Student performers follow scripts that are keyed to a particular exhibit as they play the roles of characters from history. Several performances are scheduled through the summer months, though not daily.

"Museums have just begun to catch on to interrelating theater arts with other programming," said Betty. "We've talked with groups in Cincinnati and Minneapolis who do similar programs."

The youth volunteer group is also involved in daily science demonstrations in summer, which take place at the museum store. Other demonstrations are of skilled craftsmanship. Visitors watch artisans make brooms, pottery, and baskets and weave on a 19th-century loom. Many for-sale items are actually made on the premises or by the craftspeople who do the demonstrations.

A popular annual event is "Day of the Dinosaur," traditionally the last Saturday of June. Special exhibits and activities take place at the museum, with additional fun at a park a block away. Relay races, "painting your own snake," and digging for fossils and minerals are just a few of the activities in a day that starts at 10:00 A.M. and ends at 3:00 P.M. Best of all, it's affordable, with some sessions free and others with nominal fees, from 50 cents to a dollar.

Other annual events, many of them art oriented, are held in collaboration with Owensboro organizations.

Where: 220 Daviess Street in downtown Owensboro.
When: Year-round. Monday through Saturday, 10:00 A.M. to 5:00 P.M.; Sunday, 1:00 to 4:00 P.M. Closed New Year's Day, July 4, Thanksgiving, and Christmas Day.
Admission: Free.
Amenities: Theme exhibit areas, planetarium, gift shop.
Activities: Viewing exhibits, interactive activities, science and crafts demonstrations, scheduled "Dramaworks" programs.
Special events: Day of the Dinosaur (last Saturday in June). Request a calendar of events for others.
Other: Barrier-free access.
For more information: Owensboro Area Museum of Science and History, 220 Daviess Street, Owensboro, KY 43202, 502-683-0296.

Panther Creek and Yellow Creek Parks

Wherever a park has an outstanding nature program, it is a given that an outstanding individual or group has been the impetus. So it is with Panther Creek and Yellow Creek Parks, administered by the Daviess County Parks and Recreation Department. Both parks have exemplary nature centers, and the Panther Creek Nature Trail was the first in the nation to receive an Enjoy Outdoors America award by the U.S. Department of the Interior (in 1993), while that park's nature center received the 1991 Governor's Award for Excellence for handicapped accessibility.

Park naturalist Joe Ford can take much of the credit. He is a legendary figure in Owensboro for starting the Owensboro Area Museum of Science and History, directing the facility for 21 years, and promoting knowledge of the natural sciences. The two Daviess County parks bear the stamp of this man's dedication. If you can schedule it, catch one of his talks on herpetology, ornithology, botany, local history, or folklore or join him on one of the park trails.

Panther Creek Park

This park is about five miles southwest of Owensboro in a rural area. It has ample acreage for outdoor recreation and hiking. Facilities include picnic shelters and a six-acre lake (with footbridge crossing) for viewing and feeding waterfowl and fishing for bass, bluegill, and catfish (but age restrictions apply).

An outstanding feature in the ball-diamond area is the solar-powered lighted fountain and waterfall in a base of creek stones that are embedded with fossils. It is one of more than 20,000 solar pumps worldwide. Nearby is a blacktop path with information stops where you can take a baseball quiz and identify trees, then check your answers.

The nature center provides 1⁴/₁₀ miles of elevated wooden walkways in a crisscross configuration over wetlands through which Clear Creek flows. At the center is a 30-seat pavilion, Nature's Lair, used for workshops and nature talks. Coated wire fencing assures safety for small children and wheelchair passengers. Throughout the park, 40 species of trees are marked, 28 of them in the nature preserve. More than 100 species of birds have been seen here, and the nature guidebook names 18 small mammals also observed. More than 50 varieties of wildflowers that are present seasonally are named. The lists are not complete but are provided to encourage visitors to observe and identify what they see.

Lists don't really tell the tale or give the sense of nature that you only get firsthand. They don't convey the seclusion a visitor feels among the old-growth trees or whether nature's colors today are subtle or intense.

A sign at the beginning of the boardwalk is a dedication to "The grain of the wood, music of the birds, whisper of the wind, fragrance of the woodlands, voices in the mist, dances of streams, mystery, wonder, awe of nature's fancy, unlocking our heart, freeing our imagination. Enjoy."

The mile-long Trail of Dreams follows Panther Creek, with access from the end of Sycamore Hill Trail (one of the boardwalk segments). Pass a demonstration wetland water-treatment project that uses aquatic plants to sanitize waste water, then hike to a ridge top flanked by woods on one side. The other side overlooks ball fields, playgrounds, and the natural landscaping created by wildflowers. An alternative access route from below offers a barrier-free concrete ramp leading up to a trailside viewing area. This Trail of Dreams leads to a lookout tower for even better views.

Yellow Creek Park

This park, east of Owensboro, divides its focus between ball fields and recreational sports and nature appreciation. A preserve has over four miles of hiking trails. The park also has a cross-country training course and plenty of picnic sites and open areas. Be sure to stop in the office and ask for a brochure.

The past is remembered here. At the entrance to the preserve is an iron bridge dating from the early 1800s. Two other reminders are the two covered bridges along the trail that are good vantage points for secret watching of wildlife. Curious-looking stone benches and tables are made from old limestone slabs of pre–Civil War vintage, and an old forest lookout tower was restored in 1960.

Trails are color coded: red for the Lookout Trail, blue for the Adventure Trail, and green for the Hidden Valley Trail. At the beginning, a concrete path allows barrier-free access to an observation deck overlooking Yellow Creek and goes on to a pavilion and rest rooms (the yellow-coded Challenge Trail).

Yellow Creek flows through the center of the preserve, where cascading waterfalls, small ponds, and varied terrain add interest to a nature walk. Some of the unusual features are an old cistern, a suspension bridge, an earthen dam, bald-cypress trees around a turtle pond, and old stone steps.

We see fields, too, and a dairy barn built about 1900. Around it are pecan and walnut trees. Old-growth specimens are impressive—a tall tulip poplar straight as an arrow, a giant oak, and two very mature, smooth-barked beech trees come to mind.

All in all, this trail provides a very enjoyable easy-to-moderate hike.

Where: Panther Creek Park, 5160 Wayne Bridge Road. West from downtown on State 56, then south on State 81 for 2⁴⁄10 miles, right on Wayne Bridge Road (park sign at junction) and park entrance on right after two miles.

Yellow Creek Park, 5710 State Highway 144. U.S. Route 60 east from downtown, bear right on State 144 (two miles past bypass) and continue until two-tenths of a mile past junction with State 405 (large park sign at entrance).

When: Year-round. April 1 through October 30, 7:00 A.M. to 11:00 P.M. (closes at dusk rest of year). Nature centers close at dusk year-round.

Admission: Free.

Amenities: Nature preserves and trails, playgrounds, picnic shelters, outdoor grills, ball diamonds, fishing lakes, soccer fields, telephones, rest rooms. Panther Creek has a solar waterfall/fountain, and Yellow Creek has a cross-country training course.

Activities: Walking wellness, wildlife and wildflower viewing, birding, photography, waterfowl feeding, fishing (age limits apply), picnicking, field games, spectator sports, tennis, volleyball, guided nature tours by appointment.

Special events: Request seasonal schedule.

Other: Barrier-free access. Fishing for 65 and over, 15 and under only. Pets allowed if on a short leash. Guided one-hour nature tours on Tuesday, Thursday, and Saturday by appointment (six persons minimum). Illustrated guidebooks available.

For more information: Daviess County Parks & Recreation Department (and Yellow Creek Park), 5710 State Highway 144, Owensboro, KY 42303, 502-281-5346. Panther Creek Park, 502-926-6481.

John James Audubon State Park and Nature Preserve

People with even the remotest interest in nature should not miss this 692-acre park and nature sanctuary on U.S. Route 41 in Henderson, just across the Ohio River from Evansville, Indiana.

A walk through the forest of 200-year-old trees populated by warblers and carpeted with blooming wildflowers—the same woods frequented by Audubon himself—is nothing short of a thrill.

Kentucky has good reason to celebrate this internationally famous artist/naturalist who lived from 1785 to 1851. He spent many years in the state and was in Henderson from 1810 to 1819, although he also made journeys to Europe, the British Isles, New Orleans, and other parts of the United States in his quest to accurately document birds and mammals through his paintings.

To appreciate the nature preserve fully, start with a visit to the modern John James Audubon Museum and Nature Center. The museum handsomely illustrates Audubon's life and works, while the nature center has interactive exhibits and an impressive indoor observation area overlooking feeding stations.

At the stone-turreted museum (reflective of the late 1930s when it first opened) is the largest collection of Audubon memorabilia and one of the largest collections of the artist's watercolors, oils, and engravings in the world. Guided tours are given, but a self-guided tour might be your choice.

Audubon was a charismatic individual whose greatest contribution to art was moving the illustration of birds from the previous stiff, lifeless versions that were traditionally done from museum study skins to lifelike renditions. He was said to have "pulled birds out of the glass case."

Artists, ornithologists, history buffs, and students will all find aspects of Audubon's life and work that are fascinating and informative: how he roamed the woods finding birds in their natural habitat; how he developed his innovative technique for painting them realistically; his other roles as fencing instructor, dancer, storyteller, musician, and hunting companion; and of course his four-volume *Birds of America* portfolio and accompanying ornithological biography, which took 11 years to complete. The exhibits are arranged chronologically—early days, struggling years, early success, and twilight years.

A gift shop outside the museum has books, prints, tote bags, jewelry, T-shirts, and many Audubon-related items. I couldn't resist the note cards with Audubon's illustrations of warblers.

In the nature center is a special room with views from 10 glass windows facing bird feeders outside. Binoculars hang beside each viewing station, and the room is alive with sounds piped in from the feeding area. Outside are attractors for butterflies, birds, hummingbirds, and mammals. Among the plants and feeders, some upright corncobs have been placed on a pole that is parallel to the ground. We could watch to see what animal would come and want to feed on them, then record our observations on a card that is furnished for that purpose.

Informative boards discuss nature and humanity, endangered species, what we should know about habitat destruction, and what we can do to address those concerns. One exhibit shows how a scene varies from night to day, and another shows seasonal changes. Others pose questions: How does the mourning dove get its name? How do you identify the red-bellied woodpecker? What's different about the hairy woodpecker?

Downstairs is an exhibit hall for art, photography, and other media, while on the main level is the Discovery Center. This is a place for hands-on activities and games, all relating to the understanding of birds.

For example: diversity and similarity. What are common characteristics that all birds share but that are used in diverse ways? The display points out that while ducks and woodpeckers both have feet, they are used differently and so are configured for specific purposes. The penguin and hawk both have wings, but the penguin uses its wings for swimming.

Other displays illustrate the anatomy of birds, their tracks, the web of life, feeding habits, habitats, migration, nests, and how Audubon learned about bird behaviors through observation. These things are taught using questions and answers, and in one exhibit you must jump into an oversized nest to read the questions.

The barrier-free, self-guiding Museum Trail starts from the Nature Center, skirts the observation garden, and goes for a short distance into the woods. Benches and braille markers are provided on this trail, which also leads to other hiking trails.

It is estimated that up to 1,000 species of plants, 200 species of birds, and 40 species of mammals, reptiles, and amphibians are in the nature preserve. Printed leaflets identify more than 170 bird species and many of the plants and wildflowers found here.

The system of interconnected trails totals nearly five miles, ranging from an easy walk up Warbler Road to strenuous sections that go up hills, follow the pinnacles of ridges, then dip deep into ravines beside little streams. The scenery in this climax forest, where treetops are high above, is breathtaking. You can overlook Wilderness Lake or move up close and follow the shoreline. Lush wildflowers seasonally carpet the ground. The trails are well marked and maintained.

Though the nature preserve occupies half the park's acreage, the rest of the park accommodates recreational uses such as golf, picnicking, camping, swimming, and pedal boating.

During the winter months, visitors come to hike, visit the museum, or join special nature crafts events. In summer, from Memorial Day to Labor Day, daily activities include campfire programs, crafts, and nature day camps for children. A challenge course is used by groups for team-building practice.

Park Manager Mary Dee Ellis says the spring and fall warbler migrations (with the bonus of leaf color and cool days in fall) are prime times to visit. "The people who really like us are those who stay in the cottages," she said. "Even in winter, it is nice, and if it snows, you can walk back in the woods and see animal tracks. The crowds are gone, which makes it attractive with the natural beauty of the forest being undisturbed."

And I'll tell you a secret: the cabin they request most often is #102, which has an excellent view of the lake.

Where: Entrance on east side of U.S. Route 41 in Henderson a half mile south of the Ohio River Bridge.
When: Year-round. Museum & Nature Center open 10:00 A.M. to 5:00 P.M. (closed one week during Christmas). Boat dock and beach open Memorial Day through Labor Day, from 10:00 A.M. to 6:00 P.M.
Admission: Free. Fees for camping, pedal boat rental, golf, shelters, and some special events. Senior discount (62 and over) for camping, under 16 free with parents. Modest admission fee for Museum/Nature Center with special rates for ages 6 to 12 (under 6 free).
Amenities: Museum & Nature Center, gift shop, cottages, campground, picnic areas and playgrounds, hiking trails, chal-

lenge course, golf, beach, boat dock with pedal boat rentals, shelter rentals.

Activities: Nature appreciation, wildlife and wildflower viewing, photography, hiking, tent and trailer camping, golf, swimming (own risk), pedal boating, nature and crafts workshops, daily planned recreation in summer, including Wee Nature Tales, Kids Korner, Nature Niche.

Special events: Building for the Animals (February); Project Learning Tree Workshop, Senior Nature Weekend (March); Tree Hugging on Arbor Day, Wildflower Weekend, Earth Day Events (April); Wooden Wings and Other Things (May); W. C. Handy Festival (Henderson, June); Craft Day Camp (August); Hummingbird Happenings, Fall Migration Walks (September); Big River Arts & Crafts Weekend, Fall Color Walks, Halloween Woods Walks (October); Recycled Holiday Crafts (November); Christmas for the Critters (December). For Kentucky State Parks special events brochure, 800-255-7275.

Other: Barrier-free access.

For more information: J. J. Audubon State Park, PO Box 576, Henderson, KY 42420-0576, 502-826-2247.

Henderson Tourism Office, 2961 U.S. Route 41 North, Henderson KY 42420, 502-826-3128.

Rough River Dam State Resort Park

The Historic Falls of Rough sounds like a fascinating place, which is how I discovered nearby Rough River Dam SRP, a scenic haven "far from the madding crowd," to apply the title of Thomas Hardy's 19th-century novel. It turned out to be an appropriate description.

Think about it: a man-made lake on Rough River where narrow rocky valleys and sandstone-capped outlying rocks and cliffs define the boundary between the Kentucky Coalfield region and plains to the east; a natural falls and historic old mill; interesting side trips by cruise boat or by car; and a resort park where recreational and musical events are offered most months of the year. Breathe the rural air deeply and enjoy.

What I wasn't prepared for was the bird serenade. The National Audubon Society (NAS) poster on the door of the lodge should have clued me, I suppose. Where there is bird interest, there must be birds. The poster, "No Place to Land," pointed out the problems migrating birds are facing and what people can do to help. Homeowners who landscape with native plants and provide water are filling needs that birds have for food and homes. (See the end of this section for more information about Birds in the Balance, a migratory-bird conservation program of the NAS that is part of a larger cooperative program called Partners in Flight.)

A Twilight Symphony

With an hour to spare before dinner, I started from my lodge room overlooking the lake and went down a wide gravel path bordered by railroad ties to a small dock at the shore below. Here the trail becomes a dirt path going toward the woods. A footbridge crosses a little creek, where you walk through a field for a short distance.

Blackberries were starting to bloom, as were bluebells and some beautiful white wildflowers. Springtime wildflowers add many colors to the landscape, painting splashes of yellow, white, pink, and purple. In this country, Virginia creeper seems ever-present, too.

Across another trickling brook the trail was in the woods, climbing steadily. I heard a sound and looked toward the lake. A badger, or probably a groundhog, was hastily retreating through the underbrush, showing only its dark rump as it waddled away.

Just under the crest of the ridge now, spontaneous bursts of bird sounds have become a symphony of classical jazz. A woodpecker loudly drums staccato rhythms as the cawing of crows adds a measured cello effect and flutelike trills of warblers pierce the air. This repeats for several minutes, each bird adding its own jazz riffs in the impromptu composition.

The National Audubon Society would approve, I think, and so would Itzhak Perlman.

The lodge at the park offers a cozy atmosphere and lake views from the lounge area, restaurant, and patio. The gift shop is stocked with books, T-shirts and sweatshirts, Kentucky crafts, and decorative items. The large lobby/TV room has a circular fireplace with copper-top hood as its centerpiece. Just down the hall is a game room.

The modern Falls of Rough multipurpose conference center adjacent to the lodge seats 500 people theater-style and half that many classroom-style. The large meeting room can also be divided and part of it used as a game room.

Manager Mike Paley said, "Acreage-wise, this 630-acre site is the smallest of the resort parks, though in amenities we offer more than some others. We have nice tennis courts and a par-three, nine-hole golf course that is maybe the best-kept public course in the area, with a pro shop and green fees that are very reasonable. We also have a wonderful fishing lake with lots of crappie and bass.

"The thing really unique here is that the airport is close enough to the lodge to just walk over without having to wait for courtesy transportation. Next to the 3,200-foot runway is a service building with rest rooms and a lounge. Our airport is busier than those at Barkley and Kentucky Dam Village. We get a lot of people flying in on weekends, and clubs will fly in for breakfast or lunch. Another drawing card is a concessionaire who gives short airplane rides over the area on weekends from May through October."

Renovations in 1995 and 1996 gave a new look to the main lodge and dining room, a larger swimming pool for guests, and completion of a tree-planting program in front of the lodge where a walking trail wanders among maples, dogwoods, redbuds, and other tree specimens. All cottages were modernized with new roofs, dual bathrooms, and quality construction upgrades throughout.

With several ball and tennis courts, kiddie playgrounds, a full-featured campground, a beach area near the dam with bathhouse and lifeguards on duty in summer and paddleboat rentals, and a busy marina (with pontoon boat and fishing boat rentals) open seasonally, plenty of recreational opportunity is assured.

Rough River Lake is a U.S. Army Corps of Engineers flood control operation, so the lake is drawn down in winter in preparation for spring rains. Normally, according to Mike, it is up to summer pool levels by April 15. The park marina officially opens May 1, serving a good share of the two million visitors who come to the lake each year.

Around the lake, some boat ramps and other recreational sites are operated by the Corps and by Grayson County. Visit Corps headquarters across from the park to get information about hiking trails, primitive camping, and other Corps-maintained facilities.

Falls of Rough SRP also sponsors social events and musical gatherings. In March, a well-publicized Humor Weekend draws talent from around the state. After seeing headliners demonstrate their ability to make the audience laugh or just entertain with funny songs, a Saturday workshop teaches what is funny and how to be funny. Afterward, the floor is open to volunteer stand-up comedians.

Two model airplane events are held here annually. In May, the Mint Julep Meet features radio-controlled airplanes built to scale that are judged on their flying patterns. In September, the Jimmy Doolittle National Trophy Race offers a trophy to the model that beats the competition in a race around pylons.

Two celebrations in July include a festive Fourth of July Weekend Celebration and, later in the month, the State Championship Old Time Fiddlers Contest. More than fiddling, it features all types of bluegrass instruments, plus jig dancing.

About 12 miles south of the park off State 79 is the community of Pine Knob. Outdoor comedy/dramas with music are offered on weekends from June through September. See *Dock Brown, Kentucky Outlaw,* and *Down in Hoodoo Holler* (reviving mid-1800s mysteries) and *Daddy Took the T-Bird Away,* of 1950s vintage.

Where: Fifty miles east of Owensboro. From Western Kentucky Parkway, take exit 94 and go north on State 79 (15 miles) or take exit 107 at Leitchfield, then west on State 54 to State 79 and north to the park.
When: Year-round. Campground open April 1 through October 31.
Admission: Free. Fee for golf and airplane rides.
Amenities: Lodge, restaurant, gift shop, cottages, campground, air camp, airstrip, marina, nine-hole golf course, driving range, nature trail, swimming pool, beach, recreation courts, picnic sites, playgrounds.
Activities: Fishing, steamboat cruises, boat rentals, swimming, golf, tennis, airplane rides, volleyball, shuffleboard, bicycle

rentals, picnicking, hiking, wildlife viewing, photography, daily planned recreation in summer.

Special events: Dulcibrrr, Square Dance Weekend (February), Humor Weekend (March), Mint Julep Scale Meet (May), State Championship Old Time Fiddlers Contest (July), Jimmy Doolittle National Trophy Race, Lakeshore Clean Up and Fish Fry, Kentucky EAA Sport Aviation Weekend (all in September). Kentucky State Parks special events brochure, 800-255-7275.

Other: Barrier-free access.

For more information: Rough River Dam State Resort Park, 450 Lodge Road, Falls of Rough, KY 40119-9701, 502-257-2311. Fax, 502-257-8682. Reservations, 800-325-1713.

Park Manager, U.S. Army Corps of Engineers, RR 1, Falls of Rough, KY 40119-9801, 502-582-5736.

Old Falls of Rough: Green Farms General Store, 2402 Green Farms Road, Falls of Rough, KY 40119.

Birds in the Balance, National Audubon Society, 700 Broadway, New York, NY 10003-9501.

Historic Falls of Rough

Going to the Old Falls of Rough from the park, head south on State 79, then turn west on State 110 for 3½ miles. Look for a marker that announces: "Historic Green Mill Site. General Store and Museum, ½ mile ahead." At the falls, another sign reads: "Falls of Rough, Kentucky. Population 250. 1900 census."

Mary McGee O'Neill and her family are just about the only "population" here year-round.

"I'm the one who inherited this place," she explained, then added, "Miss Jenny left it to me. I'm her first cousin twice removed."

Miss Jenny was the daughter of Lafayette Green, whose uncle, Willis Green, purchased land around the Falls of

Rough and built a flour mill in 1823. Farmers from seven counties brought grain there for milling. The mill was operated continuously by the Green family until 1968. Another family-run business on the sprawling acreage was a timbering and sawmill operation.

After inheriting the property, Mary's goal was to see it restored as a piece of living history, showing what life was like in the community during the mill's heyday.

Depending on available funding and approvals, plans are to restore the gristmill and wheat house and renovate the museum and other existing buildings, with the expectation of eventually offering a restaurant, overnight lodging, stables, and the availability of canoeing and hiking. Demonstrations of a working farm community and traditional crafts are also in the plans. Another area of concern is to preserve the marshes, swamps, and other wildlife habitats.

The old general store is a museum that has authentic memorabilia and old family papers dating back to 1795. It also has appropriate gift items for sale typical of the period or related to Native American cultures. Even as it stands, this is a fascinating place, though continuing deterioration of some of the buildings could render them unrestorable.

We walked out on the foundation of the old sawmill to view the falls. Downstream was a tower that could provide a good perspective of the falls from below. I tried to visualize the crumbling ruins as they looked when drawings were made during their glory days.

The museum is open seven days a week from Memorial Day to Labor Day and on weekends in April and May. Then in the fall. . . .

"We stay open weekends until the last colored leaf falls. After that, there's no point," Mary said.

Of course. I should have read the signs: "You may smoke inside." "You do not have to wear shoes." "Pets Welcome." "Open weekends in April unless cold and rainy."

Where: State 110 south of Falls of Rough SRP. Turn west from State 79 for 3½ miles, then go right for a half mile.

When: April through October. Saturday and Sunday in April; Friday added in May; seven days a week from Memorial Day through Labor Day; weekends again through October.

Admission: Free.

Amenities: One-hundred-seventy-five-year-old, three-story gristmill and wheat house, waterfall, bridge, and sawmill remains. Not handicapped accessible.

Activities: Learn about 19th-century folkways and history of the property through documents, memorabilia, and videos. Photography, birding, wildlife viewing.

For more information: Green Farms General Store, 2402 Green Farms Road, Falls of Rough, Kentucky 40119, 502-257-8160.

Rough River Dam State Resort Park, 450 Lodge Road, Falls of Rough, KY 40119-9701, 502-257-2311.

5

Bowling Green Area

Entering the state from the south via Interstate 65 takes you directly to the heart of south-central Kentucky, a region dominated by a vast sinkhole plain of Mississippian Age limestone and the elevated Mammoth Cave plateau where one of the nation's best-known caverns is a major attraction. With myriad sinkholes, underground streams, dry valleys, and caverns, the area well deserves the title, "Cave Country."

Bowling Green, home of Western Kentucky University, is a center of commerce and culture, with the Barren River Imaginative Museum of Science, National Corvette Museum, and nearby Shakertown at South Union—all worth a look.

For more information: Bowling Green–Warren County Tourist Commission, 352 Three Springs Road, Bowling Green, KY 42104, 502-782-0800.

Lost River Cave and Valley

The scenic half-mile-long Lost River Valley on the outskirts of Bowling Green was formed when a cave system collapsed eons ago leaving 80-foot cliffs and Blue Hole Spring, which is where Lost River rises from underground, then flows for some 350 feet in a deep channel before going into Lost River Cave. It emerges just three miles downstream where it empties into Jennings Creek in Bowling Green's Lampkin Park. Lost River is known, therefore, as the "World's Shortest Deep River."

The cave, newly opened to the public in 1995 after being closed for more than 40 years, has been a place of mystery, high adventure, and legend. Think Jesse James, Morgan's Raiders, bottomless whirlpools, secret rendezvous. Today, though, the cave and valley are being recognized for their ecological uniqueness and scenic beauty.

An ongoing project sponsored by the Friends of Lost River (with the assistance of Western Kentucky University) focuses on retaining the integrity of natural features while restoring some of the historical elements such as duplicating a historic gristmill and its undershot waterwheel (driven by water passing below, as opposed to a wheel driven by water passing over it) that was in the cave entrance. Cave Mill Dam has been repaired and metal steps replaced. Pathways, entrances, and informational signs are being constructed as funds are available. Signage tells the story of the geology, hydrology, history, archaeology, and folklore of this place.

A mile-long self-guided nature trail meanders through the valley. It was developed by the 4-H clubs of Warren County and has a trail guide with 50 numbered stops. These include specimens of 39 tree species. An impressive grove of pawpaw trees is among the features that are less commonly seen in the state. Seventy-five species of wildflowers have been identified, also.

Other things to learn along the trail include: how streams form caves in limestone; why sinkholes are prevalent in this geologic formation; how to identify trees by bark, leaves, and fruit; and uses of wild plants and identifying which are toxic. The visible land features include high bluffs, a cliff amphitheater, blue holes, water springs, and intermittent streams.

Lost River Cave is said to have the largest cave opening in the eastern United States—250 feet wide, 40 feet high, and encompassing an area of 7,000 square feet. Because water from a 94-square-mile watershed drains into it, flooding can occur, especially in spring. The tour goes into the large cave room and a smaller passage. In the cave are a waterfall, blind cave fish, crickets, white crayfish, and some Eastern pipistrelle bats. These smallest of the common bats spend summers in colonies, usually roosting in trees, but go into caves in winter to hibernate.

Nancy Shreve and Steve Capps, director and board member of the "Friends" organization, were my guides. We descended some stone steps, then followed a path on the clay surface of the cave floor. The lighting was natural and subdued, dramatizing the cave features without creating harsh or unnatural effects. It is an active cave, meaning that formations are growing. The large passage goes back for three miles, but the tour does not. Boat rides are planned that will take visitors a half mile into the cavern where an impressive flowstone formation will be visible.

As we were admiring the cave's features, young Lacey Pruitt and Kristy Hazel joined us.

"We're just in here for the first time today. It is really big," the girls said excitedly.

Big events happen twice a year, too. On Earth Day, guided tours of the cave and nature trail go on all day; and in October, an arts-and-crafts fair celebrates "Heritage Harvest." Special exhibits are in place throughout the valley, and craftspeople give demonstrations at the cave entrance.

Where: At U.S. Route 31W (Nashville Road) and Cave Mill Road. From Interstate 65, take exit 22 (U.S. 231) toward Bowling Green. Turn left on Cave Mill Road for 3¹/₁₀ miles to its dead end at U.S. Route 31W. Turn left and immediately left again into the Lost Cave property entrance.

When: Earth Day weekend (April) until mid-November.

Admission: Modest fee for adults and children.

Amenities: Cave, scenic nature trail, waterfalls.

Activities: Guided cave tours, self-guided walks, in-cave rafting trips (planned, be sure to inquire). Hiking, photography, wildlife and wildflower viewing, birding, nature study. Guided walks available on summer weekends and at other times by appointment.

Special events: Earth Day Festival (April), Heritage Harvest (October).

Other: Barrier-free access to property (in future to be extended to the cave).

For more information: Nancy Shreve, Director, The Friends of Lost River, 1928 Grider Pond Road, Bowling Green, KY 42101, 502-843-6862.

Logan County Glade State Nature Preserve

I drove all over Russellville looking for the Logan County Glade State Nature Preserve while following confusing instructions. Readers of this book won't have that problem.

Logan County Glade is actually easy to find. Russellville is about 30 miles west of Bowling Green on U.S. Route 68, and the nature preserve is on the north side of the U.S. Route 68 business route at the intersection of East Fifth Street. Look for a white sign that reads: "Logan County Health Department." Drive to the parking lot behind the health department and you will see another sign identifying the nature preserve.

This is a 41-acre tract owned by Logan County and adopted into the state nature preserves system in 1991 for protection as an extremely high-quality limestone glade that has several species of rare plants. An information board explains that the plants are remnants of prairie vegetation that used to cover what was known as the "big barrens" region to the south. The region got its name from early pioneers who observed that the land appeared barren. Native Americans had periodically set fires to burn off the trees and provide grasslands to attract buffalo.

This particular spot is on a limestone outcrop in a naturally open area of an otherwise wooded knob. The dominant vegetation is native grasses and wildflowers, with at least six species considered rare or endangered. Few glades like this are present in Kentucky or in the nation.

State biologist Marc Evans discovered this glade as he was reviewing aerial maps in an ongoing search for untouched places that would be good candidates for nature preserves. One giveaway is when the size of crown tops in a forest indicates the trees haven't been logged in a long time. Follow-up studies are done on site.

A walk on the trail in spring is to be surrounded with colorful prairie flowers. As in all nature preserves, picnicking, camping, and plant collecting are not permitted.

Serendipity on the Trail

I had just started up a gentle slope on a path covered with wood chips when I first met Alison and Frank Lyne. They immediately reversed direction to assist me in discovering the glade. Since they are artist, sculptor, and botanist (yes, three designations—two people—don't ask me to explain!) I was elated to have such knowledgeable guides.

Frank: Shooting star is the big white flower. Most are either white or pink.

Alison: They're tall, and they have flowers that are folded back on themselves.

Frank: Here are birdfoot violets. Some of these have a bicolored blossom, part deep violet and part light violet. Their leaves are finely divided—see that dissected leaf there?—and the blossoms are bigger than those of ordinary violets you see everywhere that have heart-shaped leaves.

We come to a fork in the trail where it loops like a lasso around the hilltop.

Frank: This plant community is a limestone glade. Here we see some little bluestem and big bluestem, Indian grass, and side-oats grama.

Excuse me. What?

Frank: It's called side-oats because all the little grass seeds come off one side of the stem like a little flag.

Frank pointed to a low-growing plant that had five tiny petals of electric yellow-orange. It was hoary puccoon, a member of the forget-me-not family. Beside it was purple prairie clover, a rare plant that grows only about eight inches tall in this location.

Frank: And here is a pale purple coneflower, just coming up. Besides what we see today, this place has flowers during almost all of the growing season. In the fall, there will be asters.

We didn't go all the way to the top, so we missed walking around the hardwoods and cedars that forested the knob. But this cool and sunny day was perfect for bringing out the maximum effect of brightly hued flower petals.

The shade could wait.

Where: U.S. Route 68 in downtown Russellville at the intersection with East 5th Street. Park behind the Logan County

Health Department and look for the information board near the rear of the parking lot.

When: Year-round.

Admission: Free.

Amenities: Nature trail.

Activities: Bird-watching, hiking, nature study, photography.

For more information: Marc Evans, State Botanist, Kentucky State Nature Preserves Commission, 801 Schenkel Lane, Frankfort, KY 40601, 502-573-2886.

Shooting Star Nursery, Attention: Marc and Sherri Evans, 444 Bates Road, Frankfort, KY 40601, 502-223-1679. (Catalog of native Kentucky grasses, herbs, trees, and shrubs.)

Barren River Lake State Resort Park

In south-central Kentucky, Barren River is a favorite state park—and for good reason. You might think of it as the third point in a triangle, connecting with Bowling Green and Mammoth Cave National Park—south of Mammoth Cave and southeast of Bowling Green and just a 30- to 40-mile drive from both. It is easily accessed from the Cumberland Parkway at Glasgow (exit 11). From Bowling Green, take Interstate 65 north to the Cumberland Parkway, then proceed to the park. A flashing caution-light intersection helps identify the park's entrance.

Recreational activities provide the focus of this park, with a lot of emphasis on boating and fishing. The marina rents wave runners; houseboats; and pontoon, ski, and fishing boats. Fishing is excellent for largemouth, white, and hybrid striped bass, bluegill, channel catfish, crappie, and muskie.

As you enter the park, the camping area is on the left; to the right are a playground and picnic area. Farther along, a paved walking and bicycling trail is placed beside the 18-hole golf course. Riding stables, tennis courts, sandy beach area, modern kiddie playgrounds, marina, cottages, and lodge complete the amenities. The lodge has 51 rooms, a restaurant, and a large gift shop with many crafts items.

Overnight visitors have several choices of accommodations: lodge rooms, executive cabins with two bedrooms and baths and a view of the lake, modern beach-view cottages with gas log fireplaces. Or bring your own pop-up tent or motor home and stay in the campground, which has laundry facilities and a boat ramp for campers' use but does not have a camp store. This is no problem, since many resorts and bait shops are in the area.

With the combination of woods, open fields, and lakeshore, Barren River offers excellent wildlife-viewing opportunities. Waterfowl are present year-round, but winter is the time to look for bald eagles and Canada geese. Keep a lookout on the mile-long Connell Nature Trail and the 2½-mile bicycle/fitness trail for white-tailed deer, squirrels, raccoons, groundhogs, skunks, and red foxes. Hawks, owls, and songbirds will be seen as well.

In spring, the area is a colorful explosion, with a landscape of blooming white, pink, and red dogwoods, redbuds, and fields of electric green. In fall, mixed hardwoods ringing the lake under crisp blue skies paint a different rowdy palette.

Popular annual events are the Classic Car Show in May where owners show and/or swap their antique cars; the colorful three-day Glasgow Highland Games in June; and a Beach and Boat Show, also in June.

An impoundment formed this lake into a sprawling configuration with many fingers or bays. As this is a U.S. Army Corps of Engineers lake, recreational opportunities are provided in several locations. Bailey's Pilot Point offers picnicking, boat access, and camping; and marinas are at the

Peninsula, Narrows, and Walnut Creek Recreation Areas. Visitor and camping fees apply. The lake is drawn down in winter for flood control, shrinking from 10,000 to 4,000 acres.

Where: From Interstate 65 east of Bowling Green, exit onto Cumberland Parkway, then exit south on U.S. Route 31E at exit 11 and go 11 miles to the park entrance.
When: Year-round. Campground open April 1 to October 1. Stables and swimming, Memorial Day through Labor Day.
Admission: Free. Fees for boat rental, golf, horseback riding, and shelter rental.
Amenities: Lodge, gift shop, restaurant, cottages, campground, marina, 18-hole golf course, outdoor athletic courts, stables, swimming pool and beach, playgrounds, picnic sites, two mile-long nature trails, 2½-mile bicycle trail.
Activities: Swimming, fishing, hiking, bicycling, golf, tennis, boating (rentals), horseback riding, outdoor games, photography, nature walks, daily planned recreation in summer.
Special events: Classic Car Show (May), Glasgow Highland Games and 5K Run, Beach and Boat Show (June), Christian Music Festival, Trashmasters Classic (September), Fall Festival (October). Kentucky State Parks special events brochure, 800-255-7275.
Other: Park is on central time.
For more information: Barren River Lake State Resort Park, 1149 State Park Road, Lucas KY 42156-9709, 502-646-2151. Reservations, 800-325-0057. Marina, 502-646-2151. Fax, 502-646-3645.

Park Manager, U.S. Army Corps of Engineers, 11088 Finney Road, Glasgow, KY 42141-9642, 502-646-2055.

6

Mammoth Cave
National Park

Mammoth Cave can legitimately be termed one of the
wonders of the world. In fact, since its designation in
1981 by UNESCO as a World Heritage Site and in 1990 as the
core area of an International Biosphere Reserve, it is generally
recognized worldwide on a par with Australia's Great Barrier
Reef, Egypt's Pyramids of Giza, and the Taj Mahal. As the
world's most extensive cave system, it harbors nearly 350 sur-
veyed miles of cave passageways. That's a mile for every million years, if you want to look at it that way, since the cave
has been in the making for 350 million years. It was carved by
powerful waters cutting their way to the sea as continents
shifted long before the appearance of humans on the planet.

Picture in your mind a region that is a vast sinkhole plain.
An aerial view would show fields dimpled with craterlike
depressions where the underlying limestone has eroded,
allowing surface water to run quickly underground into a
complex system of passageways. To the northwest of this plain
is the Mammoth Cave Plateau rising 300 feet. The plateau
has sandstone ridges that have been protected from erosion

and steep valleys where sinkholes and cave entrances are found. Water flows underneath the plateau from the sinkhole plain, emptying into the Green River on its way to the Ohio River and ultimately to the Gulf of Mexico.

How caves were formed is a fascinating subject. In Mammoth Cave National Park and in other caves in the vicinity, visitors have a unique opportunity to experience many types of caverns. Guided cave tours give specifics about the formations being viewed, so each tour becomes a different educational experience. Mammoth Cave offers tours every day of the year except Christmas Day. Ten tours are offered, ranging in difficulty from the half-mile Tour for the Mobility Impaired and easy quarter-mile Travertine Tour to two- and three-hour strenuous tours, and there's a 6½-hour extremely strenuous Wild Cave Tour.

In addition to cave tours, Mammoth Cave National Park offers outdoor serenity and recreation within its 80 square miles of woodlands, 30 miles of scenic rivers, and 70 miles of trails. Visitors enjoy nature walks, hiking, canoeing, horseback riding, camping, boat cruises, wildlife viewing, and scenic photography.

The national park is divided in half horizontally by the Green River. The visitors center, hotel, developed campground, and most cave entrances are on the south side. The north side has a group camp and an extensive trail system for foot and horseback traffic.

Camping has a definite appeal, and for some people this is the only way to truly enjoy an extended outdoor vacation. Others prefer cottages or the hotel, which has 108 rooms, a crafts shop, gift shop, fast food style coffee shop with indoor or patio dining, and a very popular restaurant. I can vouch for the Wild Cave Cold Plate and the best homemade cherry cobbler à la mode that I've ever tasted. Try it!

The Guided Cave Tours

Anybody's first stop at Mammoth Cave should be the visitors center, where tickets can be purchased for cave or boat tours, informational films are shown, park rangers answer questions and distribute literature, and maps and books are for sale. Signs point the way to the center no matter from which direction you approach. Park at the center or at the Mammoth Cave Hotel. They are connected by a short pedestrian bridge.

At the center, bulletin boards illustrate and explain the structure of the cave, cave mining in the 1800s, details of specific cave tours, hiking trails in the immediate vicinity, upcoming special events, and the significance of being an International Biosphere Reserve.

Inside, business is brisk at the ticket counter. By making a purchase here (instead of making a phone reservation earlier), seniors with Golden Age passes can see the cave for a discounted price. However, during peak seasons, you should probably make tour reservations before you come since tours fill rapidly. It just makes good sense to prepare in advance and not be disappointed. You may select among 10 tours for their historic interest, dramatic formations, difficulty rating (one tour is specifically for people who use wheelchairs), or opportunity to learn caving techniques. The guides are experienced and knowledgeable, each presenting a unique perspective.

Some activities are just for kids. Eight- to 12-year-olds can take a two-hour Trog Tour into parts of the cave not open to adults. Wearing hard hats and headlamps, they do plenty of crawling and learn things about caves geared to their age group. Parents can join them, though, on a three-hour Introduction to Caving trip that teaches caving basics. Another activity just for kids ages 6 through 13 is the Junior Ranger

Mammoth Cave National Park

program. Junior Rangers join ranger-led activities and record their discoveries in a booklet they buy at the visitors center.

Despite all the good stuff, environmentalists recognize some warning signs for the animal life in Mammoth Cave, which traditionally has supported 130 animal species. The constant stream of human onlookers is taking a toll. The

Indiana bat population has dwindled from 50,000 to fewer than 2,000 in the last 50 years. And a real stream—the Green River, whose waters are backing into the cave—is placing stress on threatened blindfish and endangered Kentucky cave shrimp.

The Historic Tour at Mammoth Cave

B ob Cetera, a retired schoolteacher from Chicago who guides regularly at the park, was leading the group this day. The natural entrance, at a place called Houchins Narrows, is just a short walk from the visitors center. Houchins is credited with discovering the cave in the late 1700s as he was chasing a bear down the hill (but another version is that the bear chased Houchins!). At any rate, he wasn't the first to find the cave. Prehistoric people had used it centuries before.

We go through a gate beside a waterfall created by a perpetually running spring. A rush of cool air greets us as we enter. We walk along a smooth surface, appreciating the fact that 17 miles of improved trails built in the 1930s had smoothed a boulder-strewn riverbed and are still in use today.

Bob shows us how log pipes were constructed back in pioneer days for use in extracting nitrates from the soil, with one set that brought water in and another that carried the nitrate back to the entrance.

We learn about the use of lard oil lamps in the cave and how as early as the 1880s, guides would practice torch throwing:

"They would use a 30-inch stick with a nail on the end, then tear cotton rags into strips, twist them like a plug of chewing tobacco, soak them in kerosene, and put them in a can. To light the cave, the rag torch was affixed to the end of the stick, lighted, and then thrown high against the cave wall."

Black smudges where torches were thrown remain to this day.

Some famous people have been here, adding to the folklore of the cave. Booth's Amphitheatre, for example, was named for the spot where Edwin Booth, famous Shakespearean actor in the 1860s, recited the soliloquy from *Hamlet* recognized by its beginning phrase: "To be or not to be . . ."

Three hundred and ten feet under the surface, we learn how the cave developed over hundreds of millions of years. We also learn about some of the earliest cave visitors, how scientists and geologists glean information by studying caves, and how this cave has been used over time as a treatment center for consumptive patients, a mushroom farm, and even a dance hall.

From the Mammoth Dome (192 feet high) to the bottomless pit (105 feet deep), through narrow and low-ceilinged passageways, past flowstone and interesting rock shapes, the tour holds our interest for two hours.

Bob leaves us with this thought:

"Of all the people who have had an impact on Mammoth Cave, you—the people who are coming now—will be the most important because it is now a national park. We like to encourage travelers to visit the National Park Service areas. Almost always, you'll find something interesting that relates to your heritage as an American."

Agreed.

Trails for All Tastes

We might call the park, "Mammoth Cave and More!" It is really a prime destination for a well-rounded outdoor vacation, and opportunity extends through all seasons of the year.

Uncrowded hiking, backpacking and backcountry camping, horseback riding, and nature walks are enjoyable activities at Mammoth Cave National Park.

For starters, you may wish to check out the 6½ miles of trails close to the visitors center. An excellent book, *Guide to the Surface Trails of Mammoth Cave National Park*, by Stanley D. Sides, can be purchased in the gift corner, which has books for adults and children about national parks, Mammoth Cave, nature, and the environment. Ranger-guided walks are also given on some of these trails.

One easy three-quarter-mile loop trail, which is handicapped accessible, starts between the hotel and visitors center and goes to Sunset Point. It is an elevated boardwalk for part of the way as it goes through the woods and circles a hillock. At the top is a tribute to Stephen Bishop, a world-famous 19th-century cave guide and explorer. Bishop discovered connections between major cave passages in a cave that he described as "grand, gloomy and peculiar."

The trail to Sunset Point is lighted (for returning after sunset) and has benches for resting. At Sunset Point, a wall of flagstones defines the overlook on a windy promontory that gives views of a tree-filled valley and a forested ridge beyond. From here, one can take the Echo River Trail, a 2²⁄₁₀-mile loop. An extension, the four-tenths-mile Echo River Spring Trail, ends at the Green River Ferry parking lot. Another option is to leave the Echo River Trail and continue on the Campground Trail for half a mile to—you guessed it—the main park campground.

Also accessible from Sunset Point is the winding, descending trail to River Styx Spring and the Green River. Along the way, observe how water has dissolved and shaped limestone, then enjoy the giant sycamore trees at the river's edge.

These trails are all fairly short but scenic, with sometimes steep changes in elevation as they wind down from the sandstone-capped ridge top above Mammoth Cave. Expect to see sinkholes, springs, interesting rock formations, and scenic views at the higher levels. The Echo River Trail at one point is directly above the Mammoth Dome Sink.

Another loop that starts at the natural entrance to Mammoth Cave is the 1²/₁₀-mile Cave Island Nature Trail. It descends steeply to the Green River, which means opportunity to view the river and Cave Island from a bluff. From there, walk along the river's edge and get a perspective of bluffs of Big Clifty Sandstone. An alternate trail can be accessed along the way. Green River Bluffs Trail is a 1¹/₁₀-mile self-guided nature trail (rated moderate) leading to a picnic area near the visitors center. Pick up a trail guide to learn some new forest facts.

In summer, ranger-led walks go to the Mammoth Dome Sink and the River Styx Spring, where park rangers share their knowledge of the area's wildlife and plants. Campfire and amphitheater programs also focus on nature, folkways, and Native American culture. These programs are free, require no reservations, and noncampers are welcome to attend. Monthly park bulletins give schedule information for current activities.

Other places in the park's south side combine short walks and unusual natural features. On State 70 are the Sloan's Crossing Pond Trail and the Turnhole Bend Nature Trail, with the Cedar Sink Trail near the latter location. At Sloan's Crossing hear ever-present frog serenades among cattails and lily pads and learn about the life cycle of a pond. The mile-long Turnhole Bend Trail follows an old, winding road to a deep blue hole on the Green River. This trail has narrow passages along a bluff, so caution is advised. Enjoy the Cedar Sink from an overlook or descend the eight-tenths-mile trail, passing a dense stand of cedars at the halfway point. Learn about the complex hydrology of this giant sink.

For a strictly motorized nature adventure, the Joppa Ridge Motor Nature Trail is open seasonally, depending on weather conditions. Inquire at the visitors center before attempting this route.

To learn about a fascinating historical event, take the one-tenth-mile Sand Cave Trail. It starts at a small parking lot adjacent to the sign at the eastern park entrance. A rather grisly story is told at Sand Cave: Floyd Collins, an explorer, was trapped inside in 1925 for more than two weeks and finally died there. As rescue efforts were going on, the story captured the world's attention. Curiosity seekers came, and a carnival-like atmosphere surrounded the grieving family members who were keeping a vigil in hopes of a rescue. Today, exhibits have diagrams, photographs, and the story in detail. In spring, the short walk to the cave is enhanced by the fragrance of dogwood blossoms and pine needles, trillium blooming along the path, and waterfall sounds.

Though the south side of the park gets most of the attention, it is the north side that offers miles of trails, peaceful solitude, rugged hills, deep valleys, waterfalls and bluffs, and campgrounds. The trails are ideal for backpacking and horseback riding. Maple Springs Group Camp accommodates up to 24 campers. Riders can use three campsites there from March through November. Experienced cavers can obtain a reservation to explore Ganter Cave on the Green River, hiking there from the Maple Springs area or canoeing to the site. The visitors center has information about all these activities.

Green River, Aptly Named

The placid (and beautifully green) Green River is legendary among paddlers, not for its challenges but for its scenic beauty in certain portions, especially the forested 25-mile section within the national park boundaries. Also, canoeing probably offers the best viewing opportunity of the abundant wildlife in the park.

Canoe rentals are available outside the park, and float times can vary from a half day to several days, affording options that fit almost any time schedule and budget. Canoists can begin at Dennison Ferry and take out at Mammoth Ferry (it's called Green River Ferry from the road and Mammoth Ferry from the river) or continue to Houchins Ferry for an 18½-mile float. Another recommended float starting north of the park is from just below the Nolin River Dam south to the Green River, then upstream to Houchins Ferry. *The park does not recommend floating all the way to Lock and Dam #6 because of the lack of warning signs and the danger of being sucked into the current above the dam.*

Both Dennison Ferry and Houchins Ferry have campgrounds; and free backcountry camping permits allow camping along the river except within half a mile of any ferry crossing or campground.

Fishing within the park is allowed year-round, with no license required. Black bass, bluegill, white perch (freshwater drum), crappie, walleye, muskellunge, and catfish are found in the Green and Nolin Rivers. The state record flathead, or mudcat, (97 pounds) and freshwater drum (38 pounds) were taken from the Green River, and a five-foot-long, 50-pound muskie was also caught there.

Another excellent way to view wildlife and see a portion of the park from the river is by taking an hour-long cruise on the 63-foot riverboat, *Miss Green River*, which departs several times daily year-round from its landing near the Green River Ferry.

A Green River Cruise: Another Kind of Wild

The Green River is one of Kentucky's Wild Rivers. It certainly has wildlife teeming in it, along it, above it, and on its banks. That's what I discovered when I took a sunset cruise—one of the best times of day for wildlife viewing.

The Green River was very placid, flowing smoothly and slowly even though it was seven feet above normal as we headed downstream. Water at this level, four feet above the lowest level of Mammoth Cave, backs up into the cave and causes disturbances to the complex biology of the cave's underground ecosystem, a concern to scientists.

Tall sycamore trees and silver maples graced the banks. One sycamore near the boat dock was nearly four feet in diameter and estimated to be more than 400 years old. Our guide talked about the geology of rock cliffs and caves as we passed by, pointing out that the park has more than 300 caves. One, with its opening on a cliff about 30 feet above the river, was difficult to spot. Binoculars are a helpful accessory on any scenic foray, and this was no exception. We passed a patch of cane growing at the river's edge, and the guide explained how Native Americans made torches from the stalks.

So, where was the wildlife? Everywhere!

Deer were standing still on the banks and moving along through the forest, blending with tree trunks. Turtles were in and out of the water, and water snakes skimmed the surface. Wood ducks were enjoying their own float trip one minute and flying off the next. We spotted a beaver emerging from a tree. The river is too deep for beavers to build dams here, but they dig into the banks and make their homes underground above the water level—then come out at dusk and feed on into the night. It is possible to see wild turkeys, wildcats, raccoons, foxes, muskrats, and minks on a cruise like the one I took.

Where: Main entrance is 11 miles west of Cave City on State 70; southern entrance is 10 miles north of Park City on State 255. Easy access to both from Interstate 65.

When: Year-round (central time zone). Visitors center and cave tours, every day except Christmas Day; visitors center hours, 8:00 A.M. to 5:45 P.M. Mammoth Cave Hotel restaurant and gift shop, 7:00 A.M. to 7:30 P.M.; coffee shop, 10:30 A.M. to 4:30 P.M. (summer only). Miss Green River boat tours, April 1 through October 31, with four to seven daily cruises (moonlight cruises on Memorial Day, July 4th, and Labor Day weekends). Service center, open weekends from Easter to Memorial Day, seven days a week through Labor Day, then weekends again until mid-October. Green River Ferry runs every 10 minutes from 6:00 A.M. to 9:55 P.M. (free).

Admission: Free. Modest fees for cave tours (youth price for 6 to 15 years). Discount prices for Golden Age if purchased at visitors center. Five and under, free. Inexpensive boat tours (ages 2 to 12 half price, under 2 free).

Amenities: Visitors center with auditorium; gift shops; hotel (pet kennels available), lodge, and cottages; tennis and shuffleboard courts; service center with public showers, grocery, telephone, post office, and laundry; campgrounds (primitive to full service).

Activities: Cave tours, scenic boat trips, camping, picnicking, naturalist-led campfire programs, fishing, canoeing, hiking, backpacking, horseback riding, guided and self-guided nature walks, photography, wildlife and wildflower viewing, natural-sciences study.

Special events: Wildflower Weekend (April), Founders' Day (August), Archaeology Weekend (November), Christmas Sing in the Cave (December).

Other: Barrier-free access (limited). Special tours and programs for mobility-impaired visitors. On cave tours, children under 16 must be accompanied by an adult. Bicycles are not permitted on park trails. Fishing license not required in park, but restrictions apply. Day-use horseback riders can park trailers at Lincoln Trailhead and across from Maple Springs Campground.

For more information: U.S. Department of the Interior, National Park Service, Mammoth Cave National Park, Mammoth Cave, KY 42259. Cave-tour descriptions and availability, 502-758-2328.

Advance tour reservations, 800-967-2283 (tickets also available on-site when not sold out).

Special-events information and Maple Springs Campground reservations, 502-758-2251.

Area information (including canoe rentals), 800-346-8908.

Mammoth Cave Hotel, Mammoth Cave, KY 42259-0027, 502-758-2225. Fax, 502-758-2301.

Miss Green River Boat Concession, Inc., 511 Grinstead Mill Road, Cave City, KY 42127, 502-758-2243.

Canoe rentals: Saling's Nolin Outpost (Green/Nolin Rivers), 2884 Nolin Dam Road, Mammoth Cave, KY 42259, 502-286-8323.

7

Around Mammoth Cave

Enjoying the forests, lakes, and rivers in Kentucky's Cave Country goes beyond the boundaries of Mammoth Cave National Park. In the immediate area surrounding the park are opportunities for camping, horseback riding, rappelling, boating, fishing, and canoeing, as well as learning about wildlife, history, and geology and touring other interesting caves. Some of the best places are included in this guide.

Diamond Caverns

Diamond Caverns, situated at the south entrance to Mammoth Cave National Park, is virtually surrounded by park property. The approach, going north on State 255 for a mile from Interstate 65 at Cave City, is a park-maintained corridor lined with mixed hardwoods, redbuds, dogwoods, and cedars and wide, grassy banks. This cave is one of the best decorated caverns in the eastern United States, with formations that are impressive, varied, and numerous. They include the largest single formation ever discovered.

Caves, which always have a history measured in hundreds of millions of years, naturally exude a sense of timelessness. Reading literature that was written a century ago fortifies that feeling. Formations build slowly at varied rates, but a cubic inch every 100 years in an active cave is a sort of rule of thumb. Because of this, the descriptions in old books are usually still applicable today and can provide an entertaining and informative read.

Take, for example, some observations of Diamond Cave (as it was formerly called) written in 1863 by an early explorer, the Reverend G. S. Bailey: "There is that mammoth stalagmite, 15 feet high and 25 feet through, big as a five-ton haystack, one solid stalagmite, and the largest one in the known world."

He was describing the Haystack, a formation estimated to weigh 70 tons. It took shape in the Ste. Genevieve limestone of Diamond Caverns, a rock type that is particularly pure and is well suited for cavern development.

He went on to say, "Pass onward through that great avenue full of all sorts of formations, some like icicles, some like a banner partly furled or drooping around its staff; some are like sheets through which the light of your lamp shines and shows beautiful colors."

Here, he may have been talking about the Beauty Parlor, a room full of dripstone formations such as soda straws, stalactites, stalagmites, flowstone, draperies, and curtains. The latter two form in a sheet effect, growing horizontally along an edge instead of building underneath. When bands of iron oxide are present, such formations are often called "bacon rind."

He continues: "Passing now through a kind of Gothic archway, you enter a palace of crystals, with beautiful formations covering the ceiling, floor and walls."

The sparkle seen by lantern light was what inspired the name Diamond Cave. The story goes that a young boy discovered the cave while checking his trapline and, seeing the glitter, announced that he'd discovered a diamond mine.

The caverns were opened to the public shortly after their discovery in 1859. Today, they are the focal point of a family resort that offers a lodge with restaurant and gift shop, bed-and-breakfast accommodations, an 18-hole golf course, and two campgrounds. Manager Robert Jackson, a cave-lighting engineer and master stonemason, supervised lighting projects and historical preservation at Mammoth Cave before coming to Diamond Caverns in 1995, where he quickly expanded the aboveground facilities and improved the cave's natural lighting.

The cave entrance is inside the Diamond Caverns Lodge. Visitors negotiate a hundred steps during a 70-minute tour as they descend into the mysterious, cool world below.

What you will learn on a cave tour depends on two things: what your guide knows and what questions you ask. You may find out about the history of the cave, anecdotes and legends from the past, how the cave was formed, what role water plays in a cave's formation, the geology of the cave's features, animal life, and what makes the cave unique. At this cavern, tour groups are usually limited to around 35 people.

Looking at the formations at Diamond Caverns, it is easy to understand the process by which they were created. In the cave, we see the layered limestone bedrock with vertical joints (fractures) and bedding planes, which are horizontal fractures. Water flowing from the surface to lower levels seeps through the vertical joints and onto the bedding planes. On its way, the water picks up carbon from the atmosphere, turning it into carbonic acid. It essentially becomes carbonated water!

In its carbonated form, it picks up and dissolves calcium from the limestone. A drop of water eventually reaches a place where it will drip slowly from the rock. In the process of dripping, it will evaporate, leaving a deposit of calcium carbonate in the form of dripstone, also called cave travertine or cave onyx. Depending on where the evaporation process occurs, the dripstone may be deposited on formations on the cave's ceiling or on its floor. In another form called flowstone, the deposits leave a smooth sheet that can have the appearance of flowing water captured in time.

Robert explained all this to me.

This was the only cave tour I took where large stalagmites have been sawed off and highly polished, revealing growth rings similar to ones visible on a tree stump. The cuts were made many decades ago with a two-man saw that had a diamond-tipped blade. A third man mixed sand and water, working it along the edge of the blade. As the blade moved back and forth, it polished the stone.

The rings on the stalagmite do not represent seasonal growth as tree rings do. Each ring could represent a hundred or a thousand years. Darker rings indicate periods of drought when, because moisture wasn't present, the air oxidized the minerals and darkened them. Where faster growth was taking place, the rings are lighter.

Diamond Caverns has animal life, too: cave beetles and cave crickets, white cave moths, crayfish, and salamanders. As Robert led the tour (something he seldom does because of his other responsibilities), he looked for some cave crickets.

"This one is a female, and here is a male. The female has a little, long tip at the end of her tail. She uses it to deposit her eggs into the soft, sandy soil."

"How do they survive?" was my question.

"The cave beetles eat the eggs of the cave crickets, and the cave crickets eat the beetles. It's a vicious cycle," he said, adding, "There are more cave beetles than crickets."

"Well, then, we know who's winning right now!"

Diamond Caverns also offers a wild-cave tour for young people and adults, providing an opportunity to join experienced cavers and learn caving techniques. Leading from the Sandy Crawlway, the tour goes back to a remote part of the cave where cavers see a large, deep pool, plus a stream that is home to blind crayfish; exciting, pristine formations; and old torches on the ceiling, remnants from early explorations. Notification of wild-cave events is by direct mail, and names are added to the list by request.

The lodge was renovated in 1995. Originally built in 1927, it's been updated with an eight-room bed-and-breakfast wing and an enlarged gift shop that features regional crafts. The main portion retains its traditional charm with a large reception area, several seating groups of sofas and a fieldstone fireplace. Downstairs is a game room and a homestyle cuisine restaurant.

Where: From Interstate 65, take exit 48 at Park City, turn northwest on State 255 for one mile to caverns on the right.
When: Year-round. Tours daily, 9:30 A.M. to 5:00 P.M. Restaurant open daily in summer 7:00 A.M. to 7:00 P.M., in winter opens 11:00 A.M. and is closed Tuesday and Wednesday.
Admission: Modest fee.
Amenities: Cave, lodge, restaurant, gift shop, bed-and-breakfast, two campgrounds, convenience store, and 18-hole golf course.
Activities: Tours, camping, golf, fishing, swimming.
Other: Wild-cave tours available.
For more information: Diamond Caverns Resort, Route 255, Park City, KY 42160, 502-749-2891.

Edmonson County and Nolin River Lake

It's always a welcome surprise when visiting a commercially developed area such as that surrounding Mammoth Cave National Park to find outstanding accommodations in a pleasant rural setting. For this, the Mello Inn at Nolin River Lake, just 15 miles from the park visitors center, gets my vote.

From the inn, walk a trail to the lake or hike to the top of Dismal Rock, drive less than a mile to the dam, find stables and horses nearby and ride miles of trails in the park, rent a canoe (or bring your own), fish in the lake or the tailwaters, or rappel off a cliff.

Mello Inn is a five-bedroom, Victorian-style bed-and-breakfast run by genial hosts Scott and Rhonda Mello, who will treat you as an honored guest and feed you well. All sleeping rooms have a private bath and TV, and the honeymoon suite has a Jacuzzi. The decor presents an authentic Victorian feeling, though the inn is actually very new. A full country breakfast is served in the large dining room. Guests can also gather in the Florida room decorated with cushioned white wicker furniture, or they can move outdoors to the front porch or large deck in back.

Next door is Saling's Nolin Outpost, a place to get groceries and pizza, fill your vehicle with gas, and arrange for a canoe float.

Nolin River Lake is a large, sprawling U.S. Army Corps of Engineers lake with seven recreation sites, three marinas, and three developed campgrounds scattered on its shores. The Moutardier Resort and Marina is one of these. It has cabins and a campground; pontoon, wave runner, and fishing boat rentals; and trails.

The Double "J" Stables and Campground, a licensed outfitter for Mammoth Cave National Park, is on Lincoln School Road (off State 728/1827—look for signs at the junction). Adjacent to the park, it has access to more than 70 miles of national park horse trails. Double "J" is open seven days a week. One-hour, two-hour, and half-day guided trail rides are offered, as are pony rides for small children. It also boards horses.

In summer, you may attend the outdoor drama, *The Death of Floyd Collins*, on the banks of the Green River in Brownsville City Park. It's a pleasant drive from the Mello Inn through the countryside. If you visited the Sand Cave site and the Floyd Collins Museum at the eastern entrance to Mammoth Cave National Park, you learned about the gripping historic event on which this dramatization is based. Groups can arrange for a theater package that includes an outdoor chuck wagon barbecue. The Green River Theatrical Players also perform this drama at other locations and times of year.

A Perfect Nolin River Float

As the reigning mud-caked "swamp thing" (the title I earned at Metropolis Lake), I would have much preferred an unexpected dip in the deep from a wobbly canoe. But could such a thing ever happen in placid Nolin River?

On a cool and sunny afternoon, Steve and Debby Spencer and their two boys, Beau and Tyler, Jim and Dawn Parrish and their two boys, Jamie and Josh, and I paddled three canoes from the tailwaters below Nolin Dam toward the confluence with the Green River above Lock and Dam #6. Debby and Dawn paddled one canoe, I went with Steve, and Jim brought up the rear with some of the boys who were all doing a combination of paddling and fishing.

Steve was in very familiar territory. An associate professor at Western Kentucky University, he teaches courses that emphasize outdoor recreation skills and resource management and often brings students here for floating, hiking, and study. I couldn't have asked for a more knowledgeable guide.

Our five-hour outing went fast. This is one of the most scenic Class I rivers anywhere, with new discoveries waiting around every bend. Our route took us downstream, though there's very little current (something to be appreciated on the return). We saw wood ducks, mallards, a hawk, a kingfisher, some swallows, a snake, and buzzards. We saw signs of beavers and some fish. Usually deer or turkeys are sighted on river trips, but not today.

We soon entered the park boundary, then went on down past Kyrock, an old community where asphalt was mined from natural tar pits back in the days when barges went upstream to that point. Downstream, we brought our canoes to the bank, tying onto a tangle of sturdy tree roots which gave a good foothold for clambering up to a flat-topped rock. It was time for a snack-and-soda break, then we scaled Sentinel Rock for a breathtaking view of the river below. We were at Bylew Hollow (pronounced "blue"), a box canyon below Whistle Mountain. It is half in the park, with its upper reaches on private property.

Our next stop and turnaround point was at "nameless cave," a gigantic rock shelter with many boulders. Soon, there were boy Power Rangers standing on every boulder. High above were wooded cliff tops, possible to reach on foot but presenting a nearly vertical climb. Green River was seven miles ahead, with the campers' destination, Houchins Ferry, another mile and a half "upstream" (technically, since that part of the river has no current).

On the way back, we tried to see some hieroglyphics that Steve knew were on rocks above the bank, but mostly we were enjoying a three-canoe race. It motivated the boys, and Jim's canoe came in first. His reward was having time for some serious fly casting below the dam while the rest of us caught up.

It had been a day without untimely incidents. Nobody had lost a canoe or fallen out. All our gear was intact. We could congratulate ourselves. But wait—just then Jim landed the first fish of the day, a pound-and-a half rainbow trout. Standing up in the back of his canoe, he showed it proudly, then quickly removed the hook.

Next came the most innovative way to release a fish that I've ever seen. In a flash, Jim was in the water. His paddle was floating, the fish was diving, and Jim was alternately floating and diving for his rod. The rest of us were splitting our sides laughing.

Rules of the float: wear your life preserver, keep the canoe balanced at all times, and don't show off your fish!

Steve Spencer recommends having a topo map when floating the Nolin and Green Rivers at Mammoth Cave National Park or hiking the trails. He uses a Trails Illustrated map that shows all the trails and campsites. It is available at park headquarters. For those interested in rappelling, he suggests contacting the U.S. Army Corps of Engineers for their recommendations.

Where: The locations mentioned are north and west of Mammoth Cave National Park. To Mello Inn, from Western Kentucky Parkway: take exit 107 at Leitchfield, go south on State 259 past Bee Spring, then east on State 728 to approximately five-tenths of a mile past the dam. Inn and Saling's Outpost are on the left. From Brownsville, go north on State 259 to State 728, then same as above. From the Mammoth Cave National Park north entrance, continue north on State 1352 to Stockholm and turn west on State 1827 (at Forks Country Store). When State 728 joins 1827, continue following 728 west for several miles to the inn.

When: Year-round, except Green River Amphitheater Outdoor Drama, which is Friday and Saturday nights only, 8:00 P.M. late June through Labor Day weekend.

Admission: Varies with type of activity.

Amenities: Campgrounds, cottages, trails, stables, marinas, guide services.

Activities: Camping, hiking, fishing, boating, canoeing, rappelling, wildlife viewing, birding, photography, horseback riding.

Special events: The Death of Floyd Collins outdoor drama (Brownsville, late June through Labor Day), Nolinfest (Moutardier Recreation Area, August).

Other: Mello Inn has barrier-free access. Outdoor drama has alternate rain location.

For more information: Edmonson County Tourist Commission, PO Box 353, Brownsville, KY 42210, 800-624-8687.

The Mello Inn, 2856 Nolin Dam Road, Mammoth Cave, KY 42259, 502-286-4126.

Saling's Nolin Outpost (canoe rentals), 2884 Nolin Dam Road, Mammoth Cave, KY 42259, 502-286-8323.

Nolin Lake Park Manager, U.S. Army Corps of Engineers, 2150 Nolin Dam Road, PO Box 339, Bee Spring, KY 42207-0339, 502-286-4511. (Office or campground.)

Moutardier Resort and Marina, Nolin River Lake, 1990 Moutardier Road, Leitchfield, KY 42754, 502-286-4069.

Double "J" Stables, 542 Lincoln School Road, Mammoth Cave, KY 42259, 502-286-8167.

The Green River Amphitheater, 2433 Chalybeate Road, Smiths Grove, KY 42171, 502-597-2403.

American Cave Museum and Hidden River Cave

If I were to recommend the place to start looking at caves in Kentucky, this would be it. The reason? The American Cave Museum in downtown Horse Cave is home base for ACCA, the American Cave Conservation Association. ACCA is dedicated to demonstrating, preserving, and educating, so a visit here touches many bases. Plus, you can be assured that what you learn comes from the best and most current scientific information.

Actually, the most dramatic example of a cave's complete demise and hard-fought recovery is right here. It's the story of what happened to Hidden River Cave.

For 50 years, the cave was a blight on the town of Horse Cave because of the sometimes overpowering stench that rose from the sinkhole that also formed the cave's entrance. Earlier, the river had been the community's water supply and the cave a tourist attraction. Then, as the bustling community grew and industry moved into the area, the underground river became a cesspool. The community's inadequate sewage plant was dumping into it, and industrial waste brought downriver from other sinkholes added to the pollution. It was reputed to be the most polluted cave in America. Cave animal species could no longer survive there, and many of the townspeople actually left, moving on to more attractive communities.

Unpretty as this description is, it helps one appreciate what has been called the greatest cave rehabilitation in the history of the United States, a project that took 10 years. The recovery started in the 1980s when the Environmental Protection Agency, the National Park Service, and local citizens started tackling the problem. A new sewage treatment plant was built and went into operation in 1989. By 1993, when ACCA reopened the cave to visitation along with its newly created museum, blind cavefish were again swimming in the river and Eastern pipistrelle bats had rediscovered the cave as a hospitable winter home.

David Foster, ACCA's executive director, said, "We've been open only since 1993, and what we offer is being expanded each year. Our focus is education, teaching people how caves work and how land practices affect them. People who come here can go underground to our natural environmental laboratory beneath city streets and see firsthand what goes on. They see actual experiments such as monitoring the groundwater in the cave. When they leave, they understand better how a cave was carved by groundwater, how sinkholes go into cave systems, and how water flowing from springs comes from those systems."

Visitors enter the museum at street level, then take an elevator to the ground level four stories below, where a short trail leads to the cave through a nicely landscaped nature park filled with flowers, evergreen shrubbery, and flowering trees. Our guide, Scott Turner, showed us an owl's white feather and some fur and bones on the ground. They were clues to a drama that had occurred the night before, evidence that a snowy owl had been successful in its search for a juicy mouse snack.

Standing at the cave entrance on a warm day felt like being in front of an open refrigerator. Scott gestured as he spoke, to aid communication with three Japanese-speaking tour members. They nodded their understanding as he explained the presence of fossils and how caves form as water finds cracks in the limestone and then carves it out.

We descended 174 steps to the lowest level of the tour. The newly constructed walkways will last practically forever. The planks are made of recycled plastic with the appearance and heft of wood, and the rails are of stainless steel.

The river roared past us. The water level in the cave is tied to that of the Green River four miles away and has been known to rise as much as 30 feet, depositing several inches of mud on the steps here, signaling "cleanup time" for ACCA volunteers.

Along the way, Scott had many anecdotes to tell about the area's cave wars, prior uses of Hidden River Cave, and the story of the river's pollution and subsequent cleanup. Also on the tour are the old waterworks that provided both water and electricity to the city in a much earlier time.

The next project, which should be complete by now, is to restore the old trails in the cave that were used in the 1920s and '30s.

Now for the museum tour: it starts with the anatomy of a cave system and goes on to cover history, geology, archaeology, biology, and conservation. Diagrams, photographs, real objects, drawings, and interactive models are used to depict the various subjects.

The largest display is the life-size, two-story model of a well-decorated cave interior with columns, stalactites, stalagmites, and other formations, seen from both the street-level lobby and from the lower level.

On the tour, we learn about "urban footprints"—things like cave drawings and artifacts that reveal information about early cultures. Footprint caves, mortuary caves, and ceremonial caves are three types that have been discovered.

Another subject is mining in caves. A display compares the effects of different types of lanterns and other lights. Photographs tell another tale about mining and miners. Cave onyx, bat guano, saltpeter, and prehistoric miners each had a role to play.

Caves as a water source focuses on Horse Cave, trout streams, public waterworks, and how caves furnished water in the development days of our country.

Other subjects are food and caves (how caves have been used to process and store food), therapeutic uses of caves historically, famous caves, cave safety, and cave exploration (newspaper stories and photos from the 1950s, '60s, and '90s).

Underground water is a major subject area that explains water tables, aquifers, porosity, permeability, quicksand, geysers, and implements and techniques that help people search for water.

Man's use of water and factors that influence water quality are also treated in detail. Water consumption in the eastern and western United States is compared, as are municipal methods of purifying water.

Challenges (and how to meet them) hits on hot buttons such as groundwater pollution, solid-waste challenges, pesticides, nitrogen fertilizer, erosion, and other elements that adversely affect groundwater quality.

Downstairs are exhibits devoted to Kentucky caves and people who used, explored, and visited them—how caves were used in prehistory, the early history of Mammoth Cave, tourism and the notorious cave wars, famous visitors, the Floyd Collins story, and examples of caving gear. A large photo gallery has breathtaking photographs of caves.

Another reason to come here first is the array of excellent books about caves and caving, some of which are hard to find elsewhere. As David explained, "Two kinds of people go to caves. Some just happen by and think the tour would be interesting. Others tour caves all over the country, becoming cave hobbyists. The latter group would appreciate the *Gurnee Guide to American Caves*, for example."

The gift shop selection includes books that would appeal to both groups, as well as other cave- and nature-oriented items.

"It's sort of a small nature center," David said, pointing to some bat houses.

I agreed, paid for my *Gurnee Guide*, and vowed to make a return visit.

Where: From Interstate 65, take exit 58 east for two miles (follow the billboards). Hidden Cave is accessed from the American Cave Museum on Main Street.

When: Year-round. Daily, 9:00 A.M. to 5:00 P.M. Closed Thanksgiving and Christmas Days.

Admission: Modest fees for museum or museum/cave combo. Half price for ages 6 to 12 and free for under 6. Group rates available.

Amenities: Museum, outdoor nature area, cave, gift shop.

Activities: Cave tours, exhibits, nature appreciation.
Other: Barrier-free access.
For more information: American Cave Museum, PO Box 409, Horse Cave, KY 42749, 502-786-1466. (Write American Cave Conservation Association at same address for membership information.)

Kentucky Down Under and Kentucky Caverns

It's a drizzly day in Kentucky Cave Country. Where to go? Come, join me for a walkabout in the little bit of Australia at Horse Cave called "Kentucky Down Under." Take Interstate 65 and exit 58. You're there.

We'll meet owner Judy Austin at the information center and gift shop. Interesting items here relate to zoos or to Australia or are made of semiprecious stones. Yellow rain ponchos are for sale, too. A live caged bird is a Crimson rosella from Australia named Rosie. She is mostly red with indigo throat and wing tips and areas of black.

Judy greets us. Poncho covered, we go out on the back deck and head for the discovery area. Some of the park's 40 peacocks are here, calling loudly.

"Why an outback in Kentucky?" I wonder aloud.

"I grew up in outback Australia on the sheep station," Judy explains. "We wanted to do something different with our 800 acres here to make it economically viable and still have an attraction totally different from anything else."

At the discovery area, a goat is out of its stall.

"We're still putting this together, and it's a hands-on contact area. Throughout the park, we try to tie in the message of conservation and the interrelatedness of the natural world. This is a good place to start."

I ask about the pygmy goats and white squirrel, noticing that the squirrel lacked the pink/red eyes of a true albino.

"The pygmy goats are good for kids to ride and handle, since they don't get very big. You find the white squirrels in some urban areas. They wouldn't survive in the country because they lack camouflage."

"A baby emu!"

"Right. The emu is the second largest of the flightless birds, smaller than the ostrich. Here, the hens stay on the Australian laying cycle, so they lay in the wintertime. We have to take the eggs and incubate them."

She makes a circle with her hands, showing the size of their eggs (bigger than a baking potato).

Huge cockroaches here are not from Australia but from Madagascar.

"We use them to talk about the smaller creatures that live in leaf litter and help break it down. This is the kind of activity that helps in cave-system development. They are in this area of our facility so that people can handle them."

Other things to handle are pythons, large Australian walking sticks, tarantulas, toads and frogs, snakes and turtles. Tom Trousdale, a staff member, shows an antler that has been chewed on. In the woods, rodents devour them completely, leaving no trace. Tom explains why a bison's antlers never fall, whereas deer and elk shed theirs each year.

We grab a van and head for the main gift shop from which the cave tours begin. Signs point to the different areas of the park: Tropical Bird Garden, White-Tailed Deer, Lorikeet Flight Cage, Outback Cafe, Outback Walkabout, The Wool Shed, and Bison and Elk Overlook.

Inside the gift shop are live birds in cages, Indian items, onyx, a large assortment of T-shirts, jewelry, toys, books, boomerangs, and fudge. Judy sings the "kookaburra song" to a hand-raised kookaburra in a cage. She makes a sustained gargling "whoo-whoo-whoo" noise in her throat, gradually raising the pitch. The bird responds at a lower pitch, enjoying the impromptu duet. A crowd gathers for encore after encore. In warmer weather, these birds are moved outside.

We go into a huge outdoor cage, the Lorikeet Flight Cage, to feed some colorful nectar-eating birds. The technique is to take a piece of apple (furnished) and hold it in your hand. All the birds are hand raised and people friendly, so don't be surprised if they light on your head or play with your camera. Some are bright green with a yellow collar, bright red breast, and blue head. Many come from the tropical areas of Queensland Post, and others are from islands north of Australia.

Now it's show time in the wool shed. Small children take turns milking Daisy, the cow, squealing excitedly over their accomplishment. Examples of eight breeds of sheep come out of their pens and take a pose on platforms, allowing members of the audience to come up and feel their wool. Then we go outside, line up against a fence, and watch Patches, the border collie. The handler gives her hand signals to round up a small herd of sheep. He says "lie down" and she responds immediately. "Right there" means to stay put. Patches runs the sheep between two gates and through a corridor, into a pen, then lies down at the open gate to keep them from escaping. On cue, she lets them out of the pen and brings them to the fence where we stand. A job well done for this young dog.

On to the outback walkabout area and through a double gate to stroll among kangaroos and wallabies. The red kangaroos stand six to seven feet tall, the grays reach five to six feet, and the wallabies are smaller. Some have joeys in their pouches, who will stay for six months after being born. Other animals here are the Australian bush turkey, white ibis (a water bird with black head and tail), black swans, and emus. One circular area is surrounded by a ring of piled-up brush.

It is called the "kangaroo nest" and is a safety zone to which the marsupials can escape from people.

In another pen are two camels, Alice and Burt (Alice's friend on loan from the Cincinnati Zoo).

Today, because of our schedule, we have to decide between seeing the corroboree performance that celebrates the aboriginal culture or take the cave tour. The cave tour wins, so we ask Judy about the other.

"Our show is performed three times a day. The performers tell about the lifestyle of these Australian people, their tools, how they used them, and how they lived with the land and preserved the natural resources. They were a nomadic people.

"After that, we do a welcome dance accompanied by native instruments, and the audience participates. Then we do 'dreamtime,' telling legends that explain the natural world as the aborigines saw it—for instance, why kangaroos have tails and why they hop. Finally, we demonstrate boomerang throwing."

Our route to the Kentucky Caverns cave tour takes us through the bird garden where many kinds of colorful, exotic birds are in individual cages. Plaques tell their names, their native range, and other facts.

Gene Wilkerson is our cave tour guide today. The tours leave every hour and last for 45 minutes. The tour starts inside a stone building with a look down a sinkhole that is the cave's natural opening, then the group walks to a man-made opening. The whole tour goes for one-eighth of a mile through a very colorful cave that is profusely decorated. The stalactites, stalagmites, columns, draperies, flowstone, popcorn, and cave coral are in shades of white, pink, tan, gray, and reddish brown. We hear how caves are formed, the effects of water in the cave, and why we should be concerned about groundwater pollution. One particularly interesting spot was a reflective pool that gave an optical illusion. The cave has small and large rooms, narrow passageways, steps and walkways of stone, and a great variety of things to look at.

Behind the cave is a half-mile self-guided nature trail. A longer walk is provided by a gravel road. White-tailed deer live in an adjacent thickly wooded plot and, farther along, an observation deck overlooks herds of elk and bison.

A visit to the Outback Cafe completes our tour. Screened-in eating areas have picnic tables and a view of kangaroos and wallabies. We could order bison burgers or an "Aussie" burger or other varieties of Australian or American food; but, feeling adventurous, I try the Australian meat pie and salad. The pie is in a turnover crust, and the proper way to eat it is to poke a hole in the crust with a ketchup bottle and squeeze the ketchup in. To be totally proper, one must eat it from a paper sack. Our dessert is called a hedgehog. It's an Australian brownie with a whipped topping and some slices of a New Zealand Granny Smith apple on the side. Very tasty.

Where: From Interstate 65, take exit 58 east to entrance on left.
When: Kentucky Down Under, open daily April 1 through October 31. Caverns open daily year-round except Christmas and New Year's Day. Visitors center open 8:00 A.M. Tours are 8:30 A.M. to 6:00 P.M. in summer, 9:00 A.M. to 4:00 P.M. in winter.
Admission: Moderate fee includes park and caverns in summer (park closed in winter and rates adjusted accordingly). Children's rates for ages 5 to 14; under 5, free.
Amenities: Theme park featuring Australian wildlife, farm animals, and aboriginal culture; caverns; Outback Cafe; gift shops. Free parking. In-park transportation available.
Activities: Animal feeding, border collie exhibitions, wool shed demonstration, corroboree performance, boomerang throwing. Guided cave tours.
Other: Barrier free (except caverns).

For more information: Kentucky Down Under, PO Box 189, Horse Cave, KY 42749-0189, 800-762-2869 or 502-786-2634.

Mammoth Cave Wildlife Museum

Viewing exotic animals in zoos in natural habitats has an appeal to most of us, yet there's something to be said for the kind of up-close inspection of mounted specimens, especially when they are reflective of top-rate taxidermy work and therefore truly realistic. In this respect, the Mammoth Cave Wildlife Museum in Cave City is very impressive.

The museum is the oldest and largest of its kind in Kentucky and one of the best in the Southeast, housing 500 animals and 1,100 beetles and butterflies from all over the world. They are exhibited in a 15,000-square-foot air-conditioned building that honors cave country with the "cave feeling" created by arched diorama windows and interior passageways and subdued lighting. The outside is landscaped with colorful ornamental grasses and flowering plants that attract birds and butterflies. A large paved area provides free parking.

Inside, pass through a gift shop (where you can select from toys, gemstones, and craft items) into rooms with case after glass case of exotic beetles and butterflies from around the world tagged with their common and scientific names, country of origin, and date they were collected. The butterflies are from such faraway places as Peru, Bolivia, Brazil, and Indonesia.

Passageways lead to dioramas of mammals and birds in windows on each side, some with naturalistic backgrounds and others without. The first scene has a musk ox (also called polar buffalo) and penguins, with icebergs in the background. In each display, signs give a description, history, and other interesting facts about the species on view.

Mule deer and white-tailed deer, for another example, are set in front of a wraparound photograph of woods in fall foliage and with fall leaves underfoot.

The reindeer, a close relative of the caribou, is essential to Eskimos who keep large domesticated herds and use them for milk, meat, and hides. As draft animals, they pull sleds. A mostly white specimen on display is a cross between a white Lapland reindeer of Finland and a brown Alaskan caribou. It came from an Alaskan herd and was killed and skinned by an Eskimo native especially for this collection.

Each vignette presents facts about the animals to help us understand more about how they live and survive. For instance, the heavy and broad hooves of caribou keep them from sinking in the snow as they migrate in herds that can number in the thousands. The American elk, or wapiti, never grazes at night. The large Kodiak bear found on Kodiak Island in Alaska is a subspecies of the Alaskan brown bear. Polar bear can smell a dead seal 20 miles away. You learn much more at each stop, of course.

Many other species from the United States and Canada include the snowy white mountain goat, bison, groundhogs, mountain sheep, pronghorn antelope, and prairie dogs.

Birds are displayed in great variety. Inspect the Canada blue goose, western Canada goose, mallard, Russian red-breasted goose, black-necked swan, male and female scaup, green-winged and blue-winged teal, Ross's goose, Japanese mandarin ducks, mute swans, male and female wood ducks, and hooded mergansers.

Scenes give a sense of place, too. A northern lake with a rugged mountain in the background shows off a badger, mink, and wolverine, and desert scenes harbor snakes and other desert creatures.

Here are more butterflies, arranged in a diorama setting with individual specimens laid out on the ground and, behind them, some flowering plants.

A dozen Kentucky freshwater fish specimens share a window with lobster, several crab varieties, snapping turtles, and crayfish.

Small mammals are not left out. Woodland settings make a perfect foil for squirrels, skunks, raccoons, rabbits, porcupines, armadillos, and opossums.

Specimens of marine species, such as rose coral and shells in great variety, are placed on sand, and above them, a mounted shark helps set the mood.

Exotic birds on display include the toucan, parrot, macaw, pheasant, peacock, and others. For contrast, a winter scene shows quail and grouse species. Another winter habitat shows seven species of owls.

Other animals are from Africa and Central and South America. Ocelots share a savanna setting with African lions, though it is made clear that they actually live continents apart. The cat family is well represented by tigers, cheetahs, leopards, lynxes, bobcats, jaguars, and mountain lions.

Wolves, foxes, and coyotes are all relatives, and much can be learned about them in this museum.

People who take time to read about each of the animals on display might spend a couple of hours or more here and leave with a much better understanding of animal habits and habitats.

Museum manager Gordon Hall pointed out something that bears repeating. He said, "The families who come to enjoy the wildlife displays should know that we didn't go out and hunt these animals." Many acquisitions were taken by Eskimos or other natives, and many have been in the museum since 1969 when it opened. If endangered species are represented, they were acquired at a time when they were still plentiful.

Where: From Interstate 65, take exit 53 at Cave City and go east, following State 90 to the museum on the left.

When: Year-round. Seven days a week from March through October. In March, 9:00 A.M. to 5:00 P.M.; April and May, 8:00 A.M. to 6:00 P.M.; June through August, 8:00 A.M. to 8:00 P.M., with hours until 9:00 P.M. on Saturdays; September and October, 9:00 A.M. until 6:00 P.M. Winter months, Saturday and Sunday only, from 9:00 A.M. to 5:00 P.M.

Admission: Moderate fee (children half price).

Amenities: Museum, gift shop, ample parking.

Activities: Self-guided viewing of 1,600 authentic wildlife specimens, photography, nature study.

Other: Barrier-free access. Group tours for 15 or more (by reservation only in off-season).

For more information: Mammoth Cave Wildlife Museum, PO Box 301, Cave City, KY 42127, 502-773-2255.

Crystal Onyx Cave

Crystal Onyx Cave just outside Cave City is a well-decorated cave and an underground wildlife habitat and was a working archaeological site. In early times, it was used by Native Americans as a mortuary cave, a term that visitors to the American Cave Museum will be familiar with. It therefore provides some unique perspectives to cave visitors (though viewing of human bones is not a feature of the tour). The cave has both metal and concrete steps and some places with low head room and is a half-mile round trip.

Barb Dykstra led our tour, suggesting we watch for animal life. We might see cave-adapted blind insects, some common brown bats or pipistrelle bats, cave salamanders, frogs, field mice, pack rats and wood rats, or blind crayfish.

"When we find a blind crayfish, it's an indicator that the water quality is good," she commented.

Our tour took us past cave popcorn (also called cave coral and cave grapes), banded draperies (known as cave bacon), flowstone, rimstone, stalactites, stalagmites, and columns. The cave has many beautiful formations, and it also has coral, crinoid, and brachiopod fossils. Barb gave us an excellent indoctrination on how the formations take shape over millions of years. Crystal Onyx Cave was formed vertically, with just a few horizontal passages. Iron oxide in the rock is evident by the reddish hues.

Rimstone is an interesting formation similar to flowstone but built up in ridges. According to Barb, it can even become giant rimstone dams. In slow-flowing underground streams, the calcite deposits form scalloped ridges. The rimstone we saw was a very pure calcite that hadn't discolored. Calcite is also the basis for what is commonly called "cave onyx."

We tried to find a pipistrelle bat, looking for a thumb-size, gray-brown creature with short fur. In fall, they would have long fur and look like little dandelion puffs stuck to the roof of the cave. What we did see on the ceiling was a collection of crinoid stem fossils that looked like edible chips of the "bugle" variety. Even crinoid heads have been found here, according to Barb.

Where the cave ceiling was close to ground level outside, roots of a black walnut tree were growing down into the cave. This gave Barb an opportunity for a little education session.

"Trees, like all green-growing plants, have the ability to secrete acid from their roots. That allows them to solidly anchor themselves in rock. But it also turns the rock into soil. That process is more destructive to caves than weathering erosion or earthquakes, so when the walnut tree dies it will have created an opening to the outside."

In a cave, the conversation often turns to earthquakes. Why, I don't know, since a cave is one of the safest places to be. Barb explained: "Ninety-nine percent of the destructive energy in an earthquake travels in an S-wave where the soil lies on top of the rock. In a deep layer of limestone where we are, 400 to 600 feet thick, it would take an awesome amount of energy to break the rock. Consider the great series of 1811 and 1812 earthquakes on the New Madrid fault less than 150 miles from here. One quake registered 8.8 on the Richter scale and rang church bells in Chicago. It also rang Mammoth Cave, so to speak. They say a whooshing wind came through the cave, putting out lanterns and candles. When the primary waves of the quake reached the cave, it rang with a series of booming sounds like cannons going off. Some rocks rattled and others fell, but no one in the cave was injured."

Way down in the cave, directly below where we came in, was a burial place for prehistoric people. Barb said, "Living Indians didn't come in here. It was off limits because it was an ossuary site—that is, a receptacle for the dead. The bones found here were carbon dated to 680 B.C., more than 2,500 years ago, and were from late Woodland or early Archaic peoples.

"That was before modern tribal languages. They hadn't yet developed agriculture or pottery but did have a very elaborate religious system, and one of the key features was the burials. The place where they dropped the bones was the entrance to their afterlife, and the spirits were waiting there to take them into the afterworld. The practice after death was to keep the bodies for about a year in a charnel house. When the bones were clean, they were disarticulated and bundled in a fur or a material woven of vegetable fibers, then dropped down into this cave. Archaeologists worked here in the 1970s and cataloged everything.

"So, this mortuary cave was a holy place according to their beliefs. Contrast this with Mammoth Cave, which was a ceremonial cave used by the living. We know that they did get as far as 11 miles into Mammoth Cave because their sandals and

broken bowls made of squash rind—and even skeletons—
were found."

The tour had one more level to descend. Below was the
Cathedral Room, the largest and deepest room in the cave and
a place full of colorful formations. The law of this cave tour
is "What goes down must return, but you are allowed to take
all the time you need in ascending the 98 feet to the cave
entrance."

Want to know where you've been? Outside on the blacktop
pavement is a yellow marker with a nail in the middle. It is
directly above the Cathedral Room.

Where: From Interstate 65, take exit 53 to Cave City and go
east on State 90 for two miles. Follow the signs to the cave
atop Pruitt's Knob.
When: Daily, February through December. Gift shop opens
8:00 A.M. Tours: May 1 through Labor Day, 8:45 A.M. to 6:00
P.M.; February through April and post-Labor Day through
December, 8:45 A.M. to 5:00 P.M. (extended hours offered on
busy weekends).
Admission: Modest fee.
Amenities: Caverns, gift shop, wooded campground.
Activities: Guided cave tours, RV and tent camping.
For more information: Crystal Onyx Cave, Route 2, Highway
90, Cave City, KY 42127, 502-773-2359.

Jesse James Riding Stables

For a trail ride on the eastern side of Mammoth Cave
National Park, the Jesse James Riding Stables may be the ideal
place. From Cave City, take State 70 west toward the park and
look for the stables nestled in a valley on the south side of the
highway downhill from Kentucky Action Park, an entertain-

ment complex that also has miniature golf, shops, and amuse-ment rides.

The horse trails go through the countryside, down a scenic valley, and into the woods where deer and wild turkey are numerous. Flowering trees in spring, wildflowers throughout the growing season, and vivid leaf color in fall provide an ever-changing landscape for trail riders.

Guided tours leave every 30 minutes, starting at 9:00 A.M. The shorter rides take a half hour, an hour, or two hours; and half-day or full-day rides are also available by advance reser-vation. If lunch is included, the riders stop at the top of the chair lift (on the property) and then ride it down to the on-site cafe or have a meal brought to them.

The stable provides quarter horses and western tack. It operates from March through mid-November, but, depend-ing on the weather, the season may be extended either way.

Where: State 70 west of Cave City from exit 53 on Interstate 65.
When: March 1 through mid-November (sometimes earlier and later, too). Tickets sold at café/gift shop from 8:00 A.M. Rides every 30 minutes from 9:00 A.M. until 6:00 P.M. in summer (earlier closing time in winter).
Admission: Moderate fee. Group rates available.
Amenities: Stables, with adjacent café, shops, amusement rides.
Activities: Guided trail rides from half an hour to a full day.
Other: Children must be six years to ride without adults.
For more information: Jesse James Riding Stables, 3057 Mam-moth Cave Road, Cave City, KY 42127, 502-773-2560.

8

Eastern Cave Country Lakes

Go east from the heart of the cave region and watch the karst topography of a dimpled landscape caused by sinkholes and caverns give way to wooded hills and a conglomeration of rivers all seeming to rush together in one place. Impoundments from three of them—the Green, the Cumberland, and the Obey—have formed some of the best and most scenic fishing and boating lakes in Kentucky. They're all within "hollering" distance, so to speak, so which one to visit might be a hard choice to make.

Green River Lake

Some days are really green, and so it was the morning I "saved the ducks." Heading toward Green River Lake, my car whizzed past fields of emerald green, but a movement in the grass at the shoulder of the road ahead sent up a flag of caution. I braked quickly and stopped in time to witness five green-headed ducks emerge from the tall cover, and with total unconcern, slowly waddle across the highway and disappear once again.

I was going east on State 88 from Munfordville, enjoying

the farm ponds, splashes of wildflowers, sloughs, woods, and blue sky. Coming into Green County the road is in a forest and climbing. After a while, the road gets very curvy. On this scenic route, take State 55 south just west of Campbellsville. Watch your watch: the eastern time zone dips down here in a V-shape to claim the northern half of Green River Lake. (Every other location mentioned so far has been on central time.) To get here from the south, exit Cumberland Parkway onto State 55 at Columbia.

From State 55, turn east on State 1061 south for one and a half miles and look in a field on the left for the Green River Lake State Park billboard. Following that sign takes you to a wide peninsula on the lake where you will find the campground, picnic sites, playground, boat-launching area, grocery, miniature golf, and an amphitheater.

The road to the fully equipped marina is another 1⁴⁄10 miles on State 1061, then go left. It is just above the dam and has houseboats and other boats for rent, plus groceries and supplies.

Instead of turning left, continue straight to reach the U.S. Army Corps of Engineers dam and visitors center. The road takes you over a dike and the dam spillway, then over the dam itself.

Even though it had been a green day, I wasn't prepared for the lake. At full pool, an almost iridescent green and ringed with trees, it is breathtaking. This is one of Kentucky's cleanest lakes. It is not overpressured but certainly has a presence of fishing boats, ski boats, sailboats, and houseboats, indicating its popularity.

The Corps visitors center sits high on another peninsula with excellent lake views, a picnic shelter that may be reserved, and other picnic areas. A self-guided nature walk leads to observation points and has markers identifying tree specimens.

Another interesting location is the Upper Green River Unit of the WMA on Corps property at the eastern shore of the lake. It is managed by the Kentucky Department of Fish & Wildlife Resources. A barrier-free observation tower offers opportunity to view wetland wildlife. For access, go east of Campbellsville on State 70 for 4 miles, then south on State 76 for 14²/10 miles. Where you see the "Wildlife Observation Center" sign, turn right onto a gravel road for a quarter mile.

Where: East of Mammoth Cave and south of Campbellsville off State 50, with access from the Cumberland Parkway.

When: State park open year-round; marina open March 1 through November; U.S. Army Corps of Engineers visitors center open Monday through Friday year-round and also on weekends in summer.

Admission: Park is free; fee for miniature golf, camping, some Corps-use areas.

Amenities: Campgrounds, gift shop, marina, outdoor recreation courts, trails, picnic grounds, playgrounds, boat ramps.

Activities: Camping, fishing, swimming, boating, nature walks, photography, wildlife viewing, picnicking, daily planned recreation in summer.

Special events: Arts & Crafts Festival and Corvette Show (in park, July), Kentucky State Parks special events brochure, 800-255-7275.

Other: Barrier-free access at park and dam.

For more information: Green River Lake State Park, 179 Park Office Road, Campbellsville, KY 42718-9351, 502-465-8255.

Green River Marina, 2892 Lone Valley Road, Campbellsville, KY 42718, 502-465-2512. Reservations, 800-488-2512.

U.S. Army Engineer District, PO Box 59, Louisville, KY 40201-0059, 502-582-5736.

Lake Cumberland State Resort Park

One of the most popular locations in the state is Lake Cumberland with 1,255 miles of shoreline in its 101-mile length and more than 80 square miles of surface area. It is known for its great variety of sport fish, including bass, crappie, bream, walleye, and catfish. Steep, rocky, forested hills surround it. A large population of deer and small mammals lives here, which gives excellent wildlife-viewing opportunities.

This well-developed lake area boasts several resorts and marinas, U.S. Army Corps of Engineers campgrounds and day-use facilities, and the Lake Cumberland State Resort Park.

To reach the park, exit the Cumberland Parkway at Russell Springs and go south on U.S. Route 127 past Jamestown for approximately eight miles, then left at the well-marked entrance road. (You also may want to stop at the tourist information center on U.S. Route 127 in Russell Springs.)

It's a five-mile drive to Lure Lodge through the forest on the park's winding blacktop road atop a high ridge. Suddenly, the magnificent blue of the lake comes into view through the trees. A scenic overlook allows a leisurely inspection. On a sunny day under a crisp blue sky, a picture postcard would not do it justice, but never mind. Out comes the camera, to be aimed at an inverted triangle of blue with its top edge scalloped by islands.

On we go, past the stables, a picnic area, cottages to the right, a country store and miniature golf, a road to the state dock, the golf course, and then the lodge straight ahead.

The lodge is a deluxe complex overlooking the lake, with a spa, exercise room, indoor pool, and sleeping rooms.

The Kentucky State Dock (on park property) with its full-service marina is a point of pride, offering 24-hour service and a Ship's Store that has everything from ice to karaoke equipment, with racks and racks of clothing and supplies. Rental slips are available, and boat rentals run the gamut from a 79-foot party barge to fishing and pontoon boats to wave runners. The only problem is an ever-full parking area. It is important to observe the parking regulations.

The activities center, nature center, and the head of the Lake Bluff Trail are adjacent to the lodge. The nature center is a place to get maps and pamphlets, identify locations around the lake, and learn about the area's history, the wildlife species that live here, and their habitats.

The Lake Bluff Trail is a self-guided nature trail that is a four-mile loop, although I recommend taking only the first part and returning by the park access road. The return section, across the road, seems to be little used and not well marked.

The first part, however, is a well-used trail that follows the lakeshore, climbs up hills and down valleys, goes past small waterfalls and over tumbling creeks on footbridges, and has many interesting features to observe. Listen for wood thrushes, look for the red flags of cardinal flowers, learn about fern gardens. Markers identify the forest types—oak and hickory, climax beech, and central deciduous hardwoods. A spur trail leads to a high lake overlook. Even on warm days, this shady trail deep in the forest will feel cool.

Two nearby locations of special interest are Rockhouse Bottoms and Mill Springs. Rockhouse Bottoms has Rockhouse Arch, a natural arch that was carved through a narrow limestone ridge by water action and was used over the centuries for meetings and social gatherings. Native Americans and long hunters used it in the 1700s; then in 1812, settlers named it "Rockhouse." From the park, take U.S. Route 127 north toward Jamestown, turn west on State 55, branch to the left on State 1058, then left again (south) on State 379. It is at the end of the road in a bend of the Cumberland past the community of Creelsboro.

Mill Springs is a U.S. Army Corps of Engineers recreation area east of the park on State 1275 (just off State 90 southwest of Somerset). From the park, continue on U.S. Route 127 south to State 90, then east past Monticello. State 1275 turns left, then loops back to State 90 at Mill Springs, giving you a choice of access. It was one of the first settlements in Kentucky, where a gristmill began operating in 1817. Now it has picnic facilities, rest rooms, and trails.

Where: Fourteen miles South of Russell Springs on U.S. Route 127. From the Cumberland Parkway, exit south on U.S. Route 127. The park is eight miles south of Jamestown.

When: Year-round. Dining room: 7:00 to 10:30 A.M., 11:00 A.M. to 4:00 P.M., 5:00 to 9:00 P.M. (closes at 8:00 P.M. November through March). Gift shop and grocery hours vary with season. Game room and indoor pool, open 7:00 A.M. to 11:00 P.M. Campground, open April through November. Community pool, open Memorial Day weekend through mid-August. Nature center, open daily Memorial Day to Labor Day from 7:30 A.M. to 4:00 P.M. Golf Pro Shop, open April through October (golf course open all year, weather permitting). Riding stables, open daily Memorial Day through Labor Day and weekends in spring and fall (open/close dates depend on weather).

Admission: Free. Fees for golf, miniature golf, public pool, picnic shelter rentals, trail rides.

Amenities: Lodges, restaurant, gift shop, campgrounds, cottages, meeting rooms, game room, nature center, grocery, marina, nine-hole golf course, swimming pools, spa/exercise room, recreation room, nature trails, outdoor athletic courts, picnic shelters, stables.

Activities: Camping, hiking, nature appreciation, wildlife viewing, photography, picnicking, swimming, fishing, boating, horseback riding, golf, miniature golf, tennis, daily planned recreation in summer.

Special events: Square Dance Weekend (February), Spring Fishing Unlimited (March), Tournament of Trash (September), Native American Day (October), Fall Fishing Unlimited (November). Kentucky State Parks special events brochure, 800-255-7275.

Other: Barrier-free access to some areas. Seasonal shuttle bus service to State Dock. Sign up in advance for trail rides.

For more information: Lake Cumberland State Resort Park, 5465 State Park Road, PO Box 380, Jamestown, KY 42629. Lodge, 502-343-3111. Reservations, 800-325-1709. Park fax, 502-343-5510. State Dock, 800-325-3625.

Resource Manager, Lake Cumberland, U.S. Army Corps of Engineers, 855 Boat Dock Road, Somerset, KY 42501, 606-679-6337. Generating schedule, 606-679-5655 or 502-343-4708.

Mill Springs Recreation Area (U.S. Army Corps of Engineers), 606-348-8186.

Wolf Creek National Fish Hatchery

The Wolf Creek National Fish Hatchery may surprise the first-time visitor. The main attraction, of course, is the system of indoor and outdoor raceways where each year a million rainbow trout eggs are hatched, fed to stocking size, and then released into coldwater rivers and lakes. Yet this indicates only part of what is here.

From Lake Cumberland State Resort Park, go south on U.S. Route 127 for three miles to the Wolf Creek Dam and the hatchery, which is on the right just before the road crosses the dam. Among trees and flowering shrubbery is an information kiosk, an incubator building open to visitors, and the system of outdoor raceways. Informational signs are also placed around the grounds at points of interest.

The dam was built in 1951 for flood control, hydroelectric power, and recreation; but the water deep in Lake Cumberland was too cold for the native smallmouth bass and bluegill. The changing water levels didn't help, either. They disrupted spawning activities. The solution was to stock the lake with trout, a fish that thrives in cold water.

The trout hatchery was built in 1975. It takes the water from the lake, aerates it, routes it through the raceways, then runs it into the river below the dam. By selectively drawing water from specific lake levels, the hatchery water temperature is controlled.

The eggs come from brood stock hatcheries in other states. Here, they grow into sac fry, fingerlings, and finally the nine-inch stocking size. This takes about 16 months. The tiny fish require a lot of attention, according to Jimmy Mann, one of the rangers on duty the day I visited. The smallest fish are fed six or seven times a day, and their tanks are cleaned twice a day.

Brown trout and brookies (brook trout) are also raised here. The brown trout is more tolerant of poor water quality, resulting from its being interbred from German and Scottish strains. Brook trout are technically not trout but char. They are much smaller than the rainbows and browns and must have cold, pure water to thrive.

The outdoor raceways hold the stocking-size fish. In nature, they eat insects, crustaceans, plant material, and very small fish. In the hatchery, they are fed a commercially-produced, balanced diet.

Besides touring the hatchery, you may wish to take advantage of some good fishing opportunity below the dam, where fish are stocked two or three times a week. The U.S. Army Corps of Engineers Kendall Park Campground with excellent facilities is next door, and the public fishing area below the dam also has a handicapped-accessible ramp, road, and parking area. If the fish don't bite, don't worry—the Lake Cumberland Country Store is nearby.

What a scenic area! Take a few back roads and watch for deer and other wildlife. You'll hardly be disappointed.

Just a few miles past the dam (going south on U.S. Route 127) is Seventy-Six Falls, an idyllic picnic spot on a finger of Lake Cumberland. It is popular with boaters though a little out of the way for automobile traffic. To get there, continue south on U.S. Route 127, go east on State 734, then southeast on State 1266. Its name comes from the fact that before the lake was impounded it was 76 feet high.

Where: On U.S. Route 127 three miles south of Lake Cumberland State Resort Park.
When: Year-round. Daily, 7:00 A.M. to 3:30 P.M. (outside raceways until dark).
Admission: Free.
Amenities: Visitors center, hatchery, U.S. Army Corps of Engineers campground.
Activities: Hatchery tours (group tours by advance arrangement), fishing, picnicking, camping.
Special events: Free annual fishing derby for ages 5 to 15 (June).
Other: Barrier-free access. "Handicapped only" road, parking area, and fishing ramp.
For more information: Hatchery Manager, Wolf Creek National Fish Hatchery, 50 Kendall Road, Jamestown, KY 42629-6502, 502-343-3797.

Resource Manager, Lake Cumberland, U.S. Army Corps of Engineers, 855 Boat Dock Road, Somerset, KY 42501, 606-679-6337. Generating schedule, 606-679-5655 or 502-343-4708.

Kendall Park Campground at Wolf Creek Dam (U.S. Army Corps of Engineers address above). Reservations, 502-343-4660.

Fishing derby information, inquire at Lake Cumberland Country Store, 502-343-2055.

Dale Hollow Lake State Park

Dale Hollow Lake is mostly in Tennessee but has a very distinctive state park on the Kentucky side that is especially appealing to equine enthusiasts. This remote 27,000-acre lake is one of the most beautiful in the state and is enjoyed for all kinds of water sports, including houseboating, skiing, and fishing. The lake holds the world record for smallmouth bass with an 11-pound, 15-ounce fish that was caught in July 1955. For a feeling of seclusion, set a houseboat in one of the many coves where your only view will be of nature.

Dale Hollow Lake State Park is southwest of Lake Cumberland. The major access is from State 90 halfway between Glasgow to the west and U.S. Route 127 south of Somerset to the east. The campground, sporting 144 sites, utility hookups, and three central service buildings, is open year-round. Reservations are accepted at this campground. The park marina rents fishing and pontoon boats and has an adjacent restaurant that serves three meals a day.

Hikers can enjoy 14 miles of trails rated easy to moderate, but it is the horse camp that distinguishes this park. Special horse trails have tie-up areas provided with hitching rails. During the Horse Campers Fall Roundup in mid-October, horses are allowed to camp free.

See the companion book, *Natural Wonders of Tennessee*, for more information about Dale Hollow Lake.

Where: From State 90 between Glasgow and U.S. Route 127, go south on State 449 approximately five miles east of Burkesville. Turn left on State 1206 to the park.

When: Year-round. Swimming pool open Memorial Day through Labor Day.

Admission: Free. Modest fees for swimming (noncampers) and shelter rental.

Amenities: Campground (including 24-site horse camp), marina (with fishing and pontoon boat rentals), restaurant, swimming pool, trails, picnic shelters, playgrounds.

Activities: Camping, horseback riding, hiking, swimming, fishing, water sports, picnicking, wildlife viewing, photography.

Special events: Visit with the Eagles (January), Cloggers and Line Dancers Weekend (May), Quilt Show (June), Singing by the Lake (September), Horse Campers Fall Roundup (October).

Other: Daily planned recreation in summer.

For more information: Dale Hollow Lake State Park, 6371 State Park Road, Bow, KY 42714-9728, 502-443-7431. Fax, 502-433-7453.

Nashville District, U.S. Army Corps of Engineers, PO Box 1070, Nashville, Tennessee 37202, 615-736-7161. (Lake outline map available.)

9

Louisville and Vicinity

L ouisville is a grand old port city on the Ohio River that
has developed as Kentucky's flagship metropolitan and
cultural center—certainly in terms of size and diversity. My
favorite place to stay is the Old Louisville Inn in the heart of
the downtown historic district. It has everything, including a
personal fitness trainer, and who knows who you'll be rub-
bing elbows with—could be some world-class tennis pros (as
on my most recent visit). From there, one can feel a part of an
earlier, less hurried period of history and branch out in all
directions to visit parks, museums, the zoo, natural areas,
arboretums, and botanical gardens. A Louisville base is a good
choice for people who want a wide variety of ways to experience nature.

The north-central part of Kentucky has an interesting
geology. Widely defined as Bluegrass country, this basically
oval-shaped region has at its center an upwarp (raised land
form) known as the Cincinnati Arch. As the uplift occurred,
older rocks were brought to the surface. Going away from the
crest of the arch, younger and younger rocks are exposed. The
region as a whole consists of the Inner Bluegrass (the central
part) and around it the Outer Bluegrass, bordered by the Ohio
River circling it on its northern perimeter and a series of
knobs and escarpments ringing its southern edge.

Louisville sits almost at the westernmost point, at the Falls of the Ohio River, with a scenic, crescent-shaped band of ridges, isolated rounded hills, and conical knobs to the south and west (known as The Knobs) and Muldraugh Hill, an escarpment capped with hard ledges of resistant limestone, beyond. Geode collectors find the southern Knobs to be fertile fields for exploration.

A word of advice to rockhounds: always have the landowner's permission.

For more information: Louisville Visitors Bureau, 400 South First Street, Louisville, KY 40202, 800-626-5646.

Old Louisville Inn, Attn: Marianne Lesher, 1359 South Third Street, Louisville, KY 40208, 502-635-1574. E-mail, oldlouinn@aol.com.

Falls of the Ohio

In 1792, the state boundary of the Commonwealth of Kentucky was established at the north bank of the Ohio River, giving Kentucky ownership of the Ohio, so to speak, for the portion that defines its border. The Falls of the Ohio, then, belongs to Kentucky even though access is from neighboring Indiana across the river from Louisville.

Falls of the Ohio State Park (within the 1,400-acre Falls of the Ohio National Wildlife Conservation Area at Clarksville, Indiana) commemorates dramatic geologic and historic events. It is the only place along the entire Ohio River where the river bottom has exposed bedrock; however, it is what was revealed that is significant.

In the exposed bedrock were found banks of ancient coral reef limestone teeming with fossil remnants of ancient seas, deposited during the Devonian Age nearly 400 million years ago. Actually, it is the largest exposed fossil reef of this period in the world. Today, it is a very popular 220-acre spot for studying these marine fossils (though collecting is strictly forbidden).

Just as the Devonian Age placed the fossils here, the ice age played a role in their discovery when flood waters from melting glaciers moved the river channel, rerouting the Ohio across a buried bedrock ridge.

Traditionally—before the McAlpine Dam was built with its navigation locks—the "Falls" was a series of rapids that fell 26 feet in 2½ miles. It was the only obstruction to navigation in nearly 1,000 miles of the Ohio River, requiring downriver shipments to be portaged around it. It was natural, then, that commercial establishments would spring up at this place early on and flourish and grow to be what is now the city of Louisville.

So the story here is one of geology, history, and commerce. It is also an exceptional place to view migrating birds, to hike, picnic, and enjoy the scenery.

The park's 16,000-square-foot interpretive center atop the river bluff opened in 1994 and quickly became a popular facility. In the circular two-story-high lobby is a riveting life-size diorama featuring populations that have left their mark at this place, from the prehistoric mammoth to contemporary species.

Off the lobby is a 100-seat theater where a 15-minute state-of-the-art multimedia show is scheduled every half hour. It starts with eerie music and exciting visuals that go back to a time when, as the announcer says, "warm shallow seas crept across this land and continents would not be in their present positions for hundreds of millions of years." Even small children in the audience are entranced.

The exhibit area covers a wide range of subjects with its "walking tour through time" illustrated with 3-D displays, paintings and photographs, video presentations, working models, and interactive exhibits. Geology, archaeology, cultural history, natural history, changes to the falls, mapping, and industry and commerce are covered. Visitors can learn about early explorers, the impact of the Civil War, and famous people who were here. Displays may be large (as in the very tall stratigraphic column that shows rock layers and what causes them) or small (as in the miniature village of thatched roof huts showing Native Americans engaged in traditional activities).

One of my favorite exhibits is a series of scenes of eight natural communities of birds, fish, and small mammals against photographic backgrounds that depict rocky ledges, woodland, a gravel bar, pocket prairie, sandbar, marsh, mud bank, and river.

Another subject is the extinct passenger pigeon, once the most common bird in the United States but massacred for sport. John James Audubon, who lived here for two years and sketched more than 200 birds at this location, was quoted as saying he saw a flock of passenger pigeons over Louisville in 1813 that he estimated numbered more than a billion birds. The last passenger pigeon died in the Cincinnati Zoo in 1914.

Other things to learn about are: how dams operate and how navigation locks work; industry at the falls and how a gristmill works; and pioneer woodworking tools and what they produced. You can also learn about Kentucky flatboats and Ohio keelboats. You can go inside a replica of a towboat pilothouse and a steamboat pilothouse and in both take the controls, stand at the wheel, and pretend to guide the boat.

One area in the interpretive center is for wildlife observation at a feeding station for birds and small mammals. Sound is piped into the room, enhancing the "50-yard-line" view of the activity outside as you sit on carpeted risers. More than 265 species of birds have been identified at the Falls. Another room offers views of the Ohio River below (or you can have a spectacular view of the Falls from an observation deck outside).

The gift shop has an extensive collection of books and other items related to subjects covered here.

Outside, a wide concrete ramp leads down to the fossil beds on the flats. With handholds along both sides, it is wheelchair accessible down to the lower level. Naturalist-led tours are scheduled most afternoons and weekends. They have names like Tracking Trilobites, Mollusk Mosey, Stalking Crinoids, Corals Galore, and Fossil Fun. Summer plant walks and a history hike are also given. Most of them last an hour and are fairly easy walking, though they go over irregular rocky surfaces.

The self-guided Woodland Loop Trail is also just outside the interpretive center. It is an easy-to-moderate, three-quarter-mile walk that passes through both Upper and Lower Woodlands habitats. Pick up a trail guide, which will help you identify river cane, honey locust, hackberry, cottonwood, elderberry, white mulberry, Jerusalem artichoke, wild ginger, and pawpaw specimens and learn some interesting facts about each. From the Lower Woodland, you approach the fossil beds below and are encouraged to take short side trips down to the river.

Guided fossil-bed tours are given May 1 through October 31; and from September through November, other fossil-bed tours can be scheduled through the Louisville Science Center (502-561-6103).

Fishing is also popular here, for sauger, striped bass, white bass, walleye, crappie, catfish, and other species. A year-round, double-lane boat-launching ramp is at the George Rogers Clark homesite at the end of Harrison Avenue in Clarksville. It has a special loading ramp for wheelchair boaters. You can also hike to this spot along a levee trail from the park interpretive center.

Where: From Interstate 65 at Louisville, go north and take exit zero just across the Ohio River. Follow the signs, which route traffic west on Riverside Drive to the park entrance. On the return, follow signs to Interstate 65. (Note: McAlpine Locks and Dam accessible at Louisville from Northwestern Parkway, 27th Street exit.)

When: Year-round. Daily, 9:00 A.M. to 5:00 P.M. Closed Thanksgiving and Christmas. (McAlpine Locks and Dam, 8 A.M. till dusk.)

Admission: Very modest admission, with ages 2 to 12 half price. (McAlpine Locks and Dam are free.)

Amenities: Interpretive center with exhibits, library, gift shop, wildlife-viewing room, and theater; access ramp to fossil beds; nature and hiking trails; boat ramp; picnic areas.

Activities: Viewing fossil beds and interpretive exhibits, hiking, nature walks, picnicking, fishing, wildlife viewing, birding, photography, naturalist-led one-hour hikes.

Special events: Dramatized programs and storytelling most months, some for special age groups (ask for schedule).

Other: Barrier-free access to interpretive center and some other areas. Guided fossil-bed tours, May 1 through October 31. Laser video presentation is closed captioned for deaf, provides assistive listening for hearing impaired, and audio descriptive system for the blind. Fishing requires Kentucky or Indiana license.

For more information: Falls of the Ohio Interpretive Center, 201 West Riverside Drive, Clarksville, IN 47129, 812-280-9970.

District Engineer, Public Affairs Office, U.S. Army Engineer District, PO Box 59, Louisville, KY 40201-0059, 502-582-5736. (McAlpine Locks and Dam information.)

Louisville Science Center, 727 West Main Street, Louisville, KY 40202-2633, 502-561-6103. (For additional fossil-bed tours.)

Portland Museum

It would be easy to miss this charming little museum tucked away on a quiet residential street near the Ohio River at the Falls, but that would be a shame. Portland Museum was founded in 1978 by elementary schoolteachers who wanted to make the rich river history and heritage of their town come alive for young people. Today, the museum features a light-and-sound tour, "Portland: the Land, the River, and the People," with automated mannequins representing historic characters who lived here in the 19th century—a refreshing approach that is very appealing.

Portland was founded in 1811 by General William Lytle, who wanted to build a canal around the Falls. That scheme failed, but the town prospered anyway. By 1818, the portage trail was heavily used by carriages, oxen, and travelers on foot. As taverns, shipyards, and chandlers opened up, a half dozen towns grew along this stretch of the river.

The museum also tells about earlier periods when only the Native Americans lived on the land and what their culture was like. A map of Kentucky, circa 1750, shows sacred hunting grounds and identifies places by their Indian names. A diorama of early Native American cultures depicts daily life activities such as hunting of buffalo and preparation of hides and meat.

The tour begins in the lobby, then moves to a huge table-top contour relief map that focuses on the area of the Falls while a narrator sets the scene. One by one, the mannequins tell their stories as visitors push buttons to activate each display, moving through the museum rooms at their own pace.

A woman at a ship's wheel talks about her life piloting a riverboat, her love of the river, and the feeling of freedom it gives her.

A 16-year-old boy explains what skills he had to develop for his work on the river.

Henry Shreve, "conqueror of inland rivers," had a snag boat, the *Heliopolis*, so named because it removed snags from inland rivers (thus, Shreve's "conqueror" title).

The mannequin that is Audubon speaks with a French accent. "Migrating geese were so numerous that men shot them down 30 at a time. More and more people came. Hundreds of steamboats came...." Except, at high water in spring and fall the steamboats could not pass.

A French woman talks. She followed her parents here, married, had children and lost three of them, and helped her husband build a business. "Our business is flourishing now, and our world will be alive with good music and the sounds of dancing feet."

Of course, there were local "characters," and their anecdotes are both amusing and revealing of the times.

Besides the mannequins, the museum displays implements and objects, newspaper clippings, maps and illustrations, and replicas for a fascinating look into the past.

Among the many other featured displays was one on the building of the canal, which was done mainly with picks and dynamite, and took several years.

Evidently, Shippingport, the town adjacent to Portland, disappeared in the mid-1800s, as it was repeatedly devastated by spring floods, dwindling from 600 residents in 1830. (An old whiskey bottle label has it spelled "Shipping Port.")

For more immersion in the local cultural history, visitors can enter the video viewing room and see *Witness at the Falls: John James Audubon* or *Dream of Power: The Great Mill of Shippingport*. Each lasts 20 minutes. Other videos based on events and people of the early 1800s were produced by elementary school students, who were taught animation techniques in classrooms on the museum's lower level.

The gift shop has toys and other things for children. Pencil sharpeners, for example, are diecast miniature steamboats and stagecoaches. There are geological treasures, too, and plenty of books and cassettes.

Where: 2308 Portland Avenue, Louisville. Take Interstate 64 to the 22nd Street exit. Turn west onto Portland Avenue (at the light) and look for the museum half a block down on the left.
When: Year-round. Monday through Friday, 10:00 A.M. to 4:30 P.M.
Admission: Modest fee. Discount for seniors, Armed Forces personnel, and students. Under five, free. Wednesday is "Donation Day."
Amenities: Museum, video room, gift shop.
Activities: Museum tours.
Other: Group rates.
For more information: Portland Museum, 2308 Portland Avenue, Louisville, KY 40212, 502-776-7678.

Louisville Zoo

"What's new?" That's always an appropriate question to ask at the Louisville Zoo. If you've visited before, it's likely that you'll notice some exciting innovations. Most recently, emphasis has been on providing natural habitats for the animals to enjoy and to give visitors a sense of being in exotic places. This is done by creating theme areas.

A recent one is an "Islands" area with outdoor exhibits and an indoor pavilion (following closely on the heels of the Herp Aquarium and the MetaZoo Education Center). The Islands Habitat celebrates the more than 10,000 islands in the western Pacific Ocean.

An island environment is very fragile, since it is not unusual for one or two islands to have plant and animal species that, being uniquely adapted to their isolated island home, are found nowhere else in the world. A single storm or the introduction of a new predator could wipe out an entire species. This has actually happened.

On a sobering note: more than 10 percent of the world's bird species are nearing extinction, and the majority are island species. Put another way, nearly all of the birds that have become extinct since 1600 were from islands. An example is the dodo bird, which lived on Mauritius in the Indian Ocean and became extinct in 1665.

Islands aren't the only place on earth where species are threatened, and the preservation of habitat and species is given heavy emphasis throughout the zoo. The zoo works closely with state, federal, and international wildlife agencies and organizations to save and bring back threatened or endangered species. Not all of these live in exotic places, either. Take as an example the black-footed ferret, which was nearly wiped out in the Great Plains of the United States as a result of efforts to control prairie dog populations. The species—the most endangered mammal in North America—was actually down to 13 known individuals before breeding efforts at the Louisville Zoo and four other facilities started returning some to the wild in 1991. This is an ongoing program.

Some of the newest areas at the zoo are natural habitats from other continents. When all are completed, they will represent each of the major regions of the world. An African Village and African Outpost opened in 1998. An Asian exhibit will have a tropical forest, waterfalls, and an elephant logging camp. Kentucky won't be ignored in all this. Indigenous plants and animals of the state will have a focus area, too.

Another aspect of the next-generation concept being implemented is the feeling of "you are there" in walk-through habitats. They are made as realistic as possible, even to re-

Louisville Zoo

creating natural "life dramas" that animals would experience in the wild. The animals are housed off exhibit and then brought in one by one on different days. For example, a tiger might come through one day, putting down his scent. The next day, tapirs may walk through, sensing that a predator has been there. When the tiger pays a return visit, it will be aware that the tapirs were present.

Giving animals a habitat more nearly like the wild includes providing a natural feeding situation, like feeding elephants large tree branches so they can select the ones they want, break them up, and then drag them around as they would in nature.

As the zoo's media coordinator Diana DeVaughn commented, "We don't want to have urban animals."

Of course, zoo animals have to be handled to some extent—fed and groomed, for instance. This means zoo keepers are trimming the elephants' feet and brushing the seals' teeth. Each day at feeding time, zoo visitors can watch animal-training sessions that help condition the animals to be calm and unstressed whenever they must be handled for any reason.

The zoo likes to show rarely seen types of a species, and there are many here, like the Komodo dragon, a fierce predator from Malaysia that can grow to eight feet long. It is on view in the HerpAquarium, a very modern climate-controlled structure in which exhibits simulate a tropical rain forest, daytime and nighttime deserts, a savanna, and an aquatic community. The realism includes appropriate humidity levels, authentic sounds (breaking waves, coastal birds), and natural lighting.

Sometimes experience dictates a change from what was planned, as when three species of lemurs were placed in an open exhibit. It was found that leaping lemurs had different skill levels. As expected, all could leap 15 feet horizontally, but one had Olympic-class capabilities and a couple of innovative handholds. Not wanting "Lemurs over Louisville" as the next locally popular song, the zoo ended up with just the ringtail and black lemurs sharing the spotlight in that exhibit.

Strolling around the African Veldt, the Australian Walkabout, the North and South American Panorama, the Asian Plains, or taking the tram from place to place (one ticket gives you all-day access), you will be among the more than 1,600 animals that are housed here. The zoo sits on some rolling hills near the center of Louisville but with a sense of remoteness created by the surrounding greenbelt and trees. Walking is easy on the wide and mostly shady blacktop paths. It is a very clean and well-kept zoo and a thoroughly pleasant place to spend the day. There are snack stands, a café, an education center, a gift shop, and an amphitheater where animal shows are conducted from Memorial Day through the Labor Day weekend. Also, camel and elephant rides are offered for a small additional fee.

What is the significance of this zoo? Maybe we should think of what Chief Seattle was quoted as saying in 1854: "If all the beasts were gone, men would die from a great loneliness of the spirit."

Where: 1100 Trevilian Way in Louisville. From Interstate 264 (Waterson Expressway), take exit 14 and go north on Poplar Level Road, then turn right on Trevilian Way following the zoo signs.

When: Year-round. Daily, gate hours: 10:00 A.M. to 5:00 P.M. April through August and extended to 8:00 P.M. Wednesday through Friday from June through August (closes at 4:00 P.M. September through March). Special twilight hours. Closed Thanksgiving, Christmas, and New Year's Days.

Admission: Modest fee for ages 12 to 59; reduced price for seniors 60 and over and children 3 to 11. Extra for train, tram, elephant and camel rides. Group rates. Free for active and retired military personnel and children two and under.

Amenities: Animal exhibits in theme areas, train and tram transportation, education center, café, gift shop, amphitheater, picnic area.

Activities: Animal viewing, photography, scheduled performances, summer camps and teen safaris, ZOOper Kids Classes (ages three and four), animal shows daily (Wednesday through Sunday) from Memorial Day through Labor Day.

Special events: Orchestral performances (summer), Intertribal Native American Pow-Wow (September), Halloween Party weekends (October), and others (inquire).

Other: Barrier-free access. Wheelchair, stroller, and wagon rentals. Free parking.

For more information: Louisville Zoological Garden, 1100 Trevilian Way, PO Box 37250, Louisville, KY 40233, 502-459-2181. Web site, www.iglou.com/louzoo/.

Beargrass Creek State Nature Preserve

Across from the zoo at 1297 Trevilian Way are 41 wooded acres next to Joe Creason Park that are part of the Kentucky State Nature Preserves Commission. This is a prime area for birding during spring and fall when warblers and migrating waterfowl pass through the area. More than 150 species of birds have been sighted here.

Visitors can park in a lot next to the Metro Parks Office. A mile-long trail starts on a ridge behind the office and then descends to a floodplain where walking is easy on a boardwalk among huge sycamore trees. A side trip follows Beargrass Creek and another ascends to an area where an Army camp was situated during World War I. Along the way are a great variety of plants. More than 180 species have been identified in the preserve. For success in observing wildlife, walk quietly on the trails.

The Louisville Nature Center, a nonprofit organization, provides nature programs at the preserve for the general public. It is best to contact it in advance if you are planning a trip, because information is not always available at the site.

Where: 1297 Trevilian Way, Louisville, across from the Louisville Zoo. Enter Joe Creason Park for access.
When: Daily, sunrise to sunset.
Admission: Free.

Amenities: Nature trails. Joe Creason Park has a playground.
Activities: Birding, hiking, photography, nature observation.
Special events: Seasonal workshops and hikes.
Other: Dogs, horses, bicycles not allowed in preserve.
Firearms are prohibited.
For more information: The Louisville Nature Center, PO Box
39009, Louisville, KY 40233-9009. Office, 502-429-9666.
Nature Center hotline, 502-222-9368. Nature Clubhouse, 502-
458-1328.

Jefferson County Memorial Forest

Though Louisville is in relatively flat country, just south of
the city near the community of Fairdale are some densely
forested, rugged knobs where the 5,100-plus-acre Jefferson
County Memorial Forest occupies four separate tracts of land.
It is a nature preserve administered by the county and is also
a National Audubon Society Wildlife Refuge. Three major
areas—Tom Wallace, Horine Forest, and Paul Yost—are
developed for recreation and environmental education; and a
fourth, Scotts Gap, is an end-of-the-trail destination with
parking facilities. The forest, just minutes from downtown
Louisville, is easy to reach from Interstate 65 and the Gene
Snyder Freeway.

A visit to the welcome center at 11311 Mitchell Hill Road
will get you started right, since this is the hub of activities.
You can't miss the two-story white building on the left with
its bright red metal roof and its bell tower, originally built in
1915 as the Dennis Mitchell School. Now it has offices, display
rooms, and classrooms. A T-shaped, covered boardwalk and
two outdoor patios provide additional gathering places.

Forest Ranger Steve Goodwin explained the programs.
"We have a whole array of regular and special programs, with

something going on every weekend. In the Horine section of the forest at the top of the hill is our main leadership development center and the base for our environmental education programs. Here at the welcome center, we give interpretive programs, environmental awareness programs, and others about the history of the area. Full-time naturalists are on duty at both places."

A look at the annual calendar of events shows a wide variety of activities such as Hiking with a Ranger, Project Wild Workshop for Leaders, Alpine Tower Open Climb, Arbor Day Festival, Geology of the Forest, Peeking at Shannon's Pond, Wild Edible Plants Walk, "Herp" Search, Attracting Wildlife to Your Back Yard, Family Teams Course and Campout, Stalking the Wild Turkey, Natural Dyes Workshop, Meet John Muir, Fall Wildflower Hike, Birds of the JCMF, and Trees in Winter. Some sessions are free, and others have a modest fee to cover costs.

The forest has more than 35 miles of trails over varied terrain, ranging from easy to strenuous. Some special ones include horse trails in the Paul Yost area and a quarter-mile, handicapped-accessible trail (Tulip Tree Trail) in the Tom Wallace area. The 6½-mile Siltstone Trail goes from the welcome center to Scotts Gap Road and then offers a 4-mile loop extension. Scotts Gap has a parking lot for shuttles. The popular Mitch McConnell Loop Trail at Paul Yost (for foot travel only and rated moderate) has a series of loops that can be hiked in 2-, 4-, and 6½-mile segments. Up in the 1,000-acre Horine area, which for 25 years was a Boy Scout reservation, the trail system includes a cross-country running trail.

Across the street from the welcome center is the Tom Wallace recreation area. It provides parking, a fishing pier, trails, picnic pavilion with grills, playground, archery range, and rest rooms. The self-guided Tulip Tree Trail, a loop, begins at a small parking lot off the main lot and leads to a fishing dock.

It continues up the valley into old-growth timber. This walk is especially pleasant when early spring wildflowers are blooming.

Heading back on Mitchell Hill Road, turn right on Holsclaw Hill Road to the Paul Yost area. It is in a pretty little valley where you can park, use the picnic and playground areas, and try the various loops of the Mitch McConnell Trail.

Holsclaw Hill Road continues from there, climbing up through the forest. A sharp exit to the right leads to the top of the knob and the Horine section ranger station. Assistant Forest Ranger Jack West was happy to answer my questions.

The whole forest up here is considered a wildlife sanctuary, with all plants and animals protected and no hunting allowed. The Horine section is a fee-use site, costing a dollar a day for hiking and picnicking, with an additional fee for using the family camping area. Also, six tepees located in the group area can be rented for overnight stays.

Horine is focused on education and training. During the week, corporations and organizations have meetings and workshops in the manor house on the premises. On weekends, the programs are for the public. One of the most popular is the Alpine Tower open climb. The tower is a 50-foot-tall climbing tower made from telephone poles with stone handholds. As the climbers ascend, using the principles and equipment involved in rappelling, belay teams on the ground back them up by securing the ropes. The concept, as Jack explained, is similar to rock climbing.

"When it's time to come down, the climber sits in the harness as if sitting in a chair, and the belay team feeds rope back out through the figure eight and lowers the person, like an elevator ride, to the ground."

More than 22,000 people visit each year. Besides the public and corporate programs, school groups come from many Kentucky counties to take advantage of training on the Alpine tower, the five teams courses, and a high-ropes course.

"The teams courses get people working together cooperatively on communications skills, group consensus, conflict resolution, problem solving, self-esteem building, and healthy risk taking. We do it for all age groups, from elementary school through adults," said Jack.

Of all the people who visit each year, Jack estimated that 90 percent participate in a teams course and teams-building process and the other 10 percent are hikers, campers, and picnickers.

This forest makes a great day-use getaway place for standing among giant trees, watching wildlife, hiking, or horseback riding to your heart's content—all the time breathing invigorating air. You might just see coyotes, deer, wild turkeys, raptors and warblers, raccoons, foxes, and other small forest-dwelling mammals.

Where: South of Louisville. To welcome center, take Interstate 65 south, exit west onto the Gene Snyder Freeway (Interstate 265 on the map), then take the New Cut Road exit and turn left. Continue to Fairdale and turn right at a yellow flashing light onto Mitchell Hill Road. Continue to the welcome center on the left (11311 Mitchell Hill Road).

When: Year-round, 6:30 A.M. to dusk.

Admission: Free. Modest fee for some events and some day-use areas.

Amenities: Welcome center, picnic shelters, primitive campground, rest rooms, archery range, teams courses, Alpine tower, foot and horse trails.

Activities: Hiking, wildlife viewing, birding, nature appreciation, photography, picnicking, camping, fishing.

Special events: Varied programs most weekends year-round. Schedule published annually.
Other: Barrier-free access at welcome center, special fishing pier, and in some other areas.
For more information: Jefferson County Memorial Forest, 12304 Holsclaw Hill Road, PO Box 467, Fairdale, KY 40118, 502-366-5432. Fax, 502-368-3882.

Bernheim Arboretum and Research Forest

Some people like the outdoors rugged and natural, while others prefer the beauty of an immaculately landscaped and humanly designed scene. Who's to say which is best? Nevertheless, both can be admired and appreciated at the Bernheim Arboretum and Research Forest at Clermont just off Interstate 65 about 15 miles south of the Interstate 265 junction in Louisville.

The privately endowed, 10,000-acre Bernheim property of rolling meadows and hilly knobs is Kentucky's "official arboretum" and also a wildlife refuge and conservation/education area. It is a very popular destination, offering theme gardens, scenic overlooks, 35 miles of hiking trails, a nature center and museum, self-guided nature paths, picnic areas, and a full schedule of year-round activities and special events.

A sign at the gate announces plants of special interest that are being featured in the gardens. For example, in mid-September ornamental grasses and autumn perennials may have the spotlight. It is easy to find one's way around by following a loop road that circles the middle part of the parklike grounds. Among the landscaped areas to enjoy are several that overlook 32-acre Lake Nevin. Tablet Hill sits in a grove of holly trees. Another, the Quiet Garden at the Arboretum Center, is at the eastern edge of the lake midway along the crescent-shaped shore. Views from the north shore reward you after a drive (or walk) beside native and exotic varieties of maple trees. And nature trails east of the lake follow the shoreline.

In the center of the loop drive is Big Meadow, which can be viewed from an overlook at the far end for a spectacular panorama of meadow and mature ornamental trees. Look up, and you may see a red-tailed hawk atop a tree or circling the meadow in search of an unsuspecting rodent for its lunch. Three Cedar Lakes on the eastern edge of the loop road attract waterfowl throughout most of the year. The Pines picnic area nearby has tables in the pines on ground carpeted with fragrant needles, and other tables are in a grove of deciduous trees. People can use portable grills here, but grills are not allowed in the wilderness portion because of the potential fire hazard.

The arboretum center looks out on a fountain, lily ponds, and individual flower gardens designed to show off various trees, shrubs, and perennials. The showiness of each and their exciting color combinations elicit exclamations from visitors—deservedly so.

At the nature center, you can walk a nature trail, observe wildlife, and learn about animal habits and habitats. On Sundays at 2:00 P.M. you can join a guided nature walk. The museum focuses on many aspects of nature, including how to identify trees and how to build and position birdhouses to attract a particular species. One of the most interesting objects is a portion of a fossilized tree—*Callixylon newberryi*—found in 1991 in Bernheim Forest. It is distantly related to modern conifers and is estimated to be 350 million years old.

Young couples, parents with young children, and seniors all find something to enjoy here. Beside the museum are two tall, cylindrical silos that were built in 1904 and now are a place for gray squirrels to play. In back of the museum, trails lead to a weather station, trailside shelter, deer corral, birds of prey display, waterfowl area, and a springhouse. Flower beds are strategically placed, attracting butterflies and bees.

A self-guided nature trail starts beside the deer corral, circling a transition forest (a new forest that is growing back) and then a climax, or old-growth, forest where fallen trees are found among the giant living ones. A forest is one of my favorite places to be, as it is for many of us. Do we ever tire of the fragrances, the antics of squirrels, or trees that sigh in the wind?

Outdoor excursions can provide excellent educational opportunities for children. As I walked the first portion of the nature trail, I noticed two young mothers and three small children excitedly pointing to something they had discovered under some fallen leaves. Evidently, it was time for a forest lesson, because one mother was saying, "All right. You've looked at it now, so leave it alone. This is its habitat."

With 14 trails at Bernheim, the hiking opportunity is tremendous. Leaving the landscaped grounds for the wilderness section, the forest soon closes in and rugged hills and deep ravines surround us. There are also occasional grassy areas for picnicking (some with tables and rest rooms). Each trailhead has a parking area and a sign that gives the trail name and the estimated hiking time—30 minutes, an hour, or more. Cull Hollow Trail and Jackson Hollow Trail are two popular ones at the lower elevations. Color-coded trail markers make all trails easy to follow. On a fall day with skies filled with rustling leaves driven by gusty winds and soaring birds above, the trail that beckoned me was the Tower Loop Trail at the end of Tower Hill Road. The wilderness part of Bernheim is a great place to enjoy the distinctive Knobs with their cone-shaped peaks, formed over geologic time as the resistant caprock finally eroded away.

Activities at Bernheim not so visible to the public are the ongoing environmental and research projects. For example, cooperating with the Kentucky Fish and Wildlife Service and the National Turkey Federation, Bernheim has relocated hundreds of wild turkeys to other areas of the state. Other projects focus on education, natural areas restoration, horticulture, science, and art. People who have a special interest in any of these subjects can inquire about classes and workshops.

Whether your preference is to hike to a forest lookout tower, join a moonlight carriage ride or hayride, or sit in the shady Quiet Garden watching the wind ripple the surface of Lake Nevin, you can spend a memorable day (or evening) here. I did.

Where: Just off Interstate 65 south of Louisville. Take exit 112, then go east on State 245 for seven-tenths of a mile to the entrance.

When: Year-round. Daily, 8:00 A.M. to one hour before sunset. Closed Christmas Day and New Year's Day.

Admission: Free on weekdays, moderate per-vehicle fee on weekends and holidays. Fees for carriage rides, classes, and workshops.

Amenities: Arboretum center, theme gardens, nature center and museum, picnic grounds, wilderness area, trails.

Activities: Garden and exhibit viewing, nature appreciation, photography, picnicking, fishing, hiking, carriage rides. Guided nature hikes Sundays at 2:00 P.M. Free Children's Hour (hourly) on Saturday and Sunday afternoons. Guided tours of arboretum.

Special events: Moonlight wildlife tours/programs, concerts, science demos, summer day camps (request schedule).

Other: Barrier-free access to developed areas. Regulations prohibit motorcycles, kite flying, alcoholic beverages, fishing with minnows, and pets not on a leash (ask about other restrictions).

For more information: Bernheim Arboretum and Research Forest, Clermont, KY 40110, 502-955-8512.

Otter Creek Park

After a few forays fanning out from Louisville, we soon realize that exciting places to enjoy nature are within a 30-minute drive in just about every direction. Going west on the Gene Snyder Freeway, then south on U.S. Routes 31W/60 leads to the town of Muldraugh. Turn west on State 1638 to Otter Creek Park, situated on a wooded 3,000-acre plateau that is 200 feet above the Ohio River, which borders it on the north. The park is managed by the City of Louisville.

The nature center is the first public access place on the right after entering the park. It is the structure of fieldstone and barn-red siding (hard to miss). Along the walk to the entrance are beds of ferns, pansies, and other flowers. Inside, pick up a trail map and check the activity schedule. Some typical summer activities include learning to identify poisonous and edible plants, an "owl prowl" to search for nighttime sounds and creatures, a morning hike for birdwatching and listening, and an outing that teaches about rock strata, fossils, and cave formations.

Be sure to wander through the several rooms of exhibits. Many of the interactive displays focus on wildlife, encouraging park visitors to take plenty of time to enjoy nature. Discover facts about animals of the forests, ponds, and wetlands and their habits through the seasons of the year. Other themes deal with history and folklore.

"Folk casting" (forecasting by folklore) explains how pioneers predicted bad winters and other projected weather events. When squirrels begin gathering nuts early and have unusually bushy tails, crickets are in the chimney, screech owls sound like women crying, and the woolly worms' black bands are wide—watch out! Either you're having a bad dream, or you're in for a hard winter. Plants give additional clues, as when carrots grow deeper and cornshucks and corn silks grow thicker.

And then there are recipes, like one for persimmon pudding. In many places throughout the country, a walk in the woods in the right season could yield some sweet persimmons if you beat the possums to them. What a sweet treat!

For the pudding, follow this recipe:

Start with two cups of persimmon pulp, 1 teaspoon each of baking powder and baking soda, 1 pint milk, 2 eggs, 1 cup sugar, and two cups flour. Mix and bake in a round pan at 300°F for 3 hours and let stand 24 hours before serving.

I can't comment on it. I'm still looking for persimmons!

The grounds around the nature center are aromatic and wonderful, shaded with cedars and dogwoods. Behind the center is a red barn and a cabin built nearly 200 years ago at a time in history when the motto for families was "make do or do without." Families grew most of what they needed for survival, and recycling was a way of life. There are still valuable lessons we can learn from the pioneer lifestyle.

Near the nature center at the bridle path trailhead is a parking lot where people can leave their cars and horse trailers as they ride the 5³⁄₁₀-mile trail that loops in a figure eight, with 1⁹⁄₁₀-mile and 3⁴⁄₁₀-mile sections. Riders must obtain a free map and permit, available at the camp store, nature center, or administrative building.

The hiking trail system is quite extensive. All the trails are loop trails. Most popular is the 2⁷⁄₁₀-mile Red Trail. It is easy for the most part and provides three scenic overlooks of the Ohio River, but since steep cliffs go down to the river, the spur trail to that destination is difficult. However, you can opt to stay on the bluff. The Yellow Trail is longer (3⁷⁄₁₀ miles) and connects with a rugged gorge that makes for sensational scenery and a strenuous portion for hiking. Seasonally, it is subject to flooding. The longest and most challenging trail, the Blue Trail, is 8¹⁄₁₀ miles. It circles the park but can be hiked in sections. Parts of it are also subject to seasonal flooding. Easiest to walk is the six-tenths-mile Crow's Nest Trail just outside the nature center. It's actually a self-guided nature path.

Besides the well-marked trails mentioned, the park has many old roadbeds, deer trails, and nature trails no longer maintained that can be hiked. If you want to try them, it is highly recommended that you have a topo map for orienting yourself to the terrain (you'll want the Rock Haven Quadrangle map with the northwest corner at 38 degrees north and 86 degrees west). It is very possible to get lost in these woods. It has happened!

Mountain biking is another activity here, with trails ranging from moderate to difficult. (Bikers might also check out Cherokee Park in Louisville, which has some trails designated for biking.) Since mountain bike trail designations change from year to year, it is wise to inquire before planning a trip.

With its varied topography and habitats, this park provides exceptional year-round opportunities for watching wildlife. Forests, meadows, and marshes are attractive to birds, mammals, reptiles, and amphibians. More than 170 bird species have been recorded here, and myriad varieties of plants are represented.

Though this is a public-use facility, private camps lease part of the park's acreage and these are not accessible to the public. You pass entrances to these on the way to the lodge and restaurant, which are high above the river. What a view! It could be a mural, but it's a real scene of a meandering, wide river going through farmlands. Why, I wonder, does a meal with a view taste better than one without?

There's one more place to go: down to the river's edge. Driving there means looping back to the main park road at the edge of the park. It goes past the camp store/post office and into a public-use area that has an entrance fee on weekends and holidays. This is an older part of the park. The road winds downhill past Fred's Cove, then Morgan's Cave is on the left and an old quarry is on the right. A group was practicing rappelling off the cliff as I drove by.

Another popular activity is fishing. A boat ramp is ahead at the end of this road. White perch and catfish are caught in the Ohio River, while fishermen bait their hooks for bluegill and bass (rock, smallmouth, and largemouth) in Otter Creek.

As it nears the river, the road follows a small creek on the left, and footbridges every few hundred feet allow access to picnic tables on the other side. At the one-mile mark, tall cedar trees grow right beside the road, meeting overhead like a welcoming arch. You have come to the Ohio River.

Worth a Side Trip: The Doe Run Inn

From Otter Creek Park, it is just a short drive to the historic Doe Run Inn. Continue west on State 1628, then south on State 448 for a mile. The inn was originally a mill, built in 1821 of hand-hewn timber and native limestone with walls that are two feet thick. It was converted to an inn a century later. (The old cabin near the Otter Creek Park nature center is approximately the same age.)

Besides enjoying the inn itself and the country cooking, browsing the authentic regional crafts in the gift shop, taking the walking path to the historic dam, or strolling the grounds, visitors interested in the environment may appreciate that a snail and a crayfish species living here are found nowhere else in the world.

Meals are served daily from 7:30 A.M. to 9:00 P.M. The rooms are antique filled and quaint (you won't find a TV), but for those who want to immerse themselves authentically in a 200-year-old time warp, a stay here can be a very pleasant one.

Doe Run Inn is closed on Christmas Eve and Christmas Day.

Where: From Louisville, take the Gene Snyder Freeway (Interstate 265 on the map) west, turn south at U.S. Routes 31W/60 and go 12 miles, then west on State 1638 for 2⁸⁄₁₀ miles. Park entrance is on right.

When: Year-round. Nature center open 10:00 A.M. to 4:00 P.M. Tuesday through Friday; noon to 6:00 P.M. Saturday, Sunday, and holidays; closed Mondays. Restaurant open daily 8:00 A.M. to 7:00 P.M. (extended to 8:00 P.M. Friday and Saturday). Boat-launching area closes at dark.

Admission: Free on weekdays; fees for some areas Friday through Sunday. Free hiking, parking. Fees for other activities. Free camping in wilderness areas with permit. Senior (65 and up) and group rates for accommodations.

Amenities: Restaurant, lodge, cabins, campground, self-guided nature center, general store, recreational facilities, hiking trails, bridle paths, swimming pool, miniature golf, bicycle rentals, teams course, Alpine tower, boat-launching ramp, river overlooks.

Activities: Hiking, picnicking, camping (including backcountry camping), wildlife viewing, birding, nature appreciation, photography, fishing, boating, bicycling, caving, mountain biking. For groups of 10 or more: guided cave tours, rappelling, orienteering, teams course programs, nature classes (fee charged).

Special events: Bluegrass & Barbecue Festival (May). Summer programs include: nature crafts; Creek and Stream Stroll; Star Gaze; Bees, Bats, & Micro Habitat; Mapping and Orienteering.

Other: Barrier-free access at some locations.

For more information: Otter Creek Park, 850 Otter Creek Park Road, Brandenburg, KY 40108, 502-583-3577 (Louisville) or 502-942-8686 (Ft. Knox). Horse rentals, 502-828-3070.

Doe Run Inn, 500 Doe Run Hotel Road, Brandenburg, KY 40108, 502-422-2982 or 502-422-2042.

Broadmoor Gardens and Conservatory

To discover new places while driving along, it helps to program your peripheral vision to notice anything out of sync—that is to say, not part of the natural landscape. Like a road sign. That is how I found Broadmoor Gardens, a privately owned Eden that opens to the public on weekends.

Broadmoor is about 50 miles southwest of Louisville on U.S. Route 60 and about 20 miles beyond the turnoff to Otter Creek Park. What started as a 400-acre farm owned by partners Mary Ann Tobin and Mary Bruce (Brucie) Beard was transformed into a botanical showplace that the owners now enjoy sharing with people interested in horticulture, birding, exotic domestic animals, and woodland trails.

From U.S. Route 60, turn south on Gufton-Bewleyville Road (where you see the Broadmoor sign). In a beautiful valley of fields surrounded by woodlands, the long entrance drive winds between rows of sycamore trees, decorative shrubs, and thousands of spring-flowering bulbs.

Spread before my eyes were extensive gardens with pools, fountains, and waterfalls, and glimpses of exotic animals. A white-crested peacock was perched on the roof of the conservatory, admiring its reflection in a window. Two swans were gliding on a pond, and nearby were white guinea hens, miniature ducks, and white silky chickens, whose feathers resemble fur.

The conservatory, a large room with high ceiling and skylights, has a collection of tropical plants native to Florida and Hawaii and an indoor/outdoor pool for goldfish and koi fish, which swim in and out at will.

It took nearly 10 years of planning and labor, with professional assistance, to create this paradise. Brucie and Mary Ann traveled extensively to the finest gardens in England and Europe, as well as other parts of the world for information and ideas. The result is spectacular, offering many varieties in bloom from spring through fall. A greenhouse was added in 1995. There's a gift shop, too, that is a good place to pick up garden-oriented items like birdhouses, feeders, chimes, and hand-painted clothing with nature motifs.

Each garden has a theme and a formal design. The Four Seasons Garden is divided into four quadrants and has a gazebo in the center. Clematis is very showy here. The Pastel Garden is a showplace for lilacs, irises, peonies, astilbes, butterfly bushes, black-eyed Susans, daisies, Oriental lilies, and tulips. The Moon Garden, featuring all-white azaleas, dogwoods, viburnums, daffodils, and candytufts, is said to glow under a full moon. A Shade Garden has ferns, hostas, other shade-loving plants, and interesting rock specimens. Rose and Iris Gardens share the spotlight, of course. Underplantings of tulips and other bulbs make these areas interesting in spring. Other gardens promote additional themes.

Brucie was naming the plant varieties as we walked through: phlox, euonymus, barberry, Japanese and Dutch iris, Japanese red maples, Anthony Waterer spirea, juniper topiaries that are "living statues," crape myrtle, Oriental poppies, peonies, hibiscus, coral bells. . . . It soon became obvious that a full list would fill a small book. Brucie said, "We went to a flower show in Cincinnati to find new varieties, and they didn't have a thing there that we didn't already have!"

Some plant specimens here defy traditional logic, like the aspen trees that are thriving and multiplying, though Mary Ann says they're not supposed to do that at this altitude. Columbines and blue spruce do very well here, too—but that's expected.

It should be no surprise that the garden attracts wildlife. Butterflies, bees, hummingbirds, and other birds come to dine, and deer feed on the sunflowers that are planted specifically for them. Bird feeders, bluebird houses, and butterfly boxes are placed around the gardens, too.

Not all is so formal, though. Out in the fields are masses of wildflowers from spring through fall. A hayride takes visitors through the woods and fields for an up-close look at the natural environment. The two-mile-long trail begins between the pygmy goat barn and the swan habitat, follows a woodland stretch, and then crosses a field. Deer are seen here often. Back in the woods again, the trail passes through maples, dogwoods, and redbuds—trees especially interesting in spring and fall—and a fern grotto. The ferns grow year-round because air from a nearby cave moderates the temperature. Birds and small mammals find the habitat here very much to their liking, and coyotes are in the area, too.

Guests are free to wander the property or can have a guided tour if they prefer. If you visit, ask about the farm animals. Twenty American Saddlebred horses are kept in the horse barn, which has both an indoor and outdoor training ring. Time it right, and you may get to see a new foal!

Where: From U.S. Route 31W between Louisville and Elizabethtown, west on U.S. Route 60 for 15 miles, then south on Gufton-Bewleyville Road to entrance.

When: April 1 through October 31 on Saturday and Sunday afternoons from noon to 6:00 P.M. Open weekdays by appointment.

Admission: Midrange fee (includes hayride). Discount for children and seniors. Group rates.

Amenities: Outdoor gardens, tropical plant conservatory, pools and fountains, exotic domestic animals, two-mile woodland and meadow trail, gift shop, picnic area.

Activities: Viewing formal gardens, nature appreciation, birding, hayrides, picnicking, photography.

Special events: Occasional plant sales and concerts. Inquire.

For more information: Broadmoor Gardens and Conservatory, Highway 60 East, Box 387, Irvington, KY, 40146, 502-547-4200.

Oldham Community Center and Nature Preserve

Some tourist information books have the Oldham Community Center placed at La Grange, but it is actually just across the Oldham County line from Louisville and much closer to that city. The directions given at the end will help you find it.

Oldham County has well-tended croplands and Thoroughbred farms. Apple orchards, fields of corn and tobacco, and neatly stacked hay dot the gently rolling land. At the southern end of the county, horse farms seem to take over. Until the 165-acre Oldham Community Center was established as a nature preserve in 1975 under the will of Mrs. Virginia Creasy Mahan, it was a horse farm, too.

The main entrance to Oldham, on Harmony Landing Road, goes to the administration building, other buildings, and a new nature center with exhibits. Fields, ponds, and woods dot the rectangular property. A second entrance is flanked by stone pillars, where a one-way blacktop road leads to a gravel parking lot from which people can easily access the trails, arboretum, and other outdoor features.

The center has nearly four miles of hiking trails which need no markers, since they are 20-foot-wide mowed strips between groves of trees (they serve double duty for fire control). There's also a mile-long fitness trail that circles a large field.

Gus Daeuble, Oldham's manager of building and grounds, was my enthusiastic host, even though I visited on a busy day. A school group was expected to arrive within minutes.

The conversation turned to animals of the wild. "We have deer and possum and raccoon and of course a lot of lesser animals," said Gus. "And a lot of birds are here. Also, we have a raptor rehabilitation center. Out there in that flight cage is a red-tailed hawk. Can you see him?"

"Uh . . . yes! But why is this large vulture on the ground?"

"Somebody raised him, and now he has no notion of what he is or what he's supposed to be. A vulture will fly up in the air and circle around looking for food, but not Ebenezer. He'll go sit on somebody's house and steal dog food."

Now, this is a problem with taming wild animals. Besides being illegal in most places, it completely ruins the animal and renders it unable to be returned to the wild.

Gus agreed. "Our intention, of course, is to release the rehabilitated birds. Now, the hawk I pointed to has a bad wing and can't fly. All the birds we keep are injured or have been spoiled like Ebenezer. There's a crow walking around out here named Edgar Allen Crow that was raised by someone and is about 14 years old now. He doesn't know how to be a crow, so we keep his wings clipped and let him wander around the yard during the daytime."

Rehabilitation is an ongoing program here, and the center has been very successful in releasing birds that recovered from injuries. The animals that can't be rehabilitated are used in demonstrations for schoolchildren and other groups.

That day, Native Americans were getting ready to demonstrate traditional skills, Indian lore, and plant identification. They had laid out some plants on a porch and in the yard. As three school buses of eighth-graders arrived, drums started beating. The bus doors opened and eager teenagers streamed out.

A beautiful day, a nice group, and a friendly place!

Where: From Louisville, go north on U.S. Route 42 to Prospect and turn left (north) on State 1793. Go one mile, then turn right on Harmony Landing Road. Oldham Community Center is one-tenth of a mile on the left.

When: Grounds open Monday through Saturday, 8:00 A.M. until dusk; public buildings open Monday through Saturday, 8:30 A.M. to 4:30 P.M.

Admission: Free, but donations accepted.

Amenities: Arboretum, nature center, activity room, trails, ponds.

Activities: Viewing wildlife and exhibits, hiking and nature walks, birding, photography.

Other: Special group programs. Inquire.

For more information: Oldham Community Center, 12501 Harmony Landing Lane, Goshen, KY 40026, 502-228-4362.

10

Great Bend of the Ohio

The Ohio River makes a great, sweeping curve around
north-central Kentucky, even creating a peninsular "topknot" opposite Cincinnati, Ohio. Some of Kentucky's finest
natural areas—the quiet, off-the-beaten-path kinds of places
—and other locations well known for outdoor sports such as
skiing and mountain bike riding are to be found in this northern part of the Outer Bluegrass.

General Butler State Resort Park

General Butler SRP, less than an hour northeast of Louisville,
is situated high on an isolated hill near the confluence of the
Kentucky and Ohio Rivers at Carrollton. It provides a spectacular overlook of the joining of two great waters. The hill
is a unique geologic feature formed by an uplift of limestone
and shale dating to the Late Ordovician Period some 450 million years ago—one of the few places in Kentucky where
rocks of this age were pushed to the surface. Rising 250 feet
above the surrounding floodplain in an easily accessible location, it was an obvious choice for the park system to develop
ski runs. The result has been Kentucky's only ski-resort park,
with the ski trails traditionally packed with snow from mid-
December to mid-March if cold weather holds. The ski runs

193

are used as mountain bike trails during specific festivals from April through October.

The park has six slopes on 23 acres and is open during the season from Thursday through Monday, plus holidays. A ski school instructs beginning through advanced levels, including race training and a "Ski Tots" program. Another popular activity is snowboarding, for which equipment rentals are available. The ski runs were closed in the winter of 1997–98 after several years of mild temperatures. Visitors should check year to year to make sure skiing is available.

Mountain bikers come five times a year when various competitions are held. Since this sport became a new Olympic event for the 1996 Summer Games, the regional and national competitions are gaining steadily in popularity. Richard Matthews, founder of Bike Butler, Inc., is the impetus behind the mountain biking in Kentucky, which now boasts 500 miles of trails, including many miles in the Big South Fork NRRA and the Daniel Boone National Forest (DBNF).

General Butler is a great place to see what this exciting sport is all about, and the competitions attract riders from age four through seniors. At this park, there is even a division for riders weighing more than 200 pounds. The most grueling event has to be the Off-Road Triathlon held in September. It includes a 1K swim across the park's 30-acre lake, a trail run to the ski lodge, and a 10K mountain bike race. During any of the competition weekends, recreational riders also have access to the trails on a fee basis.

A skiers' and mountain bikers' gathering place? True, but General Butler is attractive for many other reasons as well. The park is an exciting blend of natural beauty and historical presence, with special events as varied as a Bird Watch and Wildflower Weekend, an 1860's baseball game, a Traditional Irish Wake, and a gathering of barbershop quartets.

For much of that, we give credit to Evelyn Welch, curator of the Butler-Turpin Historic House and its "dependencies" (smokehouse, carriage house, vegetable garden, rose garden, stone kitchen, herb garden, henhouse, stables, barns, icehouse, washhouse, privy, and servants quarters). Though park and community-sponsored events include a Perfect Harmony Weekend for Valentine's Day, a Kentucky Scottish Weekend in May, National Trails Day events in June, and special July 4th activities, other events are connected with the Butler-Turpin historic site.

A winter encampment is held in February, featuring a weapons exhibit with flintlock rifles and tomahawk throwing.

The entire month of March is dedicated to the Irish heritage of the Butler family, descended from the powerful Butler Dynasty based in Kilkenny Castle, Ireland, since the Middle Ages. Activities include a special Butler Family Irish Celebration and Traditional Irish Wake. Music, dance, contests, and demonstrations make this a very interesting time to visit.

A Butler Bird Watch is held in April. It features daily workshops and speakers on Saturday night. It's an excellent time for birding, since chilly weather brings birds to the feeders, and viewing is easier before the trees are fully leafed. Early morning tours at the house and afternoon tours near the park lodge take advantage of the best times to see birds.

The General Butler Encampment, spanning three military generations of the Butler family, takes place the last weekend in April. It includes a style show of period costumes and a reenactment. A Revolutionary War banquet table is set up as if for a military meeting, and authentic military drills are performed.

May has a Blues Burgoo and Storytelling Contest with music, costumed interpreters, and complimentary food.

September offers learning and fun for children in a Heritage Day Camp.

October is a busy month, with Pieces of the Past (an old-fashioned quilting bee, exhibits, crafts demonstrations, and a reenactment of an 1860s baseball game), held early in the month. Later, Spirits of the Past is the Butler-Turpin version of a haunted house. People in period dress pose as historic figures; and nightly tours start at the house, where a nurse/midwife brews potions in the kitchen. From there, they go to the family graveyard. A sexton leads the way by lantern light, then tells chilling tales among the tombstones.

Several special events are related to the Christmas holidays. Antebellum tours are given from mid-November to mid-December. Each weekend in the park has special themes, with coordinated yuletide activities offered for children and adults.

A Tour Through the Butler-Turpin Historic House

I asked curator Evelyn Welch what people learn when she gives them a tour of this house, built in 1859 and completely renovated in the early 1990s. Placed prominently on a high, wooded hill overlooking meadows that seem curiously unchanged from a century and a half ago, it stands as a fine example of mid-19th-century Kentucky farmhouses.

"Our tours go through the house and the kitchen. Visitors get an overview of Gen. William Orlando Butler, for whom the park is named, and his association with the property and the house. We tell about his father, Revolutionary War Gen. Percival Butler, who came here in the 1790s and acquired this property as part of the Peachey Survey.

"The architecture of the house is a vernacular of rural Kentucky, with Greek Revival and some Italianate detail. We tell of the lifestyles of a mid-1800s family that would have owned slaves and indentured servants and how the role of the slave interacted with the people of the house—what they did for each other.

"As to the furniture and artifacts, we point out what is original to the Butler and Turpin families, describing the styles of furniture, which include Federal, Georgian, Empire, Early Victorian, and Sheraton pieces. We describe textiles, such as upholstery fabrics made of horsehair and the woven rugs found throughout the house.

"Kitchens were especially interesting. Prior to the late 1800s, they hadn't changed for almost 200 years. We tell the reason for that, and we explain cooking methods.

"The tour lasts approximately 45 minutes and is geared to both adults and children. We have special student tours, also."

General Butler SRP has all the amenities one could want for a comfortable stay, from the Woodland Trail Campground for dedicated campers to beautiful, modern cottages set in groves of trees. Either place is perfect for watching flower petals unfolding in spring, leaf color turning limb by limb in fall, the beauty of a snowy winter landscape, and enjoying birds and other woodland creatures all year long.

I like it, too, as a base from which to explore the locations mentioned next in this book.

Where: Off Interstate 71 midway between Louisville and Covington. Take exit 44 (State 227) and go west toward Carrollton for 1½ miles to park entrance on left.

When: Year-round. Golf pro shop, open March 1 through December 15. Marina, swimming pool, and beach (10:00 A.M. to 6:00 P.M.), open daily Memorial Day through Labor Day. Butler-Turpin House open daily February through December, with tours at 10:00 A.M. and 2:00, 3:00, and 4:00 P.M. (afternoon hours only on Sundays).

Admission: Free. Fee for some activities. Museum tours: adults, $2; ages 6 to 12, $1; under 6 free.

Amenities: Lodge, restaurants, gift shops, cottages, campground, museum, ski lift and lodge, nine-hole golf course, boat dock, marina (rowboats, pedal boats, and canoe rentals), swimming pool, beach, picnic shelters, hiking trails, tennis, playgrounds, miniature golf, outdoor recreation courts.

Activities: Golf, skiing (weather permitting), swimming, boating, fishing, tennis, hiking, mountain biking (during festivals), camping, photography, picnicking, daily planned recreation in summer.

Special events: Winter Frontier Encampment (February), Perfect Harmony Weekend (February), Butler Family Irish Celebration (March), Mountain Bike Championship Events (April, June, July, September, October), Kentucky Scottish Weekend (May), Off-Road Triathlon (includes kayaking, September), Spirits of the Past (October), Pieces of the Past (October). Kentucky State Parks special events brochure, 800-255-7275.

Other: Barrier-free access to lodge and some facilities. Ski and golf packages available. Senior rates (62 and over) for accommodations.

For more information: General Butler State Resort Park, PO Box 325, Carrollton, Kentucky 41008-0325, 502-732-4384. Reservations, 800-325-0078.

Ski Butler, PO Box 89, Carrollton, KY 41008, 502-732-4231. Ski information and snow report, 800-456-3284.

Carroll County Tourism Commission, Old Stone Jail on Courthouse Square, PO Box 293, Carrollton, KY 41008, 800-325-4290. Ask for free driving tour booklet and map.

Bike Butler, Inc., 4770 Squiresville Road, Owenton, KY 40359-8516, 502-484-2998 (voice and fax).

Big Bone Lick State Park

A visit to Big Bone Lick SP is a trip to the last salt sulfur spring remaining since the ice age days when salt licks in this area attracted vast herds of prehistoric mastodons, mammoths, bison, ground sloths, giant stag-moose, and primitive horses. They came southward, keeping ahead of advancing glaciers. Many of the beasts became mired in the swampy muck and died, so this eventually became a rich repository of fossilized bones.

Interesting stories of the early discoveries and discoverers can be learned at the park, which has an indoor/outdoor museum. The indoor part has displays of bones found at Big Bone Lick. Especially interesting is the comparison of mastodon and mammoth tusks. Outside, a boardwalk overlooks a field that holds a bison herd. An information board describes how, after 50,000 years of roaming the entire area between the Appalachians and Rockies, by 1800 these native animals were pushed out of Kentucky by hunters and settlers.

A wide, paved Diorama Trail leads into the valley behind the museum. Some distance ahead, a reconstructed figure of a bison and another of a giant mastodon are standing in the field, their dark, life-size silhouettes commanding the landscape. Except for the familiar 20th-century fields of goldenrod, cattails, and purple and white asters and the blacktop underfoot, we might for a split second believe we're in a time warp.

The silhouettes are part of the outdoor dioramas that make this mile-long museum trail so unusual. As we wander through fields and woods and along Big Bone Creek, with spur trails to additional points of interest, the past seems to take on a new life because we are where fascinating, earth-changing events took place.

Learn about invertebrate fossils, which were found in rocks more than 300 million years old; and identify their characteristics. And learn more about bison, the largest land mammal in North America today.

Other facts: Did you know that the great Ohio River is puny in comparison with its ancestor, the River Teays? The ice age glaciers dammed and killed the Teays, spawning the Ohio, which carved a new route to the sea.

A cutaway view of a section of Big Bone Lick shows the valley floor, the composition of land forms, and where fossil bones were discovered. We can leave the trail and walk along the edge of the creek and maybe discover some fossil remains for ourselves. What looks like just an ordinary rock may in fact be a mastodon bone!

Of course, at stops along the trail, we learn more about the salty sulfur springs. At one place, the trail leads to Big Spring. From a hexagonal boardwalk, we can look down at the spring that still bubbles to the surface much as it did millions of years ago.

Shawnee Indians came here also in pioneer times to extract salt from mineral springs and to hunt. One of the most gripping tales was of Mary Draper Ingles, a white woman, who escaped from the Shawnee in 1756 at this very spot.

Big Bone Lick also has some nice, short hiking trails. One circles the 7½-acre lake where fishing for bass, bluegill, and catfish is a popular pastime. A Kentucky fishing license is needed, as you would expect. Swimming, boating, and rafting are not allowed on the lake. Two trails go from the campground to the lake, and three trails go from the campground to the museum.

The campground, which sits on top of a hill, is one of the main attractions at this park. It is open year-round on a first-come, first-served basis. The 62 campsites are arranged in a figure eight, with a swimming pool and showers easily accessible in the middle. A covered picnic pavilion is at one end, and the miniature golf course is just outside the campground entrance, making it available to the public.

Probably the most popular special event here—and it's free—is the Big Bone Lick Salt Festival, held for three days each October. It features traditional salt making (a tedious process requiring 400 to 800 gallons of water to make a bushel of salt), a pre-1840 campsite, and demonstrations of pioneer skills such as broom making, muzzle loading, soap and butter making, dulcimer making and playing, and tomahawk and knife throwing.

Big Bone Lick State Park can also be a stop on a scenic backroads excursion that includes nearby Rabbit Hash, Dinsmore Homestead and Woods, and Boone County Cliffs State Nature Preserve.

Where: South of Covington. From Interstates 71/75, take exit 175 and go west on State 338 past intersection with U.S. Routes 42/127, then 2⁹⁄₁₀ miles to the park entrance.

When: Year-round. Museum open daily February 1 through December 31 (closed Tuesday and Wednesday in December, February, and March). Basic hours are 10:00 A.M. to 6:00 P.M., but opens 8:00 A.M. to 8:00 P.M. in summer and on October weekends. Miniature golf open April 1 through October 31.

Admission: Free. Fee for museum, camping, and miniature golf.

Amenities: Campground, grocery, museum, gift shop, buffalo herd, diorama trail, lake, hiking and interpretive trails, miniature golf, picnic grounds and shelters, outdoor recreation courts, playgrounds.

Activities: Camping, nature study, hiking, wildlife viewing, fishing, miniature golf, outdoor recreation, tennis, picnicking, daily planned recreation in summer.

Special events: Antique Tractor/Arts & Crafts Show (May), Salt Festival (October), Halloween Campout (October). Kentucky State Parks special events brochure, 800-255-7275.

Other: Barrier-free access, including diorama trail. No swimming, boating, or rafting allowed in lake.

For more information: Big Bone Lick State Park, 3380 Beaver Road, Union, KY 41091-9627, 606-384-3522.

Behringer-Crawford Museum

In the middle of Devou Park, just off Interstate 75 in Covington, is Northern Kentucky's only museum dedicated solely to this region's natural and cultural history. It is in a historic Victorian mansion built in 1848 on a hilltop overlooking the panoramic Ohio River Valley. William Behringer, who lived here, developed a collection of natural history artifacts he acquired in his extensive travels. It forms the basis for this museum, which was named in his honor in 1970. Though gathered in the 1900s, the items span a much longer period. They include fossils 450 million years old, relics from prehistoric human cultures, memorabilia of 19th-century river life and industry, and Civil War artifacts. Nature appreciation plays prominently in the exhibits and activities, too.

The museum's rooms provide gallery space for permanent and traveling exhibits; and a large, multilevel outdoor terrace is a gathering place for groups and is sometimes used as a performance stage. Nearby are two unique exhibits: a trolley, the *Kentucky*, built in 1892 and the only parlor car of its kind still existing in the United States; and the *Adventure Galley II*, a full-size replica of an 18th-century flatboat typical of those used by early settlers.

The newest permanent exhibit, in an upstairs room with a grand view of the river, is "The Ohio River: Avenue of Change." Riverboat artifacts are on display; and an authentic-looking pilothouse is set up, allowing visitors to have the feeling of actually piloting a riverboat. Displays also show the broader picture of the evolution of the river, from its early formation to its modern use in commerce and transportation. The overriding message here is that everything in nature is interdependent.

Other permanent exhibits include one about prehistoric Native American cultures from the Archaic, Woodland, and Mississippian Periods (from 12,000 to about 400 years ago). The Fort Ancient Indians were the last of the prehistoric people in this area. The exhibits include implements, points, and pottery, and explanations of how tools such as axes were made. Another display shows a tree ring dating from 1492 through 1867, a span of nearly 400 years.

Upstairs, the permanent paleontology gallery displays fossils that came from Big Bone Lick and elsewhere. A mastodon mandible from 10,000 years ago and a piece of a mammoth tusk are two examples. The typical adult mammoth was about 14 feet tall, whereas the mastodon reached around 10 feet tall. A wall mural shows a mammoth, the Ordovician Sea, and the fossils that came from there. Another illustration shows where the last ice age glaciers stopped before reaching Kentucky.

We would expect to see a Naturalist Room, and we are not disappointed. The two naturalists important in the area's history were John James Audubon and Constantin Rafinesque, who was born in Constantinople in 1783 and was the first professor of history and botany west of the Alleghenies. A 3-D display shows him giving a lecture on natural philosophy in 1826. In this room are four lithographs of Audubon's drawings (*Towhee Bunting, Song Sparrow, Least Water Hen, Yellow-Breasted Rail*) and mounted animal specimens from the region, including a raccoon, bear, fox, several raptors and other birds, and small mammals.

The Nineteenth Century History Gallery has artifacts from homes of the period and from the Civil War. In the adjoining Lawrence Duba Research Library, open by appointment, are old journals and books on the Civil War, the history of Kentucky, and Kentucky's natural heritage.

Circulating exhibits change regularly. A recent one was about archaeo-astronomy, the study of how and why ancient peoples created marking devices to track the movements of the sun, moon, and stars. Another, "Natural Setting," featured photographs taken in Boone County (the county immediately to the west) of hills, rivers, and mature forests.

The workshops and special events are mostly geared for group participation, but individuals and families can join special weekend activities at the museum. Program coordinator Betty Payne described some of these. "Many special programs are set around archaeology, like fossil hunts. Some are for parents and children together and others are for specific age groups. In summer, we have a Junior Curator Camp for older kids who go out to a dig site, plan everything, and conduct a weeklong dig. When they come back, they clean the objects, research their significance, mount them, and prepare an exhibit. It's really comprehensive," she said.

"In all the things we do, we focus on connections with this area's past, its cultural and natural history. Our crafts workshops emphasize pioneer crafts. In summer, we have a showboat workshop and then perform for the families of the participants.

"We have a tour called 'Backroads' that visits rural Kentucky areas. These are regularly booked with elder hostel groups and also through Northern Kentucky University; but groups can contact us directly to arrange a day trip."

Sometimes tours coordinate with an exhibit. For example, a feature of the archaeo-astronomy tour was how earthworks can be marking devices. A tour to the Chillicothe, Ohio, area provided opportunity for on-site observation.

Special activities often tie in with holidays. A model train show opens the day after Thanksgiving and remains up past New Year's Day. In spring, a "Waste Wizards" exhibit honors Earth Day as it features innovative and fascinating uses of waste products.

Look for more nature activities, crafts shows, and displays to be regularly scheduled in the newly expanded facilities.

Among the remodeled areas is the gift shop in a sunny corner, which has been given a face-lift to better show off the pottery, stuffed toys, books, fossil and mineral collections, and other items that make excellent souvenirs.

Covington is a charming city, but if you'd rather go directly to Devou Park before wandering its streets, just follow the directions below. Some older published instructions reflect the way things were before recent road work on the interstate changed the streets.

Where: In Covington. From the south on Interstate 75, take exit 191 (12th Street/Pike Street), go across 12th, and continue to Pike Street. Turn left (west) on Pike, then bear right on Lewis Street and continue to Montague, where there is a Devou Park sign. Turn right on Montague, which enters the park.

When: Year-round. Tuesday through Saturday, 10:00 A.M. to

5:00 P.M. Sunday, 1:00 P.M. to 5:00 P.M. Closed all national holidays.

Admission: Very modest fee. Half price for children, students, and seniors.

Amenities: Natural, historical, cultural, and archeological exhibits; library; gift shop; replica flatboat; 1892 trolley car; multilevel outdoor terrace. Seven-hundred-acre Devou Park has picnic sites, shelters, playgrounds, tennis courts, golf course, scenic overlook, and nature trail.

Activities: Exhibit viewing; nature appreciation; workshops emphasizing pioneer crafts and culture, archaeology, and nature.

Special events: Showboat Workshop (summer), Junior Archaeology Curator Camp (summer), Tall Stacks (October), Model Train Show (November to January).

Other: Barrier-free access (but no elevator). Smoking and picture taking prohibited.

For more information: Behringer-Crawford Museum at Devou Park, PO Box 67, Covington, KY 41012, 606-491-4003.

Office of State Archaeology, 211 Lafferty Hall, University of Kentucky, Lexington, KY 40506, 606-257-5735.

Boone County Cliffs State Nature Preserve

This nature preserve is an absolute jewel in a county occupying the very northwestern part of Kentucky's "topknot." On its 75 acres are land features, vegetation, and animal populations in some respects little different from the time when Kentucky was first settled and including some species found only in this part of the state. A loop trail follows two connected ridges that surround a deep, wooded ravine where a small spring-fed stream begins its journey to Middle Creek. Huge boulders, mature trees, colorful birds, and wildflowers inspired its earlier name, "Enchanted Valley."

Especially notable are the cliffs, 20- to 40-foot-high out-crops of cemented gravels that face the ravine. They were formed after powerful melting glaciers from the Kansan ice sheet forcibly washed them across the river and deposited them where they are today. Later, stream erosion cut through the area and exposed them. Some of the gravels had been pushed all the way down from northern Canada.

Both the Kentucky State Nature Preserves Commission and The Nature Conservancy place this site as one of the top ranked nature preserves in the state for its geological signifi-cance and biological diversity. For hikers, it is a very special place to enjoy in all seasons.

Joyce Bender, my guide at Lake Metropolis, shared some of her impressions of this place.

"In the fall, from the top of the cliffs, you see a carpet of colorful maple leaves just covering the ground below. And then in spring—my favorite time—the forest is a study in green with the new leaves from different species, plus carpets of tiny wildflowers adding other colors to the scene."

Late March and early April are prime months for viewing wildflowers. According to Joyce, look for spring beauty, dwarf larkspur, toothwort, squirrel corn, Dutchman's-breeches, trout lily, hepatica, twinleaf, mayapple, trillium, and violets. I was there in late summer at a time for enjoying fall wildflowers.

It is unusual to find five forest communities in a 75-acre plot, but with slopes facing all directions and dramatic changes in elevation, many tree types find just the elements they need for growth. Sugar maples dominate throughout; but the north slopes also harbor basswood and beech, and south slopes are populated by oaks and elms. Beech and oak are found on the north ridges, and elm and locust co-occupy the south ridges. The fifth type is tulip poplar, which is present near the head of the stream.

Warblers find a friendly haven among all these trees, especially in spring. The cool, moist valley floor provides habitat for several species of salamander, including the rare red-backed salamander (*Plethodon cinereus*). Squirrels and other small mammals find this an excellent playground, and their playfulness can add enjoyment to your woodland hike.

Don't expect a large billboard on State 18 announcing the preserve. Look for Middle Creek Road and a small caution sign that says, "No Outlet." Another small sign announces "Adopt a Highway Litter Control" and "1.9 miles Kentucky Nature Conservancy." Follow a narrow blacktop road lined with masses of wildflowers. Wooded hills and an occasional meadow are on both sides. You can't miss the small gravel parking lot on the left.

The trail starts out along the little stream, rising gently in the shady woods, but it soon leaves the creek and ascends sharply to the top of a ridge. At the pinnacle is a large rock. Climb it and then walk along the top of the ridge from which you see deep ravines on each side.

It was here that I met Roger and Carrie Fortney of Pensacola, Florida, who had walked only part of the trail and were returning, disappointed at not having found the cliffs. As I discovered, the 1⁷⁄₁₀-mile Main Trail has three quarter-mile spurs. The East Boundary Trail simply leads back to the parking lot; the Ridge Loop Trail goes to an overlook atop the cliffs; and the Ravine Loop Trail takes you to a viewing point at the bottom of the cliffs. Those who just stay on the main trail are missing the most exciting part! Since maps are not always available at the trailhead, it helps to contact The Nature Conservancy or the Nature Preserves Commission two or three months before your visit and request a map.

Except for one steep ascent, this trail offers easy-to-moderate hiking. The ever-changing views, interesting rock formations, and 300 species of flowering plants add up to a memorable scene just waiting for you to place yourself in the picture.

Where: From Burlington (southwest of Covington), go west on State 18 for approximately six miles, then turn left on Middle Creek Road. The narrow blacktop road changes to gravel after 1½ miles. At 1⁹⁄₁₀ miles a small gravel parking lot on the left is marked by a sign, "Boone Cliffs Parking."
When: Year-round, sunrise to sunset.
Admission: Free.
Amenities: Trails.
Activities: Hiking, birding, photography, nature study.
For more information: Kentucky State Nature Preserves Commission, 801 Schenkel Lane, Frankfort, KY 40601, 502-573-2886. Fax, 502-573-2355.

The Nature Conservancy, 642 West Main Street, Lexington, KY 40508, 606-259-9655.

Dinsmore Homestead and Dinsmore Woods State Nature Preserve

State 18 just southwest of the turnoff to Boone County Cliffs is the historic Dinsmore Homestead, a property originally encompassing 700 acres but now operated by the Dinsmore Foundation as an 80-acre living history museum site. Visitors tour the 1842 house and outbuildings for a sense of what life was like on a Kentucky gentleman's farm over a 150-year period of time. Also, the Harry Roseberry House on the property has a gift shop with regional handicrafts, books, and clothing items.

The homestead has another facet: it is a research and study center having a collection of nearly 90,000 pages of family documents such as letters, journals, and business records. This is especially significant because the farm stayed in the Dinsmore family for five generations, from the time James Dinsmore purchased the land in 1839 until 1988. Nearly all the contents and outbuildings survive. One of James's daughters, Julia, operated the farm for 54 years and kept a diary, making entries nearly every day.

The tours start at the Roseberry House, with the background and history of the farm explained, then they go to the cook's cabin, the oldest building on the property, where open-hearth cooking is demonstrated. All furniture and furnishings in the main house are authentic and represent just how the house looked when it was occupied.

Many interesting anecdotes are told. As Sis (Emma) Rogers pointed out, "The Dinsmores have had ties with all the presidents from George Washington to George Bush. One of the great-great-granddaughters of James Dinsmore was a bridesmaid in Eleanor Roosevelt's wedding. And one of the great-great-grandsons was a roommate of President Bush in college."

I asked about a stuffed specimen mounted on the wall.

"That's an elk head that Teddy Roosevelt killed. There's an autographed picture of him, too," she said.

Besides the guided tour, visitors can go on their own to see the family cemetery and a barn that is filled with old farm implements.

The most festive and lively annual event is the Dinsmore Homestead Harvest Festival on the last full weekend in September. Artists and craftsmen give demonstrations, and musicians and magicians perform. Learn about open-hearth cooking, cider pressing, sausage making, drying flowers and herbs, basketry, tatting, spinning, knitting, quilting, and silhouette cutting. A children's corner and petting zoo keep the little folks entertained. Wood-block artists and painters also show their work.

Another yearly event is a Christmas tour of the house on the first weekend in December, coinciding with a "Christmas Walk" in Burlington.

Two hiking trails have been developed in cooperation with The Nature Conservancy on adjacent property known as the Dinsmore Woods State Nature Preserve, and may be hiked daily from sunrise to sunset. This land—a 106-acre climax forest of sugar maple, white ash, and oak—has never been commercially logged. Just off the preserve on the Dinsmore property is a large population of running buffalo clover (*trifolium stoloniferum*), a federally endangered species that is present but imperiled in Kentucky and four other states.

Inquire at the Dinsmore Foundation office across the road from the museum about access to trails and parking.

Another hiking, horseback riding, and nature appreciation opportunity is across the highway a quarter of a mile south of the Dinsmore Homestead in 230-acre Middle Creek Park. This is a fairly new community park with trails that were developed in 1992 and new ones added since. You'll see the sign and the large gravel parking lot. A bulletin board describes six trails, all color coded for identification. The longest is three miles, while the others range from three-tenths to three-quarters of a mile. All trails branch from a single trailhead across a footbridge from the parking lot. Horseback riding is allowed, but no stables are on the premises. The park is open daily from dawn until dark.

Sarsaparilla at Rabbit Hash

Hannah Baird and I were sitting on wicker rocking chairs on the porch of the Roseberry House. She suggested I go to Rabbit Hash, past Bellevue and just a few miles south on State 338.

"It's such a very charming spot," she said. "The general store is always open. You can buy a bottle of sarsaparilla or Rabbit Hash beer and sit and watch the action on the river. You'll find craft and antique shops there, too."

On the way, I decided to approach Rabbit Hash from Lower River Road, which goes close to the Ohio River but is elevated above it. From that vantage point, the foreground was filled with magnificent, gorgeous, gigantic buttercup-yellow flowers, and beyond were barges and pleasure craft going upriver and down. It was a perfect prelude to a Rabbit Hash experience.

It is said the town got its name during the 1847 flood when, with food generally in scarce supply, the townspeople nevertheless had an abundance of rabbit hash.

The Rabbit Hash General Store, built in 1831 and operating continuously since 1880, is beside the river. When I visited, picnic tables under big trees and more splashes of tall buttercup-yellow flowers provided a setting that no hungry traveler or landscape painter could resist.

I browsed through the many items for sale, bought an old-fashioned sarsaparilla in the distinctive Rabbit Hash bottle, and turned to leave.

On the inside of the door was a sign:

"Purchase your Rabbit Hash Museum membership here. Active membership, $5. Inactive, $10. Rabbit Hash Historical Society."

Where: Approximately 6½ miles west of Burlington and one mile east of Bellevue on State 18. Museum parking on right. Trailhead parking, a quarter of a mile farther on left.

When: Office hours, year-round Monday through Friday, 9:00 A.M. to 5:00 P.M. Museum open April through mid-December, Wednesday, Saturday, and Sunday, 1:00 to 5:00 P.M. Trails open year-round, sunrise to sunset.

Admission: Moderate fee. Children half price, senior discount, special family rate.

Amenities: Well-preserved 1842 homestead with carriage houses, barn, family cemetery, cook's cabin.

Activities: Homestead tour, hiking, birding, nature study, picnicking, photography, horseback riding (no stables).

Special events: Dinsmore Homestead Harvest Festival (September), Christmas Home Tour (December—part of the Burlington "Christmas Walk"). Old-Timer's Day (September, in Rabbit Hash).

Other: Group tours by reservation.

For more information: Dinsmore Homestead Foundation, PO Box 453, Burlington, KY 41005, 606-586-6117 or 6127.

Cynthiana/Quiet Trails State Nature Preserve

Decisions, decisions—so many places in Kentucky to appreciate nature, but where do you go this time? You might (as I did) enjoy a restful weekend northeast of Lexington. Using the historic Seldon Renaker Inn in Cynthiana as a base, I found great variety in nearby places: Quiet Trails to the north, Blue Licks to the east, and Paris (and an arboretum) in the very heart of Thoroughbred farm country to the south, each within a 30-minute drive.

The Seldon Renaker Inn, built in 1885, is operated as a bed-and-breakfast by Jim and Juanita Ingram, Cynthiana residents who are well versed in local anecdotes and the history of this community. Juanita's deluxe Continental breakfast is a memorable treat. The inn's location right in the middle of town is perfect for those who appreciate a small-town atmosphere without unwanted "touristy" add-ons. Antique buffs will like to know that Cynthiana, established in 1793, has the second-largest collection of cast-iron-front buildings in Kentucky.

Quiet Trails State Nature Preserve is near the little community of Sunrise on the Licking River 15 miles from Cynthiana. Other preserves mentioned so far have featured wetlands, prairie, and other habitats. This one is a place to study and appreciate the natural heritage of the rich Bluegrass region. Its 110 acres offer a great diversity of birds, maturing oak and hickory trees, and wildflowers.

More than three miles of main trails and connectors go on top of ridges and into ravines, passing through woods and fields, and beside ponds and barns to the banks of the river, and then follow it for three-tenths of a mile. Migratory songbirds are attracted to this place in spring and fall, and bluebird boxes along the trail encourage this species to stay awhile. A keen woodsman's eye can spot resident mammals like gray squirrels, cottontails, raccoons, and other small creatures, but no one could fail to notice the great splashes of colorful wildflowers in fall.

The spur trail along the river is an excellent place to observe waterfowl during their seasonal visits, especially herons, horned grebes, and spotted sandpipers. Also, 20 species of mussels have been found in this part of the Licking River.

Where: Cynthiana is on U.S. Route 27 about 30 miles northeast of Lexington. To Quiet Trails, go north from Cynthiana on U.S. Route 27 for 10½ miles, then east on State 1284 for 2⁷⁄₁₀ miles to Sunrise. After the four-way stop, continue on Pugh's Ferry Road (a very narrow road) for 1⁸⁄₁₀ miles and look for the preserve on the right.

When: Year-round during daylight hours.

Admission: Free.

Amenities: Self-guided trails, wildlife observation blind, fact sheet/species list.

Activities: Hiking, birding, wildlife viewing, photography, nature study.

Special events (Cynthiana): Earth Day Celebration (May), Woodford County Horse Farm Tours (July).

For more information: Quiet Trails State Nature Preserve, c/o Kentucky State Nature Preserves Commission, 801 Schenkel Lane, Frankfort, KY 40601, 502-573-2886. Fax, 502-573-2355.

Cynthiana Chamber of Commerce, 117 Court Street, Cynthiana, KY 41031 (walking tours and maps, Monday through Friday, 9:00 A.M. to 4:00 P.M.), 606-234-5236.

Seldon Renaker Inn, 24 South Walnut, Cynthiana, KY 41031, 606-234-3752.

Blue Licks Battlefield State Park/ Nature Preserve

From Cynthiana to Blue Licks, the best route to take is east on State 32 (Pike Street in Cynthiana) to U.S. Route 68, then left for about 10 miles to the park. State 32 winds through pastoral farmlands in rolling country. Nearer Blue Licks are more hills and fewer farms. On U.S. Route 68, I pass a sign, "Fallen Rock Zone," and think that this is somewhat more comforting than the ones that say, "Watch for Falling Rock." Obviously, any rock I will encounter here will have already fallen.

Enough semantics, though.

You can't miss the park entrance on U.S. Route 68. To the left is the campground area and on the right the nature preserve. A sign tells about "Pioneer Pursuit," which refers to what is known as the last battle of the Revolutionary War, fought here August 18, 1782. The British and their Shawnee Indian allies, following a buffalo trace, crossed the Licking River at Blue Licks ford where they ambushed Kentucky militia forces who were following. The defeat, though, energized George Rogers Clark to strike the final blow of the war by destroying the Indian towns along the Ohio River.

The Buffalo Trace Trail in the park's 15-acre nature preserve is where the pioneers pursued the British-led Indians. This particular trace went all the way from the salt springs at Blue Licks to the Ohio River. If you come in fall, you have a chance of seeing the federally endangered Short's goldenrod (*Solidago shortii*), one of the world's rarest plants, in bloom. Its smooth leaves distinguish it from other goldenrods. It is speculated that buffalo may have carried the seeds in their fur and dispensed them along the trail; and, by continual trampling and grazing, they maintained the open habitat the plant requires.

Until 1997, the only remaining examples on earth of Short's goldenrod were within a two-square-mile area at Blue Licks. That year, several clumps of the seedlings were planted on rocky fossil beds at the Falls of the Ohio near where they were first discovered (in 1840).

Another interesting aspect of Blue Licks was brought to light during the past 100 years. Several digs unearthed a mastodon tusk and bones of prehistoric animals that perished at the licks. Some of them are on display in the park's very well-maintained Pioneer Museum, an attractive stone building that holds two levels of exhibits. It is what the museum at Big Bone Lick should be, and we hope soon will be.

The history of Blue Licks goes back 300 million years when primitive seas were receding and leaving salt deposits. Over time, ice age animals visited, man arrived on the scene, the pioneers came, and later, it was a popular resort. The same salty water that attracted mastodons brought the 19th-century tourists.

Among the prehistoric relics are mastodon teeth, vertebrae, jawbones, tusks, and other fragments. Other artifacts prove the presence of Native Americans through the Woodland, Adena, Mississippian, and Fort Ancient cultures. Adventurers came and then, pioneer settlers. Weapons, implements, and domestic artifacts have been preserved from those times. The museum's lower level has a great abundance of artifacts from the Civil War, from Indian households, and from pioneer households.

A seven-minute video tells about the Battle of Blue Licks.

"Genuine Blue Licks Water" is displayed in several different bottles that were sold by the Blue Licks Springs Company. Wooden crates were used for shipping the water, and each bottle was wrapped with straw to keep it from breaking in shipment. Wrapped, they look like little straw brooms.

I was inspecting a walking stick made from a convoluted ash root carved to resemble a snake.

"That is quite artistic," I commented to curator Louella Moore.

"Yes, and over here is a taffeta wedding dress. That's from 1900 to 1905, and it was designed by a dressmaker," she said.

Louella has a real love for her work. For more than 20 years, she has eagerly welcomed visitors and, relating anecdotes from the past, has provided insight into the pioneer culture behind the items on display. A visit to this museum with Louella as your tour guide is the most enjoyable way to see it. I promise.

Though this isn't a resort park, the campground has 51 sites; and two double cottages just above the banks of the Licking

River are very modern, with satellite TV reception and large decks overlooking the river. They have everything except telephones, but that can sometimes be a plus.

Where: Forty-eight miles northeast of Lexington on U.S. Route 68.

When: Year-round. Campground, museum, miniature golf, and gift shop open April 1 through October 31. Gift shop, 9:00 A.M. to 4:30 P.M. Museum open 9:00 A.M. to 5:00 P.M. (doors close at 4:30). Swimming pool and miniature golf open Memorial Day through Labor Day. Golf also open weekends in April, May, September, and October.

Admission: Free. Very modest fees for museum (discount for children; under six, free), camping, swimming (six and under free with adult), and miniature golf.

Amenities: Cottages, campground, pioneer museum, gift shop, meeting facility, hiking trails, swimming pool, miniature golf, picnic grounds, shelters, playground.

Activities: Camping, hiking, swimming, miniature golf, nature appreciation, exhibit viewing, photography, staff-led recreation on summer weekends.

Special events: Campers Appreciation Weekend (April), Guided River Trail Walks (National Trails Day, June), Blue Licks Reenactment Celebration (August), Car Show (September), Halloween Campout (October), Crafts Fair (November). Kentucky State Parks special events brochure, 800-255-7275.

For more information: Blue Licks Battlefield State Park, PO Box 66, Mount Olivet, KY 41064-0066, 606-289-5507. For handicapped accessibility, call 800-255-7275 (TDD equipped).

Kentucky State Nature Preserves Commission, 801 Schenkel Lane, Frankfort, KY 40601, 502-573-2886. Fax, 502-573-2355.

Nannine Clay Wallis Arboretum

Paris, the seat of Bourbon County, is truly the heart of the immensely picturesque Thoroughbred country. Within the county are approximately 90 Thoroughbred horse farms, including Claiborne Farm, which produced the legendary Triple Crown winner, Secretariat. All the horse farms are closed to the public; however, some are open only by appointment.

Among the stately 18th- and 19th-century historic properties in Paris is the seven-acre Nannine Clay Wallis Home and Arboretum, headquarters of The Garden Club of Kentucky, with four acres devoted to the arboretum. It is just a block off Main Street at 616 Pleasant Street (a two-way street, unlike Main Street).

For tree study and as an example of how one could landscape and plant for beauty and wildlife habitat, this is a premier site. The grounds have six theme areas: a Walk Garden, Perennial Garden, Wildflower Garden, Bird Border, Shade Garden, and Rose Garden. Throughout are magnificent tree specimens representing 55 species. The trees have markers, but even more valuable is the excellent illustrated study guide visitors may borrow as they stroll the grounds. The guide gives scientific and common names; descriptions with tips for growing and use; a glossary; and drawings of the leaf, fruit, and crown. A foldout map identifies the location of each tree.

The beauty of an arboretum is that each tree is given room to grow and branch out fully. Many of the trees here are mature and, I suspect, near their maximum size, and new trees are added each year through a Gift Tree program sponsored by the garden club—so this place just gets better and better.

The on-site hostess is Gertrude McMahan, who lives in the 18-room mansion. During the life of Nannine Clay Wallis, the home became known for its hospitality. It was especially open to teachers and schoolchildren, and that is still the case. The public is welcome to walk the grounds and visit with Gertrude, who says, "I've always worked around a lot of people. I'd be lost without them."

Christmas is a special time. "Everybody is invited on December 1, 2, and 3 no matter on what days they fall. We have all kinds of crafts and greenery and things to sell," said Gertrude.

Naturally, birds, butterflies, and squirrels find this an attractive refuge. Stone benches, birdhouses, birdbaths, a small lily pond, an outdoor pavilion, and a carriage house provide different views and quiet spots. "I think people will enjoy coming here and seeing the beautiful trees and flowers," said Gertrude. "Schoolchildren come. Their teachers bring them, or they come on their own. Sometimes they are here until dark, getting leaves and bark."

I had a chance to observe that. I had just finished a tour of the grounds, lingering over the rose garden which was in bloom and was standing under a monstrous black walnut watching squirrels cavort on the lawn.

Two girls and a boy, about 10 years old, came in from the street, walked around the yard inspecting things, then trooped to the front door and went on inside. I had the sense that they were "coming home."

Where: In downtown Paris at the corner of Pleasant and Seventh Streets, one block east of Main Street. If heading north on Pleasant, turn right on Seventh Street and drive into the parking lot on the left.
When: Grounds open daily, year-round.
Admission: Free.
Amenities: Arboretum with theme areas.
Activities: Nature study, photography, wildlife viewing.

Special events: Christmas Open House (December 1, 2, and 3).
Other: Illustrated study guide and map of grounds available for use while on the property.
For more information: Nannine Clay Wallis Arboretum, Garden Club of Kentucky, Inc., 616 Pleasant Street, Paris, KY 40361, 606-987-6158.

Paris/Bourbon County Chamber of Commerce, 718 Main Street, Paris, KY 40361, 606-987-0779.

11

Frankfort and Lexington

"Kentucky Bluegrass" is legendary, often associated with the entire state. Yet, the inner Bluegrass region is a relatively small portion of Kentucky centered around Lexington, Frankfort, and Paris. Under the rolling terrain and fertile soil that is noted for producing strong Thoroughbred racehorses are thick-bedded limestone rocks of Ordovician, Silurian, and Devonian Periods of the Middle Paleozoic Age (that is, from 490 to 350 million years ago). These are the oldest rocks in the state that were brought close to the surface. Not all is rolling pasture land, though. The Kentucky River has sliced a deep gorge through a portion of the area south of these two major cities, creating breathtaking scenery.

To tailor your trip to your special interests, contact the Frankfort and Lexington visitors bureaus to get a wealth of information. The places listed here should please nature enthusiasts, but more opportunities wait in the wings for your discovery.

Other places to consider for overnight stays are the historic towns of Midway and Versailles, both presenting a small-town atmosphere in Woodford County between Frankfort and Lexington. Take historic walking tours, ride the Bluegrass Railroad Company's nostalgic train through Bluegrass farmlands and along a scenic gorge, and visit the Toy and

Train Museum. The Sills Inn (in Versailles) gives easy access to the locations mentioned in this section. Other lodging is available in Woodford County homes dating back to the 1700s. Call 606-873-5122.

For more information: Frankfort Visitor Center, 100 Capital Avenue, Frankfort, KY 40601, 800-960-7200.

Lexington Convention and Visitors Bureau, 301 East Vine Street, Lexington, KY 40507, 800-848-1224 or 606-233-1221.

Woodford County Chamber of Commerce, Main Street, Versailles, KY 40383, 606-873-5122.

Sills Inn, 270 Montgomery Avenue, Versailles, KY 40383, 800-526-9801 or 606-873-4478.

Kentucky Game Farm/ Salato Wildlife Education Center

The Game Farm and Salato Center at the headquarters of the Kentucky Department of Fish and Wildlife Resources is rapidly becoming the number one tourist destination in Kentucky's capital, Frankfort. It would be impossible not to find this place, since signs everywhere around the county announce the distance to "Game Farm Lakes."

The Game Farm is a 132-acre property right on U.S. Route 60 three miles west of downtown and very accessible from Interstate 64, with grounds that are open to the public, two fishing lakes, and ample free parking for visitors.

Phase One of an ambitious expansion was completed in 1995 with the opening of the Salato Wildlife Education Center, and Phase Two is well underway. It includes outdoor classrooms, trails, observation areas, and habitats for raccoon, river otter, mountain lion, bobcat, deer, bear, turkey, and buffalo;

and elevated walkways for viewing aquatic life in streams and ponds. Phase Three will expand visitor parking and the recreation area at the front of the property, adding more trails in natural habitat areas.

Even though Phase Three will be done in stages and isn't expected to be complete until the year 2000, it is simply an enhancement to the very fine existing outdoor recreation area. The long entrance drive with specimen trees dotting the landscape goes past a wildlife observation area and a small lake. You can walk to both from the paved visitor parking lot.

A kiosk helps orient visitors to wildlife appreciation with posters about flowers, the river otter, birds, reptiles, amphibians, protecting habitat, and a diagram showing a lake ecosystem. From here, paths go down to the lakes, to a model wetland, a picnic area, and a "backyard" with wildflowers and bird nesting boxes and feeders. A blind is provided for people to sit in and observe the birds. The lakes hold catfish, crappie, largemouth bass, and bluegill, making them equally attractive to waterfowl and fishermen. The lake is also a popular place for hikers, who enjoy the mile-long circular trail at lake's edge and often bring their dogs on leashes. The trails will be expanded through the woods and will have outdoor study stations where wildflowers and trees are explained.

On the back part of the property in habitat areas are some of the animals mentioned and a variety of birds, including bald eagles. Some were illegal pets confiscated by the agency, and others were injured and cannot be released into the wild. During Phase Two this area is taking on an entirely different character, allowing the animals to have the kind of homelike atmosphere they deserve. Instead of looking at a black bear in a cage, visitors see it in a natural habitat.

The Salato Education Center is truly a gem, an 11,000-square-foot building demonstrating the theme, "Reconnecting People and Nature—for Life." It is faced with a native limestone veneer and natural wood decking. It is completely handicapped accessible and has all the modern conveniences any visitor could need. The exhibits, classrooms, and activities allow expansion of popular programs that are offered year-round.

A "welcome wall" is the first thing you see. It is a place to check out current and upcoming happenings. Overhead displays of mounted native bird and fish specimens lead to three large aquariums that contain Kentucky fish species typical of different regions, from the Appalachian foothills to the floodplains near the Mississippi River.

A three-dimensional map of the state shows Kentucky's topography and river systems. Touch a computer screen to get more information, such as the location of state parks.

One wall is devoted to Native Americans, recognizing them as the first stewards who knew how to care for the land and the creatures who lived on it.

Other exhibits deal with crucial environmental issues, such as restoration efforts for river otters and peregrine falcons.

Laura Lang, wildlife administrator for the Salato Center, said, "What we hope to accomplish is that people coming here will learn why wildlife is important and what they can personally do to help nurture it. It may be as simple as not mowing around the fence in their yard so that rabbits, insects, and birds can have a nice fencerow habitat. Or it may involve consciously planting native plants that produce berries and nuts. They can also look at bigger issues like conserving wetlands across the state. Or recycling motor oil (instead of pouring it on the ground) to help preserve underground water quality."

Introductory videos tell about the department and how it hopes to improve wildlife habitat across the state and protect their quality of life. Other videos are tapes of the popular

Kentucky Afield television program on KET, sponsored by the department.

Visit the comfortable Watchable Wildlife room where window walls allow you to observe and identify the animals and birds outside. You may get hints on how to attract wildlife to your yard. Similar observation areas look out on landscapes featuring plants native to four major Kentucky habitats: an eastern forest, a prairie, a meadowland, and a wetland. Nearby, observe live bees in a hive that is in a tree trunk, also visible through a glass window.

Rotating exhibits assure that there is usually something new each time you visit. All have outdoor themes and relate to Kentucky. The gift shop continues the outdoor emphasis with an offering of books, art prints, patches, and souvenir items.

The center also has indoor and outdoor classrooms for programs and workshops geared for specific age groups from preschoolers through adults. Leadership training, hunter education, wildlife appreciation, and conservation are just some of the broad categories covered. "HabiTOTS" is a program that teaches three- to five-year-olds about native animals and the food, water, and shelter they need to survive. It takes the form of a monthly story hour about "Busy Bees and Other Insects" and "101 Ways to Eat Worms" and other subjects.

One of two special annual events is the Free Fishing Week held in June for children through age 15. More than 300 participants usually attend. The kids fish for bass and bluegills and learn casting techniques, responsible angling etiquette, and similar skills and subjects; some win door prizes.

The other annual event is Conservation Day, on a Sunday afternoon usually in September but sometimes in October. Nonstop activities include archery, air gun shooting competitions, a fishing derby, hunting dog demonstrations, fly-tying, habitat-restoration displays, and a "Concert for Conservation" musical program.

Where: From Interstate 64 in Frankfort, take exit 53B and go north on U.S. Route 127 for 1½ miles, then left on U.S. Route 60 for 1⁷⁄₁₀ miles to the entrance on the right.
When: Year-round. Grounds open daily, sunrise to sunset. Salato Center open 9:00 A.M. to 4:00 P.M. Tuesday through Saturday; 1:00 to 5:00 P.M. on Sunday; closed Mondays and legal holidays.
Admission: Grounds are free. Very modest fee for Salato Center; ages 5 to 15, half price; under 5, free.
Amenities: Fishing lakes, natural wildlife habitats, trails, picnic area, education center, gift shop, outdoor animal exhibits, public rest rooms, phones.
Activities: Wildlife viewing, birding, fishing, photography, nature study, hiking. Also, workshops and special programs for children three and up, families, and adults; and hunter-education courses.
Special events: Kids Fishing Days (June), Conservation Day (September or October).
Other: Barrier-free parking (limited) and access.
For more information: Visitor Programs, Salato Wildlife Education Center, Kentucky Department of Fish and Wildlife Resources, #1 Game Farm Road, Frankfort, KY 40601-3909, 502-564-7863.

Buckley Wildlife Sanctuary

Considering the detailed directions to this place, one might conclude it is hard to find. Well, only to someone unfamiliar with Frankfort. I admit that on my first try I exited too soon from U.S. Route 60 and found myself at a dilapidated old distillery on the Kentucky River. I tried again, and Tim Williams, the manager of the National Audubon Society's Clyde E. Buckley Sanctuary, was waiting when I arrived, late.

The sanctuary is on 275 acres, mostly wooded but with open fields, ponds, sinkholes, and wetlands, too. One hundred and fifty-eight species of birds, 23 species of amphibians, 16 species of reptiles, and 37 species of mammals have been recorded here. Three interpretive walking trails lead through varied habitats. Self-guiding trail booklets identify places of interest on each trail. The objective of the sanctuary is twofold: to create and maintain diversity of wildlife by encouraging native plants and animals and to teach the general public about them.

Tim showed me the display barn, which was built in Civil War days (the 1860s) and had been a tobacco barn. Now, it has displays and a contour map of the sanctuary, which gives an excellent overview of what is to be discovered here. Elk Lick Branch, which flows into the nearby Kentucky River, has cut a gorge that divides the property. The part south of the river is closed to visitation. Other displays use "matching" games and interactive techniques to test a visitor's knowledge of birds, other animals, and plants.

Near the barn is a bird blind with one-way glass for private viewing of feeders and the birds that visit. Hummingbird feeders are put out in summer until sometime in September. When cold weather comes, it is time for suet feeders. Birds otherwise are fed mixed seed, sunflower, cracked corn, millet, milo, peanut bits, and thistle seed.

The sanctuary is heavily visited by school groups. It is not unusual for two dozen schools to visit in a week's time. When I was there, the area was being prepared for a big event the following week. Students in grades kindergarten through three, from six schools, would be coming each day for four days; and high school students from Lexington and Frankfort would wear costumes representing endangered species as they acted as guides. Live animals would be brought in for demonstrations. And that is a typical week!

The biggest special event of the year is Fantasy Forest in October. It features costumed "critters" who interpret the world of animals, a horse-drawn hayride, and straw bales around a bonfire where banjo music, fiddle playing, magic acts, and storytelling take place. The nature center and gift shop are open, and refreshments are available.

As for vacationing families, I asked Tim what they would do on a typical visit.

"A family would come in, park their car, put their admission in the wishing well, then they might want to head out on a trail," he said. "If they walk the one-mile trail that goes through the forest and up around a 1½-acre pond, they could look for wildlife.

"In fall, they will see a lot of color in the trees and some interesting spiderwebs. They'll see asters, goldenrod, and common snakeroot. As they hike, they'll see evidence of animals being here: holes in trees, seeds that have been gnawed on here and there, plants that have been chewed or broken off. They're liable to see some white-tailed deer and wild turkey, and they're certainly going to see a lot of insects like praying mantises, grasshoppers, beetles, and butterflies. The monarchs will be heading south. They'll see and hear birds, too.

"At the pond, they'll probably see some bluegill and bass sunning themselves at the top of the water. They may see a butterfly or grasshopper not make it over the pond but land in it instead, which will please the hungry fish.

"As they come back off the trail, they might want to stop here at the bird blind. They can turn the speaker on to hear the birds. The blind has a heater, too, for use in winter. If they've brought a picnic lunch, they can use our picnic tables and get a cool drink of water from the fountain. A unisex rest room, which is always unlocked, is on the back porch of the nature center.

"In the afternoon, after watching the birds, they might want to grab another self-guided booklet and head out on another trail."

For groups, Tim's staff plans programs to meet specific needs, ages, and interests. Though the facility isn't wheelchair accessible yet, programs can be adapted for mobility-challenged people. They might not walk the trails but would enjoy slide shows and visiting the nature center.

The nature center is an old farmhouse that's been renovated. The main room has displays and exhibits—bird nests, fossils, examples of edible and medicinal plants, and an indoor beehive.

I couldn't find the queen bee, so Tim gave me a quick lesson:

"The best way is to look around at everything, and there'll be something that just looks out of place. A queen cell looks like a peanut. Here she is! Now, there was a drone or two in here. Drones are the boys, and they're big, too, but shaped different from the queen. Here are capped-over worker bees, which means they have a wax cap covering them. Capped-over drones would look like a bullet. And here is honey, capped. Nectar doesn't yet have a cap. By the way, a queen will lay about 1,500 eggs a day."

We moved into the next room.

"Oh, this is great. You'll love this," said Tim.

I sensed I was about to have a Buckley Nature Center experience.

"Have you ever seen the Toad Abode?"

I admitted that I hadn't as I looked at the toad sitting on a shoe box lid.

"This is one of the things I do with the kids. I'm just going to show you what this toad does for a living. I'll put a mealworm in front of it. You see, the worm has to move. The first thing the toad does is make sure its food is moving, thus alive."

"She's not doing anything. Maybe she's not hungry."

"She's always hungry."

"Oh, look. It just . . . disappeared!"

"Its tongue went out and grabbed it. Pretty nifty, huh?"

We fed the toad two more worms, then two at once. I never saw its tongue move.

"What it does, it shuts its eyes and its tongue goes out, and its eyes go down in their sockets and push that off its tongue and down its throat."

So . . . sleight of tongue. A new kind of magic!

We ended the afternoon on the front porch, talking about Clyde E. Buckley and his wife, Emma, who willed their estate to be used as a place where the public could experience nature. Emma lived to be 102.

"She walked around out here in her late 90s," said Tim, who has been here as manager for over 20 years. "She'd hold my arm and walk. We would walk trails and then sit on this porch. She would rave about the porch with its big oak beams and the limestone flagstone full of fossils. It's a nice place to sit and watch birds.

"She would sit here and talk about her experiences and always ask me if the kids were using the place, and what kinds of things were they learning."

Where: Ten miles south of Frankfort. From U.S. Route 60 heading south of Frankfort, continue past the Interstate 64 interchange for a quarter of a mile, then turn west (right) onto State 1681 where a sign points to the Buckley Preserve. This is not a crossroads. (Coming from the opposite direction, heading north on U.S. Route 60, you see State 1681 coming in from the east. Get in the left-turn lane, and when you are in sight of the Interstate 64 overpass ahead, look for 1681 west.) State 1681 goes to Millville, about 2½ miles. When you reach Millville, the road dead-ends. Directly in front on a telephone pole is a green arrow pointing left: "To Buckley Sanctuary." Turn left on State 1659 and go 1⁷⁄₁₀ miles. On the right is a ball field and playground and beyond that another green arrow pointing right. Turn right onto State 1964 and go exactly one mile. Make a clear right turn (another green arrow is on a tree ahead) and go a half mile (this is Germany Road), at which point a road splits left. Do not take it. Go straight ahead for seven-tenths of a mile to the Buckley entrance, marked with a large sign.

When: Year-round. Closed Monday, Tuesday, and holidays. Trails, bird blind, and display barn open 9:00 A.M. to 5:00 P.M. Wednesday through Friday and until 6:00 P.M. Saturday and Sunday. Nature center and gift shop open 1:00 to 6:00 P.M. Saturday and Sunday or by appointment.

Admission: Very modest day-use fee. Ages 16 and under, half price. Additional fee for special events.

Amenities: Nature center, gift shop, interpretive trails, display barn, animal-observation station.

Activities: Nature study, hiking, photography, wildlife viewing, birding, picnicking.

Special events: Wildflower Search, Buckley's Birdathon (April), Hawks & Owls (June), Magic in Nature (July), Living Dinosaurs (August), Wish Upon a Star (September), The Eagle Lady, Fantasy Forest (October), Audubon Christmas Bird Count (December).

Other: Pets, hunting, fishing, and camping not allowed.

For more information: Clyde E. Buckley Wildlife Sanctuary, 1305 Germany Road, Frankfort, KY 40601-9240, 606-873-5711.

American Saddle Horse Museum

You may have seen this horse on a trail, pulling a surrey, jumping a fence, in the showring, or in famous paintings as the mounts of Generals Ulysses S. Grant and Robert E. Lee. If you've seen an American Saddlebred in any of these scenarios and noticed its presence and style, you're sure to recognize the breed the next time. Its special look comes from a happy attitude, readiness, and alertness. Usually 15 to 16 hands high, it carries its head high, ears forward, neck gracefully arched, and moves with a stylish gait. The American Saddlebred differs from other breeds in conformation, temperament, and heritage. It has everything a potential owner would want: stamina, elegance, and personality.

The place to learn all about this breed is the American Saddle Horse Museum at the Kentucky Horse Farm in Lexington.

As I drove up the long entrance road, several flocks of Canada geese were passing overhead, 30 to 40 in each flock. Their honking was pure music in the fall air.

Coming from a horse-loving family, I knew this would be a special day. My mother owned and trained quarter horses, and my favorite pastimes as a teenager were taking trail rides and riding in rodeo parades. So the sign in the museum lobby only fired my enthusiasm: "You're going to have fun in the American Saddle Horse Museum. To show you the world of the horse America made are special exhibits, exciting shows and computers to use. Savor the excitement of the horse show and find the horse that's made for you."

A short award-winning multimedia show, "Saddlebred for America," gets the visit off to a good start. It has up-to-date information from the world of the American Saddlebred, including clips of the current five-gaited grand champion.

The development of this purely American breed goes all the way back to the Middle Ages and the ancient English Pacer, forerunner of the Narraganset Pacer, a breed contributing to the blood lines of the Standardbred, Paso Fino, Morgan, and the American Saddlebred. The Narraganset was the horse Paul Revere rode on his famous midnight ride.

The other important name is Denmark, foaled in 1839, the Thoroughbred stallion known as the foundation sire of the modern American Saddlebred. Ann E. Kraft, my museum guide and a former co-owner (with Lynn Zaske) of the 1990 two-year-old, three-gaited world's champion American Saddlebred, Demons Begone, took the story from there:

"In the 1800s, there were basically two stallions that most of our horses trace back to: Denmark and Harrison Chief. Thoroughbred stallions are bred to standardbreds, trotters, or pacers, some with Morgan ancestors but especially those descended from the Narraganset Pacer.

"The Narraganset has a four-beat lateral gait, each foot hitting the ground individually in the lateral motion. While most breeds walk, trot, and canter to move forward, ours have the natural inherited ability to do two additional gaits, the slow gait and the rack. It's very smooth to ride. Not all American Saddlebreds inherit the two extra gaits, but if a horse is from two registered saddlebred parents, it can be legitimately registered, too."

The museum presents the history of the breed in dioramas, touch-screen videos, an art gallery, and interactive settings. Find out the many ways horses were invaluable in decades past. Walk through an actual horse trailer. Take a computer quiz to see what you've learned at the museum or use the computer to find out where saddlebred farms are located in your state and the dates of upcoming events.

Also, learn about famous horse farms and become acquainted with celebrity horses such as "Mr. Ed." According to Ann, probably the first celebrity saddlebred was Columbus, a horse Buffalo Bill Cody rode in his Wild West Show. It was trained by Tom Bass, an African-American trainer from Missouri considered the father of saddlebred trainers. He developed the bit that is still in use today and was well known for training dressage or high school horses. He trained Columbus to canter backwards, which was how Buffalo Bill always made his entrance.

Since the museum is also headquarters for the American Saddlebred Horse Association, it has information about events all over the country.

The association sponsors an annual youth camp that emphasizes riding and handling. Giving a child a horse can be a good way for the youngster to learn the responsibility of feeding and caring for the animal and gain confidence that comes from taking on a big animal and showing it well. Equitation competitions always evaluate the ability of the rider to ride and show the horse correctly, as well as the performance of the horse itself.

A four-day tour called "Saddlebreds in the Bluegrass" is held annually in July. It includes a visit to the horse park and museum, visits to eight saddlebred farms in the Lexington area, and a horse show. The museum has details.

An excellent assortment of books, videos, clothing items, jewelry, and many decorative objects, all with saddlebred motifs or emphasis, is available in the museum's gift shop. You can also request a mail-order catalog by calling 800-829-4438.

I do highly recommend visiting the museum on its own or as a prelude to seeing the Kentucky Horse Park. Getting caught up in the fascinating story of Kentucky's only native breed (and the oldest registered American horse breed) lends a perspective not gained fully elsewhere.

Where: On Kentucky Horse Park grounds in Lexington. From Interstate 75, take exit 120 (Ironworks Pike, State 1973) and go east for less than a mile to the horse park entrance on the left.
When: Year-round. Daily, 9:00 A.M. to 5:00 P.M., with exceptions noted: hours extended until 6:00 P.M. Memorial Day through Labor Day. Closed Monday and Tuesday from November through March. Closed Thanksgiving Eve and Day, Christmas Eve and Day, New Year's Eve and Day.
Admission: Modest single admission fee (or discounted combination price for both museum and horse park). Senior discount; ages 7 to 12, half price; 6 and under, free. Season pass available.
Amenities: Interactive exhibits, touring exhibits, multimedia shows, art gallery, gift shop.
Activities: Viewing exhibits.
Special events: Annual tours, youth camp. Request current information.
Other: Barrier-free access.
For more information: American Saddle Horse Museum, 4093 Iron Works Pike, Lexington, KY 40511-8434, 606-259-2746.

Horse Tales and Tails

A deep affection for the American Saddlebred resides in many hearts, but devotion can occasionally take a bizarre twist, as in this true tale related by Ann Kraft.

"John Hunt Morgan, considered Lexington's most famous citizen, led a Confederate cavalry group known as Morgan's Raiders during the Civil War. One time, he left his favorite saddlebred mare, Black Bess, in Tennessee when he had to return by ferry to Kentucky. He never saw her again, but in 1911, the townspeople decided to build a statue at the old Lexington courthouse to commemorate him and Black Bess. The sculptor, however, made a decision to place Morgan on a Kentucky Saddler stallion. In his view, a mare wasn't a fitting mount for a general. This doesn't set well with our people, so even today—on April Fool's Day, Halloween, or when Kentucky plays Tennessee—some UK students usually run down there and paint the horse's 'extra parts' red or orange, depending on the situation. It's their version of a protest!"

What's behind the practice of setting a horse's tail? Is it humane?

"Originally, tail setting was introduced on carriage horses to free up the muscles of the hindquarters. In laymen's terms, a tail has very strong muscles running down the tailbone that pin the tail to the buttocks and can clamp down hard. On show horses, to make them aesthetically pleasing—to create a waterfall tail and allow it to rise in balance with the head—two of these muscles are surgically nicked. Now the horse is more comfortable and has better freedom of motion.

"Also, to train them for the ring, which requires a lot of stamina as they go through their paces for maybe 45 minutes, we jog them. We put them in harness with a crupper underneath the tail to hold the harness on. If the horse were able to clamp down on the crupper, he would 'goose' himself and take off flying. You'd have 1,200 pounds of horse taking you for a ride not of your choice.

"As for being humane, they wear well-padded tail sets in their stall to keep the muscles limber. These sets are all cotton, soft, and are changed every day. The horses are well cared for, in a stall with bedding, are fed and exercised appropriately, get all their shots—the whole nine yards. The tail heals quickly, and they can do everything with it except clamp down. These healthy and happy animals can even swish flies to their heart's content."

Kentucky Horse Park

If you're interested in horses, plan to come early and stay late. This internationally renowned park in Lexington, sitting on more than 1,000 acres of land neatly divided by white rail fences, is truly amazing. The estate has a long history dating back to the late 1700s. In the early 1800s, Caneland (as it was then called) was the first farm in this section where Thoroughbred horses were raised. Now it could be described as one of the world's top equine facilities for shows and competitions. Or call it a stunning museum that covers 58 million years of the horse on this continent. Or a showplace that is a working horse farm. Or an ongoing tribute to Thoroughbreds and all the other major breeds.

After parking in the ample lot, you might take a minute to enjoy the immaculate landscape here: wildfowl and wildflowers, swans, and fountains. A life-size bronze statue of Secretariat and another of two foals are prominent here, but just inside the entrance is the statue of Man O' War, the greatest Thoroughbred racing champion of all time, winning 20 of 21 starts and setting three world records before retiring. People are surprised to learn that though Man O' War was foaled, stood at stud, died, and was buried in Kentucky, he never raced in the Bluegrass State!

The daily schedule is a busy one. The visitors center has event information and hospitality personnel to answer any questions. Straight ahead are the theaters. The introductory film, which is shown every 30 minutes, brings the audience an up-close look at horses, from the thrills of the track and the showring to the still beauty of pastures at dawn. It was shot in wide-screen format at more than 50 locations around the world.

A pleasant way to get oriented to the park is by taking a 15-minute horse-drawn tour, which is included in the price of admission. The park owns several draft horse teams. My team was a pair of hefty Percherons, standing more than 17 hands high, who pulled an authentic reproduction of a trolley of the pre-automobile era.

As a kid, I used to hang out at the fairgrounds stables every year during the local county fair, so visiting the horse barns here seemed a quite natural thing to do. One barn holds the draft horses and at least one resident chipmunk, who, at sight of me, quickly scurried through a doorway to the feed and harness room.

Most people really enjoy the Parade of Breeds barn. It is in a horseshoe shape, and soothing music is piped in. Privately owned horses representing more than 40 breeds are stabled here. Plaques identify the animal and its owner, give its height/weight/age, its daily menu, and its performance level. For example, the Lippizan was a stallion, 15¹⁄10 hands, 1,150 pounds, 15 years old, trained for a particular level of dressage. His menu called for measured grain feedings morning and afternoon and a hay supplement once a day.

Since people who own horses are usually caught up in the enjoyment of a specific breed, they may not have knowledge of some of the others. These were new to me: Russian Don, Peruvian Paso, Teton American Cayuse Indian pony, and the Friesian. The smallest horses being shown when I visited were American miniature horses, only 36 inches high.

Each day at the park has special events. The Parade of Breeds takes place at the Breeds Barn. It is a narrated performance, with horses groomed and costumed authentically.

Other events on a given day might be a steeplechase, a horse show, competitions, or a crafts fair. Polo events are predictable: every Sunday at 3:00 P.M. from June through September. I happened to be here during the three days of the year that the National Finals Sheepdog Trials were held. The 100 top dogs from the United States and Canada were showing off their best skills of herding and penning sheep as they followed the voiced instructions of their trainers.

Another interesting activity is watching the harness maker and the farrier (the one who shoes the horses) at work. Posters on the walls in each of these shops aid in explaining the terminology of things like saddles and bridles. The hackamore, for example, comes from the Spanish *jaquima* and is a bridle that has no bit. It is used, especially in the West, to break broncos. In the farrier barn, shoes of various types are displayed, as are instructions for shoeing a horse.

The International Museum of the Horse is unique in the world, a two-story gallery complex with multimedia and interactive displays for adults and children. At the start, a ramp ascends gradually alongside a curving wall. On the wall is a time line that tells a story in photos, text, and with artifacts. It covers the period from 35 B.C. up to the U.S. equestrian team in the 1976 Olympics. Opposite this wall is a companion story that illustrates the chronological history with major artifacts and full-scale tableaux, beginning with the eohippus of 58 million years ago. In all, this is the most complete equestrian history ever assembled. It's all here: Man O' War, circus horses, rodeos, the horse doctor, Indian ponies, the Royal Canadian Mounted Police, and so much more. Upstairs, a breed wall shows photos of 62 breeds and interactively gives information. It also has "The Horse in Sport Gallery," where you can discover 35 uses of the contemporary horse, and "Calumet Farm: Five Decades of Champions," with 560 trophies and 35 paintings.

Housed in the same building are the William G. Kenton Jr. Gallery of equine paintings, photographs, and sculptures; the W. Paul Little Cultural and Learning Center (and research library); and the Winner's Circle Gift Shop, which could be described as an elaborate boutique carrying anything horse-related you could imagine.

The park also has its Clubhouse Restaurant, featuring luncheon menus of soups, salads, sandwiches, side dishes, and Kentucky specialties such as burgoo and country ham.

Sometimes it's hard to leave for reasons you would not suspect. I headed out, noting the sign: "Caution. Children, people, horses, ducks, geese, and swans have the right of way." A swan was sitting in the middle of the road, and geese were wandering through the area. As I waited, I mulled over the possible next-day headline:

"Famished Woman Detained by Swan at Kentucky Horse Park."

Nope. Too ordinary. Happens every day.

Where: In Lexington. From Interstate 75, take exit 120 (State 1973, Ironworks Pike) and go east for less than a mile to the main entrance on the left. Campground entrance is past main entrance.

When: Year-round. Open daily from 9:00 A.M. to 5:00 P.M., mid-March through October. Closed Monday and Tuesday, November 1 through mid-March. Closed Thanksgiving Eve and Day, Christmas Eve and Day, New Year's Eve and Day.

Admission: Moderate fee. Discount for ages 7 to 12. Discounted combination ticket for horse park and American Saddle Horse Museum. Additional charge for some activities and special events. Admission covers: Film showings, museum, horse shows and daily events, gift shop, art gallery, all display barns, horse-drawn tour, walking farm tour, Parade of Breeds, restaurant.

Amenities: Visitors center, International Museum of the Horse, restaurant, gift shop, library, dressage complex, harness maker's shop, farrier's shop, draft and carriage horse barns, all-breed barn, outdoor show arena, polo fields, steeplechase course, resort campground (with 260 sites, many amenities, planned recreation), picnic pavilion.

Activities: Horse-drawn shuttle (10:00 A.M. to 4:00 P.M.), guided museum tour (3:00 P.M.), Parade of Breeds show (11:00 A.M. and 2:00 P.M.), Hall of Champions presentation (10:15 A.M., 1:00 and 4:00 P.M.), film, *Thou Shalt Fly Without Wings,* every half hour (9:30 A.M. to 4:30 P.M.); also (for additional fee), surrey excursion, horseback trail rides, pony rides, carousel.

Special events: More than 60 events. National and international competitions, including Kentucky Rolex Three-day Event (dressage/cross-country/jumping, April), High Hope Steeplechase (April), Egyptian Event, Paso Fino Festival of the Bluegrass (June), Junior League Horse Show (American Saddlebreds, July), Rocky Mountain Horse Show, National Finals Sheep-Dog Trials (September), U.S. Open Polo Championships (October).

Other: Campground permits are for up to 14 days; checkout at noon.

For more information: Kentucky Horse Park, 4089 Iron Works Pike, Lexington, KY 40511, 800-568-8813 or 606-233-4303 (both TDD equipped).

Campground information, write campground director at same address or call 606-259-4257 or 606-255-2690.

Equine classes and short courses, 800-568-8813, ext. 206, or 606-259-4206.

AAEA painting and sculpture workshops (at the park): Liz Dubenitz, Administrative Director, American Academy of Equine Art, PO Box 1315, Middleburg, VA 22117, 703-687-6701.

Show-horse information: The United Professional Horsemen's Association, Kentucky Horse Park (address above), 606-231-5070.

Lexington Children's Museum

Children up to about age 13 enjoy visiting the Lexington Children's Museum to learn about science, nature, and lifestyles of people around the globe. I had fun observing firsthand the enthusiastic exclamations from little voices as youngsters went from room to room. As museum director Roger Paige pointed out, "We offer the kinds of things parents who are traveling want to find for their children to do."

Since the museum is in the middle of downtown in Victorian Square (a complex of boutiques and restaurants in revitalized turn-of-the-century buildings), it is easily accessible. Victorian Square has its own parking garage that offers three hours of free parking.

The first display visitors see is about how water erosion carves valleys and how to fight it by planting trees. Behind a large glass wall, bare soil has been piled up and is being washed down by a stream of water, simulating erosion. This gets us in the mood for the next stop: the Natural Wonders gallery, one of the permanent exhibits on the museum's main floor.

Natural Wonders teaches about the ecosystem and Kentucky's flora, fauna, and geology. It has artifacts, questions to answer, and games. Special activities include making fossil rubbings and playing a natural history matching game. Also, try on a turtle shell or put together a fossil skeleton and guess what the animal was.

Another permanent area is Around Our Town. Here, we get acquainted with the services towns provide and jobs people have. Explore the workings of a bank, fire station, and the like. You can learn something about each place. Get in a delivery truck or "visit" the newspaper.

Heartscape (Explore the Heart and Lungs) is a gigantic walk-through heart and lungs which explains how these two bodily organs work and how oxygen is supplied to the body from the lungs.

In the Bubble Factory, children walk inside a huge bubble. Is a bubble really round? Find out. Experiment stations are provided for making real bubbles and working out answers to bubble questions.

Beginnings is for ages one through three, a place to crawl through big blocks, investigate a playhouse, and play with water. There's even a "walking piano" where you walk on the keys to play notes.

The museum likes to be a gathering place for activities. An example of this is the animation gallery, which teaches the science of animation and how stop-action and claymation are done. Children can actually make little figures, put them in front of a backdrop, and imagine what they'd look like on TV. They also learn how to make zoetrope "movies" that accomplish the sense of movement as objects are spun around.

Around Our World provides a place to learn about other cultures and their music, games, dress, customs, and environment. For instance, to learn about Kazakhstan, we can put on a folk costume, enjoy folk tales with universal themes such as "victory of the humble over the powerful," and play guessing games about Russian art, music, and poetry.

In another area, learn about artifacts that are found in the ground. The exhibit teaches that in digging up objects we need to relate them to other things to find the answer to puzzles.

An astronomy corner, Kentucky Skies, has a collection of photographs. The museum and the Bluegrass Astronomy

Club jointly sponsor programs at the University of Kentucky Arboretum or Raven Run Nature Sanctuary for stargazing, usually at night. This monthly activity is free to the public.

For those who want to walk on the moon, the Physics and Space: Explore the Universe corner is the place. We can walk on a moonscape model and pretend to be astronauts.

Energy Class (about the sources, uses, and conservation of energy) is new, and it's different in that energy stations are placed in each gallery. In the Physics and Space corner, the physics of energy and space travel are emphasized, while in Around Our World the topic is international aspects of energy. Some countries have fewer energy resources than others, which leads to conflicts; so what will the visitor (playing the role of international arbitrator) do? Which options should be implemented? All energy stations are computerized and interactive, allowing realistic statistics to be used in solving problems.

Another area is about teeth. Walk inside a huge mouth, lift up a baby tooth, and see the permanent one erupting underneath. Also, learn about animal teeth. Turn a crank to make an animal's jaw move its natural way.

Special events—demonstrations, activities, and workshops —are tied to themes of the exhibits. During the summer, when peregrine falcons are nesting on the tops of downtown buildings, such programs might focus on habitats of endangered species. The museum displays an exhibit about the falcons and the nesting activity. It includes photographs, but the most interesting aspect is the opportunity to view the birds. The state installs a video camera to monitor the birds' progress as they are fledging (that is, learning to eat on their own and catch food on the wing). The museum gets a live feed that allows visitors to watch the action in real time. The museum also keeps a rolling cart on Main Street, parked just below the building where the falcons are nesting. It is "decorated" with binoculars and information and is manned by elementary school children who have learned about the birds and can answer questions.

The biggest special event of the year is Museum-Go-Round, held on Memorial Day weekend. Four blocks of Main Street are closed for this street festival hosted by the museum and the city. Programs, games, singing, and dancing take the spotlight.

The museum store is in the shopping complex adjacent to the museum entrance and is open additional hours. It has an extensive inventory of nature and science toys, puzzles, books, and games.

Bringing Back the Peregrine Falcons

In 1993, the Kentucky Department of Fish and Wildlife Resources (KDFWR) joined in a federal program of rescuing the peregrine falcon population from the brink of extinction through a process called hacking. The goal was to remove these birds from endangered/threatened status by 1997. One of the locations where hacking took place in 1993 and 1994 was downtown Lexington. Ten birds were released each year for two consecutive years into a protective environment until they were able to fly. In Lexington, the two-year survival rate was 75 percent. KDFWR hoped that at least one breeding pair would return to Lexington when they were ready to raise their own young.

Peregrine falcons are about the size of crows (but with a 3½-foot wingspan) and are the swiftest of birds of prey, capable of diving at 200 miles an hour to catch small birds in midair. Historically, one race of peregrines nested in Kentucky on cliffs above the Rockcastle River in Laurel County and on other cliffs along the border with Virginia—and possibly along the Kentucky River gorge in central Kentucky. They were even seen in western Kentucky in the 1930s, nesting in cypress trees. These birds disappeared completely from the eastern United States.

The ones hacked in Lexington (and those hacked subsequently near Herrington Lake on the Dix River east of Harrodsburg) were brought here from Wyoming. Louisville does have a nesting pair that it is believed were hacked somewhere within 100 miles, but otherwise only a few that migrate through each year between Alaska and the Gulf Coast are seen.

Since these young birds have no parents to protect them from the great horned owls, they would soon fall victim to that predator if they were released in traditional habitat areas. In cities, this is not a problem. The rooftops give them the height they need and also feel natural. There are some hazards, though. One Lexington bird flew down an elevator shaft and starved to death; another was hit by a car; and a third collided with a building.

Look to the skies in April for a bluish-colored bird with a black cap, white chin, and yellow legs and feet. Likely as not, it will be whizzing by.

Where: Victorian Square in downtown Lexington at Broad and Main Streets. Main Street is one way going west, and eastbound traffic is routed on Vine Street. From either, go north on Broadway, turn right on Short Street (one block north of Main), then right again into the covered parking lot for Victorian Square. A pedestrian walkway goes over Broadway; elevators serve all floors of the mall.

When: Year-round, daily. Monday through Friday, 10:00 A.M. to 6:00 P.M.; Saturday, until 5:00 P.M.; Sunday, 1:00 to 5:00 P.M. Closed Mondays during the school year. Closed Easter,

Thanksgiving, and Christmas. Open Labor Day but closed rest of week.

Admission: Very modest fee; children's rate; under two, free.

Amenities: Galleries with science and nature themes, museum store, toddler play area, birthday room, educational resource center, recycle arts center.

Activities: Interactive exhibits, games, puzzles, experiments, art and learning activities.

Special events: Museum-Go-Round (Memorial Day weekend). Inquire about others.

Other: Barrier-free access. Parking garage offers three hours free parking with stamped ticket. Museum store publishes annual Nature and Science gift catalog.

For more information: The Lexington Children's Museum, Victorian Square, 401 West Main Street, Lexington, KY 40507, 606-258-3253. Museum store and recycle arts center, 606-258-3258. Fax, 606-258-3255.

For fact sheet and pamphlet about peregrine falcons: Peregrine Falcon, KDFWR, I&E Division, #1 Game Farm Road, Frankfort, KY 40601, 502-564-4336.

The Lexington Cemetery

Nationally recognized as one of the most beautiful cemeteries in America, the Lexington Cemetery is well worth a visit from several perspectives: learning about the cultural and political history of this region; admiring the lakes and gardens, more than 200 species of trees and 179 known species of birds; and discovering facts about some of Kentucky's most distinguished or unusual historical figures.

Seasons are clearly defined here, with masses of ornamental cherry trees, dogwoods, magnolias, and crab apples in spring; formal flower gardens in summer (one of the gardens covers nearly three acres); flaming maple, sassafras, and sweet gum in fall; and frosty, snow-covered evergreens and bare-branched deciduous trees on wintry days. Visitors are welcome to take self-guided tours of the grounds. Three tour pamphlets are available.

The arboretum tour (using a green tour guide titled *A Tree Walk in The Lexington Cemetery*) identifies 41 tree species, all marked with metal plates. Many are quite old. In fact, an American basswood is possibly the largest of its kind in the United States. The cemetery was established in 1849, and the trees were allowed to grow naturally. No fertilizers or insecticides were used, nor have the trees been pruned. Most of these trees are the best specimens to be found in the area. The tour starts at the Henry Clay Monument and can be taken in two parts or as a whole.

While on the tree walk, you may wish to have in hand the bird checklist prepared by the Audubon Society of Kentucky. Year-round residents commonly seen include the American kestrel, killdeer, belted kingfisher, downy woodpecker, tufted titmouse, Carolina wren, northern mockingbird, northern cardinal, and American goldfinch.

The historic tour, Walk Through History, goes through parts of the oldest sections of the cemetery. The tour guide tells many fascinating anecdotes about Lexington's history and citizens, tales that are probably not found in textbooks.

The Tour for Children offers an oversized illustrated map showing 45 stops. The tour is a mixture of learning about people, burial customs, and natural features such as sinkholes and cypress knees. Games, riddles, and quizzes are included. A Scavenger Hunt (things you identify, not collect!) and a bird-watching game are two of the activities.

Where: 833 West Main Street (on U.S. Route 421) in Lexington on the outskirts of downtown.

When: Year-round, 8:00 A.M. to 5:00 P.M. daily. Office open weekdays, 8:00 A.M. to 4:00 P.M.; and Saturday, 8:00 A.M. to noon.
Admission: Free.
Amenities: Nationally recognized arboretum. Information office, self-guided tour booklets, and bird checklist.
Activities: Historic Tour, Children's Tour, Tree Walk, birding, nature appreciation.
Other: Some guidelines for a visit to this private property: Children under 18 must be accompanied by an adult; bicycles and motorcycles not permitted; pets must be on leashes; picnicking, drinking, sunbathing, and sports activities not permitted. Behavior should respect those buried here.
For more information: The Lexington Cemetery, 833 West Main Street, Lexington, KY 40508, 606-255-5522.

Raven Run Nature Sanctuary

The Lexington Parks and Recreation Department administers this 374-acre sanctuary south of the city, bounded by Raven Run Creek and its Middle and North Forks, Chandler Creek, and, at one glorious overlook, by the Kentucky River Palisades. The approach to Raven Run is a country drive through farmlands and fenced pastures, contributing to the anticipation visitors feel as—having escaped from the city—they near the preserve.

This is a mother lode of nature where nearly 400 species of plants have been observed, as well as mammals such as white-tailed deer, gray foxes, small rodents, and other creatures typical of this Bluegrass region; and at least 205 species of birds. The habitats include meadows, cedar glades, forests from successional to mature, ponds, and streams. Among the plants are 300 species of wildflowers.

Even the parking lot here is surrounded by flowers—quite a few beside the road, too. I heard a crow calling in the distance in a voice that is best appreciated by another of its species. Among the trees and in grassy areas nearby are picnic tables.

To the right is the Freedom Trail, a barrier-free paved walkway that can be somewhat challenging, since it has grades up to eight percent. This trail leads to a meadow ecosystem, a cedar thicket, and a stream ecosystem, crossing two bridges along the way. It goes in serpentine fashion downhill to the river, making three interconnected circles. Benches for resting and little wheelchair turnouts are placed strategically. A white line helps the visually handicapped remain on the trail. People can call ahead before visiting if they need a guide to assist them.

Most visitors will head for the nature center, intending to hike some of the nine miles of trails in the wilderness portion of Raven Run. Reach the center by a 200-yard trail from the rest rooms at the edge of the parking lot or continue on the entrance road (on foot) for roughly the same distance. It is important to pick up a trail map at the nature center. The series of main and connecting trails, though color coded and marked, can be confusing, and a map will help new visitors keep their bearings. Since hikers need to be off the trails a half-hour before closing time, they should plan their day to get back in time.

At the trailhead behind the nature center is a signboard that explains the sanctuary, trails, regulations, and points of interest. It also depicts bird nests, paper wasps, hackberry gall, and other nature facts. Inside the center, with soothing music playing on the radio, I looked around the room at animal pelts, stuffed animals, tree identification samples, and other hands-on displays and exhibits.

An activities schedule is published quarterly and available to the public on request. Among the summer lineup of events is a twice-monthly "learn to camp" program for all ages, which is suitable for the handicapped as well. It involves an overnight stay in a safe and supervised setting. For a nominal fee, tents, meals, and most of the equipment are provided, though participants are encouraged to bring their own sleeping bags.

Stargazing, sponsored by the Lexington Children's Museum, is an evening program on the first Friday of each month through October. It is a free program for all ages (handicapped, too), and no reservations are necessary.

Monthly early morning bird walks start at 6:30 A.M. on scheduled Saturdays for those who have made reservations. One caution: don't be late. Since this is earlier than the regular hours, the gate is closed again at 7:00.

Another activity with reservations required are the tree walks guided by a park naturalist on some Sunday afternoons. People learn to identify dozens of trees by studying their leaves, twigs, fruits, and other characteristics.

Wildflower walks on Saturday mornings through several seasons give opportunities to observe the changing floral landscape. Spring wildflowers are found on the cool, moist forest floor, whereas in summer the gaily colored meadows—though baked by the sun—are an irresistible attraction.

Then there are the free nighttime walks held on the full moon and attended by hundreds of people. Some have themes, as the Night Insect Walk and Bug Pageant in July, a nationally recognized event sponsored by the University of Kentucky's Department of Entomology.

Two of the most popular trail destinations are the Kentucky River Palisades overlook, presenting views of one of Kentucky's three undeveloped limestone gorges (where I decided to go), and a series of cascades on Raven Run Creek where the north fork comes into the main stream. Features of historic interest include old rock fences, a lime kiln, and the remains of a gristmill. The stone foundation of old Evans Mill, built in 1820, is near the cascades.

My hike took me along the Red Trail (also referred to as the Boundary Trail) past a field of goldenrod and a profusion of flowers with gold, red, green, white, and purple hues, then into the woods. The September morning air was fresh from misty rain of the previous day. Sound carries a long distance in the woods when the air is damp, and every rustle of leaves or darting of squirrels and birds is heightened. The dirt path changes elevation but not too steeply. For a time, it follows an old stone wall. Numbered markers coordinate with the trail guidebook. Coming upon the lime kiln told me I was still on the right track.

Suddenly, red trail-marker arrows were pointing in opposite directions. I'd about decided to take the uphill route (it makes sense that the overlook will be on higher ground), when along came Josh Huffman and Roy Stephens, from Lexington and Pine Knot, respectively. Both said the overlook was their favorite place in the preserve. They were headed there, so I joined them.

Soon, we were standing on a large boulder looking down at the Kentucky River 100 feet below. The water was very calm, except for the wake of an animal swimming across. It may have been a duck or a muskrat, but we couldn't see it clearly. The view was spectacular, with a sheer rock cliff just to the left of us and the far hills beginning to show fall colors.

The shadows were lengthening. I headed back while my two hiking companions continued on toward the cascades. The quietness of the woods was punctuated by birds' trills and sudden thumps. A fox squirrel ran across the path in front of me, its red-tinged fur making identification easy. A leaflet,

"Mammals of Raven Run," has illustrations of some forest creatures that live here: raccoons, Virginia possums, muskrats, gray and fox squirrels, groundhogs, and the Southern flying squirrels.

One other item of interest: on Jacks Creek Road near the entrance is a historic brick house built around 1804. Visitors to Raven Run are welcome to go inside.

Where: Southeast of downtown Lexington. From downtown, take Richmond Road (an extension of East Main Street), then right onto U.S. Routes 24/421 (Old Richmond Road). Go 3³⁄10 miles, then turn right onto Jacks Creek Pike (State 1975). Raven Run is another 5²⁄10 miles on Jacks Creek Pike, which turns off State 1975 onto State 1976 (just follow the yellow center line and the signs). Alternately, take Tates Creek Road (State 1974) as follows: from the New Circle Road beltline, take exit 18 and go south for about 9½ miles, then left on Spears Road (State 1975). You will be turning right onto Jacks Creek Pike.

When: Year-round. Daily, June through October; Wednesday through Sunday at other times. Trails close 30 minutes before park closure. Access sometimes limited. Hours vary with season, but basically 9:00 A.M. to 5:00 P.M. (until 7:00 P.M. June through August, until 6:00 P.M. May and September). Closed Thanksgiving Day and Christmas Day. Heavy rains can cause park to close.

Admission: Free. Small fee for some events.

Amenities: Nature center, barn, trails, ruins of old gristmill, rest rooms.

Activities: Hiking, birding, photography, nature study, picnicking (in designated areas only).

Special events: Wildflower walks, night hikes, stargazing, early morning bird walks offered seasonally.

Other: Special six-tenths-of-a-mile, barrier-free trail and access to nature center (some events barrier free). Pets not allowed. Fires are prohibited.

For more information: Raven Run Nature Sanctuary, 5888 Jacks Creek Pike, Lexington, KY 40515-9536, 606-272-6105 (for information and to receive the newsletter).

Lexington-Fayette County Division of Parks/Recreation, 545 North Upper Street, Lexington, KY 40508, 606-288-2900.

Shaker Village of Pleasant Hill

It would be quite impossible (outside of a science-fiction tale, I suppose) for anyone to actually go back nearly 200 years. Yet, there is a place here and now where you can step into a 200-year-old rural community that—though the inhabitants are long gone—has been perfectly preserved. It's the Shaker Village of Pleasant Hill, between Harrodsburg and Lexington, a National Historic Landmark and the only place of its kind where all buildings open to visitors are original. The village, comprising 2,700 acres and 33 buildings set in one of the most scenic parts of the Bluegrass, sits on a rolling plateau two miles from where the Dix and Kentucky Rivers meet.

The Shaker colonies that flourished in the 19th and early 20th centuries were models of community life devised by a devout and visionary religious group who believed in celibacy, equality of race and gender, and freedom from prejudice. They ultimately became better known for the perfection of their craftsmanship—especially furniture—than the ritualistic dance that gave them their name. The people who lived at Pleasant Hill so long ago kept detailed diaries. Now, hosts and hostesses dress as Shakers and explain (and demonstrate) the Shaker way of life.

Visitors tour the grounds and exhibition buildings, eat authentic Shaker food in the Trustees' Office (a dining hall), purchase Shaker reproductions and well-made Kentucky crafts—and some even spend the night.

This is a very popular tourist destination for all the reasons mentioned, but nature enthusiasts get bonuses.

Hour-long river cruises on a scenic and little-traveled part of the Kentucky River depart five times a day. Special narrated "River Ventures" tours are given on the first Saturday of each month, and a monthly Sunday afternoon "Downriver Discovery" tour locks through Kentucky River Lock No. 7. The lock-through is uniquely available on the *Dixie Belle*, since, with a river closed to commercial traffic, the locks are not normally open.

Naturalist-guided hikes include three series, each given on three consecutive weekends: Wildflowers Along the River (in April), Late Summer Nature Walks (September), and Late Autumn Along the River (October and November).

Each hike usually takes 4½ hours, and each has a special focus. For example, the late fall series, "Mammals and More" teaches how mammals live and survive in winter and how you can find their signs; "Trilobites and Other Links to the Past" makes a fossil search into the Kentucky River Gorge past layers of sedimentary limestone; and "Patterns in Nature" shows how to recognize woody and herbaceous plants after the leaves have fallen. The tour guides are specialists in biology and geology from colleges and state agencies.

Visitors may also hike to the river on their own along the 1826 Shaker road. Another trail from Shaker Landing leads past woodland wildflowers to a waterfall nearby. And at the landing are some remains of old buildings and a display that gives more insight into the importance of the river to the Shakers.

If visitors walk the village streets with a careful eye, they will see what a casual glance misses. Here's a hint: look at the stone paving in front of the steps of the West Family House to discover the fossil remains of a cephalopod, a snakelike marine creature of 450 million years ago. My source for this information was the guidebook, *Walking Tour of Shakertown*.

A Kentucky River Cruise Aboard the *Dixie Belle*

O n a virtually uninhabited stretch of the Kentucky River, the 150-passenger stern-wheeler makes daily excursions through a scenic tree-lined gorge. Except for an occasional fishing boat and the ever-present wildlife, the passengers and crew have the river to themselves.

As we depart from the landing, a vulture is overhead, gliding on thermal air currents, and turtles are sunning themselves on the banks. The captain starts pointing out places of interest, like the Kentucky River palisades that come into view. He also tells about the wildlife along the river.

It is not unusual to see great blue herons, green herons, osprey, woodpeckers, muskrats, water snakes, ducks, kingfishers. Mammals are plentiful, too. Wild turkeys, opossums, groundhogs, deer, and wildcats are in the area, and coyotes are frequently heard at night. Black bears may be on their way. They are moving westward, and sightings have been reported at the headwaters of the Kentucky River east of here. Also, some were relocated from east Tennessee to the Big South Fork NRRA.

The forest through which this river winds has water maple, sycamore, walnut, hickory, beech, basswood, redbud, and dogwood trees. In spring, the banks are a fairyland of white and pink, and at the peak of fall color, they reflect a true spectacle with myriad shades of red, gold, and yellow.

The fish population in the Kentucky and Dix Rivers, Herrington Lake, and the tailwaters of the dam includes rainbow and brown trout; largemouth, smallmouth, black, and hybrid bass; and a variety of catfish, walleyes, sauger, white crappie, perch, carp, and gar.

The pilot's narration includes the geologic and natural history of the river, information about paddle wheelers, and local anecdotes.

Where: On U.S. Route 68, 25 miles southwest of Lexington and 7 miles northeast of Harrodsburg.

When: Daily, year-round. Village tours, 9:00 A.M. to 6:00 P.M., April 1 through October 31. Reduced hours November 1 through March 31. Craft sales shops, 9:00 A.M. to 5:00 P.M. (until 7:30 P.M. April through October). All facilities closed December 24 and 25. Riverboat excursions, 10:00 A.M., plus noon, 2:00, 4:00, and 6:00 P.M. April 28 through October 31.

Admission: Moderate fee. Discounted tickets for youths (12 to 17) and children (6 to 11). Under 6, free. Combination tickets available for Village Tour and Riverboat Excursion. Group rates.

Amenities: Exhibition buildings, gift shops, dining facilities, 80 lodging rooms, meeting rooms, trails, stern-wheeler riverboat.

Activities: Self-guided walking tour of village; living history demonstrations; music, dance, and craft demonstrations; daily riverboat excursions; nature appreciation; photography; wildlife viewing.

Special events: African-American Shaker History Weekend (February), photography workshops (March, September), intergenerational workshops (March, July), watercolor workshop (April), Wildflowers Along the River, Threads of a Culture (April), Dixie Belle excursions (daily, April 28–October 31), River Venture (monthly, May through October), Downriver Discovery (monthly, May through October), nature hikes, Harvest Festival, archaeology workshop, Bike Trek to Shakertown (September), Fall on the Farm (September, October), Autumn Life on the River (October, November).

Other: Barrier-free access. Advance reservations necessary for Trustees' Office dining and for overnight lodging. (Overnight guests have access to additional trails.) Conference facilities and services available.

For more information: Shaker Village of Pleasant Hill, 3501 Lexington Road, Harrodsburg, KY 40330, 606-734-5411.

12

The Mountain Parkway

First, a word about the sprawling Daniel Boone National Forest (DBNF), which has a presence in 21 eastern Kentucky counties from north of Morehead to the Tennessee line. It is managed as seven ranger districts. Major highways that traverse the forest are Interstate 64, the Mountain Parkway, the Daniel Boone Parkway, Interstate 75, U.S. Route 27, and U.S. Route 421. Additional access is provided by excellent state roads. Hikers who have the time and inclination may hike the entire length of the 257-mile Sheltowee Trace National Recreation Trail that starts at the northernmost tip of the forest and connects with all major developed areas, ending in Tennessee. A popular 45-mile round-trip is from the Clear Creek Recreation area near Cave Run Lake and south to the system of loop trails at the Red River Gorge Geological Area, then returning by the same route.

Kentucky's Bert T. Combs Mountain Parkway, splitting from Interstate 64 at Winchester and going east through the DBNF and on to the Licking River at Salyersville, has opened up some premier destinations to easy access from Lexington and Louisville. In Kentucky, traversing the mountainous eastern region's two-lane roads poses more problems than a visitor might expect because coal trucks must use these roads, too. No matter how courteous the drivers are (and they are!), they can't always pull off to let you by. You could spend two hours going 20 miles.

Kentucky's answer is to provide a system of excellent four-lane roads between major mountain destinations. The Mountain Parkway is the best way to reach the Natural Bridge State Resort Park and the Red River Gorge Geological Area.

For more information: Visit the Red Caboose at the exit 33 rest area off the Mountain Parkway, 606-663-9229.

Write Forest Supervisor, Daniel Boone National Forest, 100 Vaught Road, Winchester, KY 40391, or call 606-745-3100. (Information, including "Recreation on the Daniel Boone National Forest" brochure.)

Pilot Knob State Nature Preserve

If you're up for a short but strenuous hike, one of the best views you'll find anywhere is between Winchester and Clay City just off the parkway. From a 730-foot high knob, you'll see a panorama of three regions: the Bluegrass, the Knobs, and the Cumberland Plateau. It is said to be the spot from which Daniel Boone first glimpsed the Bluegrass on June 7, 1769.

It's not hard to find if you follow these directions. I took State 15 from Winchester going southeast. Five miles before reaching Clay City, Hidden Valley Road goes to the right and Brush Creek Road goes to the left. On the left also is Roadside Marker #132, identifying Pilot Knob. Go 1½ miles on Brush Creek Road to a small parking lot and trailhead.

Pilot Knob is a 308-acre preserve in a second-growth oak and hickory forest. However, along with changes in the elevation and direction of sunlight exposure, other forest types are encountered. At the summit are stunted old-growth chestnut oaks and pitch pines, and at other places, you'll see tulip poplar and red maple. Near the summit is a rock outcropping of conglomerate sandstone that had been quarried in the early 1800s. The interpretive trail is a 1½-mile round-trip.

It is always advisable not to hike alone in wilderness areas because of various hazards. At Pilot Knob, you should watch out for poisonous snakes. It helps to stay on the trail and be alert around the rock outcrops.

The best reward is in the fall, when from the knob a crazy quilt of color is spread out before your eyes.

Where: From Clay City, five miles northwest on State 15 and right on Brush Creek Road to the end.
When: Daily, sunrise to sunset.
Admission: Free.
Amenities: Trail to 730-foot-high knob.
Activities: Hiking, nature appreciation, birding, wildlife viewing, photography.
Other: Hunting and camping not permitted.
For more information: Pilot Knob State Nature Preserve, c/o Kentucky State Nature Preserves Commission, 801 Schenkel Lane, Frankfort, KY 40601, 502-573-2886. Fax, 502-573-2355.

Natural Bridge State Resort Park

The name, Natural Bridge, comes from a sandstone arch within the park that is famous as a long-standing tourist attraction in an area noted for geologic wonders. Within a five-mile radius are many exciting formations—at least 150 natural arches, plus numerous rock houses, pinnacles, sheer cliffs, and balanced rocks.

The park itself is one of the state's most visited and a favorite of many people that I met in Kentucky. Its location in the middle of the DBNF and its proximity to the Red River Gorge Geological Area add to its appeal, but without these, it would still be a top spot for hikers and nature lovers.

About half of the park—943 acres—is a State Nature Preserve that protects the habitat for rare and endangered plant species such as the state-endangered small yellow lady's slipper and the federally endangered Virginia big-eared bat. The terrain is rugged, with vegetation changes from ridge tops to valleys—pines and oaks are on the dry ridges, and hemlocks and tulip poplars are lower down. The valley floor is host to ferns and wildflowers that thrive in a cool, moist environment.

For people who like to be out on the trails, this is the place. The 18 miles of trails, which close at sunset, range from 3/10 of a mile to 8½ miles. Many are interconnected, allowing options and variety for those planning a particular day's hike. Getting an early start and allowing some extra time is a wise plan when hiking the longer trails through the preserve.

The park's Hemlock Lodge overlooks Hoedown Island Lake. I stayed there one September and listened to the honking of passing geese in the mist above the lake. As the mist lifted and the sun peeked over distant hills, I watched rows of ducks swimming below, making music and patterns like a college band at halftime—a drum major swimming alone, one line coming toward me, two others going to the right, and a fourth line receding. Happy ducks on the water executing

a perfect peel off. All that was missing was a bass drum (a jumping fish would do).

At the end of the lodge are trails to the nature and activity centers and to the Natural Bridge. Balanced Rock Trail goes by an extraordinary and much-photographed rock formation and is the steepest trail in the park. Most people taking this trail choose it as their return route.

The Original Trail is the one I took. It winds through rhododendrons and huge hemlocks, large overhanging boulders, and sheer rock faces. The trail was built in the 1890s by the Lexington and Eastern Railroad during the height of logging operations. It climbs more than 500 feet and ends beneath the span of the Natural Bridge. The climb to the top of the bridge follows a fissure in the rock. Going across the top, the words form automatically: "Wow, what a view!" It seems one can see forever.

Then my route took me along Battleship Rock Trail to Devil's Gulch and Lookout Point. This is a high, level trail with great views and places that compel one to stop and look. The trail goes past the top of the sky lift. This is another way to get to the top, by the way. Besides the ease of ascent, you have some awesome views. Up here are mostly younger trees but also a few tall pines. This area was burned several times by forest fires caused by cigarettes dropped carelessly from the lift.

Lookout Point is a prominent cliff offering a view of the Natural Bridge made immortal by photographers.

Devil's Gulch Trail was temporarily closed, so my descent would have to be by way of the Needle's Eye stairway. First, though, on to Lover's Leap. This is the highest cliff in the park, and presents a dizzying, 360-degree view. Deep woods cover the steep mountainsides in all directions.

After successfully negotiating the Needle's Eye descent, I

explored the Salt Mine and Rock Garden Trails. Though the sky was now cloudless and the sun shone brightly, the forest floor was shady under big trees, and ferns covered the ground.

"One of the most outstanding things about Natural Bridge," said park naturalist Wilson Francis, "is the plant life. Winter visitors see a lot of green. The forest is rich with hemlocks, some quite old, and white pine. Of the five counties that have large numbers of native white pine, four are right here together. It's the steep terrain and cool, dark canyons that let those trees hang on. We have loads of rhododendron and mountain laurel. You can also find yellow birch here and some southern plants like big-leaf magnolia."

Other plants of this forest include 50 varieties of ferns and an absolutely stunning assortment of spring wildflowers, including orchids and lilies. Late April and early May are usually the height of the spring wildflower season.

Wildlife viewing is inhibited to a degree by the dense forest. Hikers often see squirrels and woodchucks. In early morning and late evening, woodland birds are heard, though they're not easily spotted visually. Because hunting is allowed in the surrounding national forest, woodland mammals are quite shy.

Another interesting and easy-to-walk trail begins at the park's Whittleton Campground, following Whittleton Creek along the grade of a narrow gauge logging railroad built in 1898. A walk to the large Whittleton Arch at the base of a sandstone cliff is a two-mile round-trip from the campground. This trail also connects the Red River Gorge and Natural Bridge Trails.

Natural Bridge has four naturalists on its summer staff and two year-round. Daily programs are offered from Memorial Day through Labor Day. A summer day's activities might include an hour-long guided tour of the Natural Bridge, where a naturalist would talk about plant communities and rock formations. Two or three junior naturalist activities for kids 6 through 12 would include creek walks, cave tours, and nature-crafts activities, when kids collect things from nature and use them in making displays. Evening programs usually meet in a lodge room or the activities center (a convention hall that seats 200) and feature guest speakers or slide shows on natural history, logging history of the park, or railroads.

For pure recreation, square dancing is a weekend activity during the summer season, and folk or bluegrass concerts are offered regularly.

The nature center has displays of mounted wildlife specimens collected over the years. They include bears, a mountain lion, deer, and foxes. Other displays focus on iron manufacturing, logging, and saltpeter mining (which went on here during the War of 1812). All relate to the history of the area.

Nature-related special events include a Herpetology Weekend in either April or May. According to Wilson, "We have more salamanders in April and more snakes in May, so we kind of go back and forth in our scheduling." Other events are a Wildflower Weekend in May, a Mushroom Foray in September, and a Nature Photography weekend in winter.

Another place worth mentioning is the Miami Valley Serpentarium, near the park on Natural Bridge Road. It wasn't open when I visited, but it is highly recommended—run by a nonprofit organization dedicated to educating the public about reptiles. Staff members present programs at Lexington Children's Museum and Raven Run Nature Sanctuary. At the serpentarium, in a show that blends science and entertainment, visitors are introduced to 60 specimens from around the world, including cobras, mambas, pythons, and rattlesnakes. They'll tingle your spine, I suspect.

Where: Southeast of Lexington, Interstate 64 to Mountain Parkway, then exit 33 toward Slade and State 11 to park entrance.

When: Year-round. Dining room serves three meals daily. Campground, open March 1 through November 30. Sky lift, snack bars, nature center, miniature golf, open April through October 31. Pedal boats and pool, open Memorial Day through Labor Day. Park closed the week of Christmas.

Admission: Free. Fee for some facilities.

Amenities: Lodge, gift shop, cottages, campground, dining room, meeting rooms, open-air dance patio, sky lift, snack bars, 20 miles of trails, nature center, pedal boat rentals, swimming pool, miniature golf, tennis, picnic grounds, playgrounds, canoe access. Shelter rentals available.

Activities: Hiking, camping, sky lift rides, swimming, tennis, photography, fishing, wildlife viewing, naturalist-led interpretive programs (year-round), outdoor games, miniature golf, picnicking, weekly square dances (April 30 through October), daily planned recreation in summer.

Special events: Shindig in the Mountains (May), National Mountain-Style Square Dance & Clogging Festival (June), Mushroom Foray (September). Kentucky State Parks special events brochure, 800-255-7275.

Other: For barrier-free information, 800-255-7275. TDD equipped.

For more information: Natural Bridge State Resort Park, 2135 Natural Bridge Road, Slade, KY 40376-9999, 606-663-2214. Reservations, 800-325-1710. Fax, 606-663-5037.

"Hoedown Island" Square Dance Information: Richard Jett, PO Box 396, Campton, KY 41301, 606-668-6650.

Miami Valley Serpentarium, 1275 Natural Bridge Road, Slade, KY 40376-9701, 606-663-9160. Modest admission charge. (Open daily 11:00 A.M. to 7:00 P.M. June through

August and on weekends other months, except November through February, when it is closed.)

Red River Gorge Geological Area

The Red River Gorge Geological Area surrounds the middle section of the river for which it is named and actually comprises some 26,000 acres. It is an easy hour's drive from Lexington via the Mountain Parkway and only a 30-mile round-trip from Natural Bridge State Park.

Why do visitors come? Its geological features are legendary: some 100 sandstone arches (also called bridges) and many sheer cliffs, rockhouses, chimney rocks, and lookout points. Scientists say it is unsurpassed in the number of plant species (555) found in comparable-sized areas in Kentucky. Rock climbers, hikers, backpackers, and canoeists know it well. Students of geology, botany, and biology find it of great interest. It is also a fascinating place for cultural history buffs. Auto touring on the most famous scenic drive in Kentucky makes for heavy traffic on weekends, so be warned.

If you start at Slade (Parkway exit 33) and go north on State 15 for a mile, then right on State 77, you'll be entering the gorge area through the Nada tunnel, which was built in 1911. It is narrow, but not too narrow for today's vehicles. The first load of logs to go through jammed in the tunnel in 1912 and had to be dynamited free! Follow the signs toward the Gladie Creek Historic Site and visitors center. You'll then be on State 715, which loops around and finally rejoins State 15 several miles east of Slade.

Throughout your visit, be on the lookout for spectacular rock formations. The gorge has such variety and richness in its geology, flora, and fauna. With this, plus the changing seasons, each visit is certain to have unique aspects. Parking areas are provided near the most-visited interesting places, and markers give information about forestry practices such as timber harvesting.

The gorge has its own extensive trail network (officially, the 36-mile Red River Gorge National Recreation Trail). In addition, the Sheltowee Trace National Recreation Trail passes through the geological area. Ask the Stanton Ranger District for a hiking guide to the gorge area and the trace. Topo maps are strongly recommended.

While on the trails or along streams, watch for squirrels, raccoons, chipmunks, beavers, muskrats, minks, foxes, groundhogs, skunks, opossums, vultures, various songbirds, owls, woodcocks, grouse, rarely seen eastern ribbon snakes and corn snakes, plus other denizens of the upland forests. Come in late April or through the summer and fall to identify the wildflowers. You're sure to be met with dazzling displays. Among the rare varieties present here are purple gerardia, pink azalea, spreading pogonia, crane-fly orchids, climbing fern, and white-haired goldenrod (*Solidago albopilosa*, which is federally endangered and present only in Menifee and Powell Counties of Kentucky and nowhere else in the United States).

Canoeing the Red River through the gorge is another popular activity and a way to get an entirely different view. According to my paddling friends, the middle section is probably the most desirable all around. The upper section is undoubtedly the most scenic but has fluctuations in water level that can turn your float into a hike or, on the other hand, make you join the ranks of the demolished-canoe club (which adds dozens of new members each year). On its best days, it is a beautiful Class II or III+ whitewater, generally runnable from late December to late May. I suggest Bob Sehlinger's guide (see Reading Guide). The Middle Red River, rated Class I, begins at the State 715 bridge and ends at Raven Rock at the

State 77 bridge. It passes through some very fine scenery and is usually runnable from late fall to early summer.

If you look in the Red River's waters and see darters, you know the water quality is excellent. Fishing is good for small-mouth bass, spotted bass, rock bass, Ohio muskellunge, catfish, and longear sunfish. Fishermen may want to check with the U.S. Army Corps of Engineers to see if Swift Camp Creek, a tributary to the Red River, is currently being stocked with trout.

The Gladie Historic Site is of special interest because of the restored log house that was built around 1880, later moved half a mile to its present location and reconstructed around 1914. It has been fully restored and is used as an interpretive site for exhibits that tell the story of the gorge: its history, the logging industry, geology, and botany. Also displayed are pioneer implements and other objects of daily life.

Visitors can enjoy several activities at Gladie, including seeing a sorghum vat and mill, watching a small herd of bison from an overlook, inspecting an old moonshine still, viewing an old-fashioned herb garden, and looking at a collection of old farm implements kept in a barn.

Adjacent to the eastern edge of the developed part of Red River Gorge is the 13,000-acre Clifty Wilderness Area, a part of the National Wilderness Preservation System. It is rugged and undeveloped and should only be accessed by people who possess significant woods skills. Recreation opportunity includes hiking, backpacking, horseback riding, camping, fishing, hunting, and canoeing. More than 750 different flowering plants and 170 species of moss grow there.

For additional roaming within a few miles of the geological area, you may wish to visit some of the historic iron furnaces that are open to the public. They date back to the early 1800s. One of these, Cottage Furnace, is just off State 213 south of Stanton. Another, Fitchburg Furnace, is between

Beattyville and Ravenna just off State 52. Both places have Forest Service–maintained picnic areas. Several other furnaces are along the line dividing Powell and Estill Counties.

Where: Two entrances. Western entrance (the most used) is north of Slade. Take exit 33 from Mountain Parkway, then State 15 north to State 77, and east on 77 to entrance. Eastern entrance is on State 715. Take exit 40 from Mountain Parkway and go north on State 715.

When: Year-round. Gladie Historic Site Information Center open seven days a week from April to October (10:00 A.M. to 6:00 P.M.) and weekends during fall and spring. Koomer Ridge campground, open Memorial Day weekend through fall foliage season.

Admission: Free. Modest camping fee (half price with Golden Age Passport).

Amenities: Visitors center, gift shop, wildlife-viewing blinds, outstanding geologic formations, exhibits, reconstructed historic house, trailer/tent fee campground, boat ramp, canoe access sites, extensive trail system, picnic sites, adjacent Clifty Wilderness Area.

Activities: Hiking, camping, backpacking, nature study, wildlife and wildflower viewing, birding, photography, horseback riding, cross-country skiing, fishing, canoeing, interpretive programs, Koomer Ridge Amphitheater programs on Saturdays from Memorial Day through Labor Day.

Special events: At Gladie: Bluebird Workshop, Gladie Wildlife (April), Gladie Wildflower Walk (May), National Trails Day (June), Bike Tour (July), Apple Butter/Cider Festival (September), Sorghum Festival (October), Gladie Creek History (November), Christmas Open House (December).

Other: Many places not barrier free. Closed to off-highway vehicles. Often crowded on weekends. Additional camping in Daniel Boone National Forest (DBNF).

For more information: District Ranger Station, USFS, 705 West College Avenue, Stanton, KY 40380, 606-663-2852. (Information, including cross-country skiing trails.)

Forest Supervisor, Daniel Boone National Forest, 100 Vaught Road, Winchester, KY 40391, 606-745-3100.

Wild Rivers Coordinator, Division of Water, Department for Environmental Protection, 14 Reilly Road, Fort Boone Plaza, Frankfort, KY 40601, 502-564-3410.

Two addresses for topo maps: Kentucky Department of Economic Development, Maps & Publications, 133 Holmes Street, Frankfort, KY, 40601, 502-564-4715. Kentucky Geological Survey, Publications Sales, Room 104, Mining & Mineral Resources Building, University of Kentucky, Lexington, KY 40506-0107, 606-257-5863. ($2 for each quadrangle; free "Index to Topographic Maps for Kentucky.")

13

I-64 Will Take
You There

Interstate 64, bisecting Kentucky from east to west, goes through the northern part of the Daniel Boone National Forest and gives easy access to some outstanding parks and natural areas in Carter and Greenup Counties. If your approach is from the east, from West Virginia or eastern Ohio, you'll be entering Kentucky just south of Ashland and heading toward the DBNF.

Jesse Stuart State Nature Preserve

Greenup's favorite son was Jesse Stuart (1906–1984), who lived in nearby W-Hollow, taught school, and became Kentucky's poet laureate and a world-acclaimed author for his novels, short stories, and poems about Appalachian Kentucky. Two of his best-known works are the autobiographical *The Thread That Runs So True* and the novel *Taps for Private Tussie*. For young readers, *The Beatinest Boy* is a perennial top choice. Stuart's writing is a true slice of Americana that authentically portrays rural Greenup County and the people who lived there.

Seven hundred and thirty-three acres of his homeplace 3½ miles from Greenup is a state nature preserve that also preserves the way of life that he observed and wrote about. Since trail guides are not always available at the preserve, it would be a good idea to obtain one from the Ashland Convention & Visitors Bureau at 207 15th Street.

On the preserve are pastures, old fields, and a second-growth oak and hickory forest. The 4½ miles of trails take us along ridge tops and down in the hollows. We walk through pastures to Op's Cabin, a small white clapboard building where Stuart did much of his writing. Here, we might see deer. I had a close encounter with a snake along the trail in some foot-high grass, not seeing it but hearing a warning rattle. Coon Den Hollow is a short loop and another place to watch for wild turkeys and all the small mammals that frequent these woodlands.

Beyond Op's Cabin, the trail goes to Seaton Ridge, a place called Laurel Ridge in Stuart's writings. From Op's Cabin, we can alternately return by way of Shingle Mill Hollow as we loop back to the trailhead. Typical of the area, migrating songbirds are more numerous in spring and fall. Hawks can be seen year-round, and wildflowers change with the seasons, from late spring through fall.

A pilgrimage here (and most visits end up being pilgrimages even though they did not start out that way!) could actually start in Greenbo Lake State Resort Park, which has a Jesse Stuart Library, or in Ashland where the Jesse Stuart Foundation has its headquarters in the Ashland Oil Tower building at the corner of Bath and 13th Streets. The foundation arranges tours that depart by bus from Greenbo Lake State Resort Park and visit places mentioned in Stuart's writings.

Finally, a word about Greenup. This little town on the Ohio River is a charming place, as a walking tour will reveal. The public library on Harrison Street has brochures that identify 69 buildings, many of Greek Revival architecture dating from the mid- to late-1800s. Alongside the river are public picnic grounds and a boat-launching ramp.

Two excellent covered bridges are in Greenup County. Would-be authors of runaway bestsellers, take note. Bennett's Mill Bridge is five miles north of Lynn on State 7 (west of Greenup), and the Oldtown Covered Bridge crosses the Little Sandy River between Oldtown and Hopewell. On other country drives, you might discover some of the 20 or so old charcoal furnaces built from 1818 to 1856.

Where: From Greenup (14 miles northwest of Ashland on U.S. Route 23), turn onto State 1 from U.S. Route 23 and go south 1⁹⁄10 miles to W-Hollow Road (also State 2433). Continue 1½ miles to the nature center parking lot on the right.
When: Year-round, daylight hours.
Admission: Free.
Amenities: Trails, historic buildings, handicapped parking marked.
Activities: Hiking, wildlife viewing, birding, photography, nature study.
Other: Barrier-free access. Visitors are asked to stay on trails and not intrude on private-use areas.
For more information: Jesse Stuart State Nature Preserve, c/o Kentucky State Nature Preserves Commission, 801 Schenkel Lane, Frankfort, KY 40601, 502-573-2886. Fax, 502-573-2355.

Ashland Convention & Visitors Bureau, 207 15th Street, PO Box 987, Ashland, KY 41105, 800-377-6249.

Jesse Stuart Foundation, 1212 Bath Avenue, 12th Floor, PO Box 391, Ashland, KY 41114, 606-329-5232 or 5233. (To book guided tours or order merchandise.)

Greenbo Lake State Resort Park

Greenbo Lake isn't exactly billed as the park for wildlife, but I saw more animals here than at most other locations. The entrance is on State 1 just a few miles south of the Jesse Stuart Nature Preserve. Coming from Interstate 64, exit at Grayson (exit 172), then go north for 15 miles.

The long entry drive sits astride a wide ridge top and after a mile or so reaches the historic Buffalo Furnace where iron was produced between 1851 and 1875. Kentucky ranked third in U.S. iron production in the 1830s but slipped to 11th place by 1865. When the ore and timber were depleted, that signaled the end of the furnace era. About 20 vertical feet of an old stone stack is all that remains here.

A picnic area overlooking Buffalo Branch is across the road from the furnace ruins. An earthen dam impounds three clearwater streams, Buffalo Branch, Claylick Creek, and Pruitt Fork Creek, to form the beautiful three-fingered Greenbo Lake. Fishing is good here, they say, for trout, bass, and catfish. The marina, open April 1 to October 1, rents pontoon boats, pedal boats, rowboats, canoes, and motorboats— enough variety to please most water sports enthusiasts. Large motors are not allowed, though; a 10-hp limit is observed.

The wooded hills surrounding the lake are mixed hardwoods and pine, while higher on the surrounding ridges are stands of oak and hickory. Drive slowly to the lodge, for deer are plentiful. One of their favorite places seems to be the grassy area surrounding the tennis courts. At least a half dozen were grazing (hardly noticing pedestrians or traffic) as my car crept by. Below, on the opposite side of the road was the Buffalo Branch finger of Greenbo Lake, the beach area, a fishing pier, and a collection of ducks and Canada geese gliding on the lake's surface.

Acorns were falling, and gray squirrels with flowing bushy tails scampered to retrieve them. I watched one through the binoculars as he took a nut and, in small spurts, traveled about 30 feet to the base of a road sign, where he dug quickly, buried the nut, and then piled the dirt up around it. Squirrels are much better at hiding things than finding them again. I wouldn't be surprised to see a new tree there in a few years.

Near the lodge is the trailhead for two park trails and a signboard that identifies eight Kentucky trails, showing the trail systems marked on topo maps. The 3,300-acre park offers more than nine miles of trails. A major Kentucky trail—the Michael Tygart Trail (MTT)—begins here and continues for 24 miles to the Jenny Wiley Trail system, a 163-mile trail that begins on the Ohio River at South Portsmouth and ends at Jenny Wiley State Resort Park at Prestonsburg.

To sample a section of the Michael Tygart Trail, you can start from this trailhead and go for 1½ miles to the park road that leads to the campground and boat dock, then walk on that road to return to the lodge. This would be an easy hour-long walk.

The Michael Tygart Loop Trail circles through the park, starting at the boat dock and follows the lake's shoreline into Pruitt Valley, passing by some old, abandoned 1800s-era homes. Then it ascends a small hill, follows a pasture, joins a gravel road, and returns along the MTT, heading back into the park on top of a mostly wooded ridge for a total of seven miles. An overnight shelter is located on the return section. Spring and fall (late April, early May, and the last half of October) are suggested as the best times to use this trail. Wildflowers are more abundant then, and you won't be bothered by the tall weeds that can detract from the scenery in summer.

Walking the Fern Valley Nature Trail

On a blue-sky-with-puffy-clouds day, a nature walk through the woods, beside a lake, up and down hills, and with the promise of seeing the birds and mammals of the forest is hard to resist. So why try? Armed with the illustrated guidebook that visitors may borrow from the park headquarters, I was ready for adventure on the 1¹/₁₀-mile Fern Valley self-guided interpretive trail.

It starts out above the lake, with patches of water reflecting through the trees. This is Jesse Stuart country, and he is fondly quoted in the trail book. As the wind shakes the leaves, big drops collected from the previous night's rain come noisily down through the trees.

Soon, the trail is climbing higher and the lake is more visible. The guidebook identifies a fallen beech tree as animal habitat. Sure enough, one log is the residence of a chipmunk, who scurries into his hideaway. A white-tailed deer bounds away, jumping with its tail straight up.

Halfway up the hill is a pitch pine tree (other species here are Virginia, white, and shortleaf pines). Another deer escapes, even though I'm following the advice to "walk softly, be quiet, make no sudden moves, and cast your eyes about."

Hounds are yelping in the distance, which probably is making the deer skittery. The dogs make quite a commotion, their voices carrying clearly across the lake.

On the descent toward the lake, one can take the regular trail or a shortcut. Down in the hollow is a giant white oak. Another very young, perhaps half-grown, deer looks at me curiously, ears up and wide apart. It has to stretch its neck to see me over the undergrowth.

Squirrels chatter and songbirds loudly trill, then crows raspily join in. Having had a grand view of the lake from above, we now follow a stream and then the lakeshore, but we're still in the woods and the path has narrowed. The trail booklet tells about the pines that were planted here in 1960. A nice breeze is coming off the lake, and clouds are forming in earnest. I listen for the wind in the pines, that sighing moan I'm trying to remember from girlhood days in northern Minnesota. To me, it's something like the songs of whales I've heard in recordings.

At the last marker is a bench for viewing the lake at leisure, then the trail rises gently and ends with wooden steps and a handrail. I am back at the lodge.

The lodge has all the amenities of a first-class resort park, with restaurant and gift shop, meeting rooms, and 36 sleeping rooms with balconies overlooking the lake. It also has a library dedicated to Jesse Stuart. His photo is just as I remember him during an interview in 1971, when he was a guest on my radio show—horn-rimmed glasses, hair parted to the side. The library has a memorabilia collection, books by Jesse Stuart and others, for children and adults. Some are anthologies. They may be read here or checked out by lodge guests.

Daily naturalist-led programs are offered only in summer at this park (between Memorial Day and Labor Day).

Where: North of Grayson on State 1. From Interstate 64, take exit 172 and go north for approximately 15 miles to park entrance.

When: Year-round. Campground open April 1 to October 1. Marina open April 1 through October 31. Gift shop open 8:00 A.M. to 7:30 or 8:00 P.M. in summer and 10:00 A.M. to 6:30 P.M. the rest of the year.

Admission: Free. Fees for golf, miniature golf, bicycle and shelter rentals.

Amenities: Lodge, gift shop, dining room, Jesse Stuart library/reading room, 225-acre lake, marina, hiking trails, self-guided nature trail, bathhouse and swimming beach, miniature golf, outdoor athletic courts, bicycle rentals, stables, picnic areas, and playgrounds.

Activities: Boating, fishing, nature walks, hiking, camping, swimming, tennis, golf (on privately owned course nearby), miniature golf, basketball, bicycling, horseback riding, picnicking, wildlife viewing, photography, birding, daily planned recreation in summer.

Special events: Tri-State Railroad Show, Artifact/Arrowhead Show (March), Antique Car Show (April), Spring Outdoor Weekend (May), Jesse Stuart Weekend (September), Greenbo 5K Challenge (October). For Kentucky State Parks special events brochure, 800-255-7275.

Other: For handicapped accessibility information, call 800-255-7275 (TDD equipped).

For more information: Greenbo Lake State Resort Park, HC 60, Box 562, Greenup, KY 41144-9517, 606-473-7324. Reservations, 800-325-0083.

Two addresses for topo maps: Kentucky Department of Economic Development, Maps & Publications, 133 Holmes Street, Frankfort, KY, 40601, 502-564-4715. Kentucky Geological Survey, Publications Sales, Room 104, Mining & Mineral Resources Building, University of Kentucky, Lexington, KY 40506-0107, 606-257-5863. ($2 for each quadrangle; free "Index to Topographic Maps for Kentucky.")

Grayson Lake

This is a prime recreation spot for boating, fishing, picnicking, camping, and hiking among natural beauties surrounding a 1,512-acre lake impounding the Little Sandy River and some of its tributaries. The lake has excellent fishing waters and a scenic shoreline that has steep sandstone bluffs 50 to 150 feet high and waterfalls flowing into the lake on its upper reaches (upstream from Bruin Creek). The land area is managed by the U.S. Army Corps of Engineers and two state agencies. Of the total 17,142 acres, more than 10,000 (including the lake) are managed as a WMA under the care of the Kentucky Department of Fish and Wildlife Resources. The Grayson Lake

State Park includes Rolling Hills Campground, the Bruin Recreation Area, and some undeveloped land in the area of Clifty Creek. The day-use area around the dam, nearby Camp Webb Refuge, and the state park are closed to hunting.

At the dam is the Corps' Grayson Lake Information Station. I found out from ranger Bernita McCloud that the Corps has a demonstration program for attracting wildlife and produces instructional handouts on things like building bluebird boxes, squirrel nesting boxes, and bat boxes. Illustrated leaflets for young readers are on numerous subjects, including "Water Safety for Kids" and "Junior Ranger Track Pack" (identifying animals by their tracks).

An unusual collection here—unusual because each specimen can be handled by visitors—is the display of mounted animals. All the animals were roadkills or died in some other similar way but were in good enough shape for mounting. Up-close, touchable specimens are a rarity. We are allowed to pet a sharp-shinned or red-tailed hawk, a barn owl, gray fox, beaver, red fox, raccoon, and bobcat. A countertop display has a snakeskin, bird nests, butterflies, insects, and leaves (with descriptions of trees from which they came).

Bernita also told me about the 1¾-mile interpretive nature trail near the dam at Shelter #4. It was developed in the late 1950s and qualified for the National Trail Register. Footbridges make it easy to negotiate as it meanders along the river in a meadow setting, then rises into a cliff-line section where hemlocks and rhododendron are dominant, continues into a hardwood forest, and loops back. The hiker sees a wide variety of birds, wildlife, and vegetation. Hidden from view on the back side of the trail are planted food plots that attract deer and other wildlife.

Other food plots are below the dam on the river bottomlands. They are accessible to everyone. The goal is to educate the public in planting for backyard habitats that shelter and feed wildlife.

The nature trail, which begins next to the Area #4 picnic grounds, is considered a 60-minute walk. This allows an easy pace. The trail begins as a wide path following the creek past silver maples, water willows, and box elders. On the opposite bank are cliffs and rock overhangs. Moving away from the river slightly, we are in a moist environment perfect for sycamores, Christmas ferns, walking ferns, and New York ferns. The trail climbs a few steps up a short bluff to a picnic table and shelter, then goes across a footbridge into a world of rhododendron, hemlock, mountain laurel, and holly.

More steps, another bench, and we have left the river and gone into a forest of white, black, and red oaks. At Marker #14, the trail is following a path made by white-tailed deer. We have been striding to the occasional sound of a waterfall as smaller streams rush toward the Little Sandy. Should we look up, hoping to see squirrels leaping from one branch to another or look about, watching for deer standing like statues in hopes we will not see them? Maybe we should just investigate the wildflowers along this part of the trail.

Soon we go down through a fissure in a large rock, then make a long, steady climb (with a bench at the halfway point) to a picnic shelter. Now it's time to begin the descent. We're out of the woods, with a meadow to the right and more wildflowers.

My return trip was in a misty rain, which didn't seem to bother a pair of cardinals as they whizzed by. Nor did it bother me. Nor did it bother the fisherman casting for trout in the tailwaters below the dam, where the fish are stocked in spring and fall.

Driving on toward the state park, the road takes us over the Clifty Creek Embayment, WMA access points, the entrance to the state park, the Bruin Area swimming beach (where lifeguards are on duty from Memorial Day through Labor Day), and a three-lane launching ramp. The lake is fished for bass, crappie, catfish, sunfish, bluegill, and muskie.

Park activities center around camping and water sports. Also, a historical outdoor drama, *Someday*, is quite an attraction during June and early July weekends. It is based on the experiences of Hiram Rice, a Confederate officer during the Civil War when families often had divided loyalties and resulting conflicts.

Where: Seven miles south of Grayson. From Interstate 64, take exit 172, then go south on State 7 past Grayson to the Corps of Engineers visitors center at Grayson Lake Dam. State Park is approximately 12 miles from Interstate 64. WMA is accessible from States 7, 1496, and 986.

When: Year-round. Corps of Engineers Recreation Area, open 7:00 A.M. to 10:00 P.M. (fishing hours are unrestricted). State park camping, April 1 through October 31. Swimming beach, open Memorial Day through Labor Day.

Admission: Free. Fees for camping, boat rentals, and some other activities.

Amenities: Visitors center, marina, launching ramps, campgrounds, wildlife viewing area, interpretive nature trail, picnic grounds, playgrounds, beach, boat rentals.

Activities: Camping, fishing, boating, swimming, hiking, nature study, wildlife viewing, birding, photography, picnicking, boating, canoeing, hunting (on WMA).

Special events: *Someday* 1860s musical outdoor drama (Grayson Lake State Park, weekends from late May through early July, 8:30 P.M.).

Other: Barrier-free access and fishing pier.

For more information: U.S. Army Corps of Engineers, Huntington District, PO Box 2127, Huntington, WV 25721, 304-529-5452.

Grayson Lake State Park, Route 3, Box 800, Olive Hill, KY 41164-9213, 606-474-9727. (*Someday* reservations and information, 606-286-4522.)

Grayson Area Chamber of Commerce, PO Box 612, Grayson, KY 41143, 606-474-5596.

Kentucky Department of Fish and Wildlife Resources, #1 Game Farm Road, Frankfort, KY 40601, 502-564-3400. (WMA and hunting/fishing regulations.)

Carter Caves State Resort Park

Carter Caves has several distinctions that make it one of the hottest (or "coolest") state park destinations in Kentucky for the dedicated nature enthusiast. Its mountain setting with caves, unusual geological formations, challenging hiking trails, two nature preserves, and a lake and floatable stream provide an unbeatable combination. And, despite its easy access and modern facilities, it retains the charm of old days and old ways—even a Strange Music Weekend that is quickly becoming legendary.

I think I had the best cabin on the property, #247. It was in a thicket of hardwoods and hemlocks in a secluded spot below the roadway and next to a path leading to the 3¼-mile Red Trail. This trail loop goes by Fern Bridge (a 120-foot-wide sandstone arch over a wildflower-laden valley floor), Raven Bridge, and the park's most massive arch, Smokey Bridge (220 feet long and 90 feet high). On the way to these spots are views of the idyllic Smokey Valley Lake below.

The park trails are hilly, with high places and sheer drops. Hiking by oneself is not advised, and parents should always accompany their children on the trail. Be sure to have water and plan your hike to end during daylight hours (unless you're backpacking on the nine-mile Simon Kenton Trail that connects with the Jenny Wiley Trail to the east).

If Raven Bridge is your major interest, the easiest way to get there is by the seven-tenths-mile Blue Trail, which starts at the lodge, leads along a ridge top to the bridge, then connects with the Red Trail for a return loop on a lower level in the valley. An even shorter loop is possible using the connecting half-mile Yellow Trail (though with this loop you won't see Raven Bridge).

Natural Bridge Trail is a half-mile loop that starts at the welcome center and goes down a valley to the foot of Natural Bridge, crosses under it, then climbs to the top. Surprise! A highway is on top of the bridge. It is the entrance road to the park over the only natural bridge in Kentucky that supports a paved highway.

The park's most scenic trail may be the Cascade Trail, located in one of the two natural areas, Cascade Caverns State Nature Preserve. It passes some extraordinary geologic features such as the Cascade Natural Bridge, the Box Canyon (a 60-foot-high, sandstone box-shaped wall), and the Wind Tunnel. It is hilly and difficult in places but only three-quarters of a mile in length. The northern edge of the natural area is on steep north-facing slopes along Tygarts Creek. Mountain maple and Canadian yew are two northern species that grow here.

The Green Trail offers a different kind of hike. It starts near the welcome center and goes through Cave Branch Valley, roughly paralleling the park's entrance road, then up into Horn Hollow where quite a few cave entrances can be seen. It is hilly, requires a stream crossing, and is not a loop (so retracing one's steps is required). In spring, the reward is total immersion in wildflowers.

Besides the woodland mammals common to all similar places in Kentucky, bears and bobcats are sighted here each year. Poisonous snakes are not so common, but poison ivy is! In the low-lying areas near the lake and streams, you may see river otters and minks, beavers and muskrats.

Another way to enjoy the woods is to take a guided trail ride. The stables, nicely landscaped with greenery and with a blazing campfire to greet us, is open from April 1 through October 31. The standard trail ride lasts 45 minutes and goes through a beautiful section of woods on a fairly level trail. Stables manager Gerald Kiser, looking every bit the cowboy with a red bandanna tied around his neck, led the trail ride I took. His horses were well mannered, outfitted with Western tack, and the trails were in excellent shape. We were introduced to our mounts, given instructions on reining the horses (they are not trained to neck rein), told to keep a horse's length between us and the rider in front, and off we went.

We came to a spot in the trail where Kiser told about staring down a bobcat. He had stepped away from the motorized vehicle he uses while doing trail maintenance and suddenly found himself face to face with the surprised cat. About four minutes later (which he said seemed much longer), he had won the face-off, and the cat had backed away.

The stables are at the edge of Tygarts State Forest, an 800-acre property that lies basically north of the park. Simon Kenton Trail goes through it, and a primitive campground is planned on a new 7½-mile park trail that just barely skirts inside the forest.

My tour guide at this park was Sam Plummer, a naturalist and caving specialist. We drove down a narrow, winding road to the boat-launching ramp. Cattails and lily pads decorated the lake here.

"Smokey Lake is a 45-acre man-made lake that is used for boating and fishing," Sam said. "On the upper end are beaver dams. Lots of times you can see ducks swimming along, and there are plenty of raccoons. This is a trophy-bass lake with a 20-inch limit, though one that size hasn't been caught.

"Right after it became a trophy lake, a man came down determined to catch one," Sam added. "On the last day of fishing he finally landed a big bass; but it was only 19½ inches, so he couldn't keep it."

"I guess he couldn't figure out how to stretch a bass," I said.

Next, we headed for Cascade Caverns. It is the county's largest cave, with many formations and an underground waterfall; and this is the only state park that offers cave tours. To get there from the park, go toward U.S. Route 60 and turn right on State 209 to the entrance.

Sam, who is an avid caver, a member of ESSO (Eastern States Speleological Organization), and who has practically grown up in caves, was in his element.

The tour took us through several chambers, including The Square Dance Hall; the enchanting Lake Room with the water's mirror surface reflecting trees outside; and a large room featuring King Solomon's Hanging Gardens, a stalactite assemblage. We skirted past breakdown; crossed a tiny stream, James Branch; and stopped on top of an underground natural bridge to look down Cascade Avenue, the longest passageway in the cave, and listen to tumbling waters. An impressive example of flowstone was on one wall.

We also peered out from the natural cave mouth where James Branch splashily exits the cave amid fallen boulders and stillwater pools. The opening is 60 feet high and about 150 feet wide.

Some little brown bats were flying up high.

"They're little, they're brown, and they're bats," Sam said sagely.

"You're beginning to sound like a tour guide now. So tell me, how should people decide which cave to visit?"

"If you want to see beauty, I would recommend this Cascade Tour. For a more history-oriented tour, I suggest the Saltpeter Cave Tour. If a person likes to get wet and muddy, either the Bat Cave Tour or one of our 'crawling tours' in Saltpeter

Cave will satisfy that craving. They last about two hours and are limited to 15 or 20 people. You have to sign up in advance. Then the 'X' Tour is a scenic tour much like this one but half the walking distance. If you have time limitations, that would be a good choice."

Our tour continued to the Dragon Room and a view of the upper end of Cascade Avenue, then a short walk outdoors to another entrance and the cave's underground waterfall.

It was a very interesting tour and guide and, more important, I passed all of Sam's quizzes on identifying underground formations!

Of the 40 or so known caves in the park, tours go regularly to the three caves Sam mentioned. (Published literature says there are 20 caves, but naturalists know of many more.) Experienced cavers who own proper equipment may tour Laurel Cave on their own, and the wild-cave tours Sam mentioned go into Bat Cave in summer but not in winter when about 10 percent of the total known population of federally endangered Indiana bats hibernate there. Bat Cave is a Kentucky State Nature Preserve.

Naturalist-guided activities go on year-round, but several choices are offered each day during the summer. A typical week's schedule provides nature walks, a Smokey Bridge Walk, Bat Cave wild tours, Saltpeter Cave crawling tours, Saltpeter Cave lantern tours with storytelling, Tygarts Creek canoe trips, Caving for Kids, junior naturalist programs, kids' games, relay races, crafts activities, scavenger hunts, concerts, sing-alongs, square dances, ice-cream socials, and productions of Theatre in the Park.

If mountain music is one of your special interests, don't miss the humorous Strange Music Weekend. Come in late August for this three-day festival and stay at the campground, cottages, or lodge. You can even bring an instrument and join a "jam."

Strange Music started several years ago and is now a highlight of this park's special events. It features performances and contests. Not only is the music strange, but strange instruments can range from washboards to vacuum-cleaner hoses or other objects one's imagination might produce, adding a unique blend of sounds to accompany guitars, fiddles, and the like. Cave tours are also conducted on this weekend.

Where: Off Interstate 64 west of Grayson. Take exit 161 onto State 182 and go north, cross U.S. Route 60 and continue for three miles to the park.

When: Year-round. Stables open 10:00 A.M. to 6:00 P.M. April 1 through October 31. Boating and swimming begin Memorial Day.

Admission: Free. Fees for cave tours, golf, miniature golf, boat rentals, public swimming pool, horseback riding.

Amenities: Lodge, restaurant, welcome center, gift shops, cottages, campground, caves, golf course, nature trails, nature preserves, rental boats, swimming pool, stables, tennis courts, picnic grounds, playgrounds.

Activities: Camping, cave tours, hiking, backpacking, nature study, geological study, golf, miniature golf, tennis, boating, fishing, swimming, wildlife viewing, birding, photography, horseback riding, picnicking, boating, canoeing, guided canoe trips, daily planned recreation in summer.

Special events: Great Escape, Crawlathon (January), Mountain Memories (March), Spring Wildflower Weekend (April), Pioneer Life Week (July), Becoming an Outdoorswoman, Strange Music Weekend (August), Fraley Family Mountain Music Weekend (September), Storytelling in the Cave (October). For Kentucky State Parks special events brochure, 800-255-7275.

Other: For barrier-free information, 800-255-7275. TDD equipped.

For more information: Carter Caves State Resort Park, Rural Route 5, Box 1120, Olive Hill, KY 41164, 606-286-4411. Reservations, 800-325-0059.

Cave Run Lake in the Daniel Boone NF

The 670,000-acre Cave Run Lake is one of the best publicized and most visited locations in the DBNF. Because of the extensive outdoor recreation opportunities, it's hard to imagine anyone having a boring time here. It has easy access from Interstate 64, and campgrounds and resorts provide accommodations from primitive to luxurious.

Where to start? Try the visitors center, 2½ miles south of U.S. Route 60 on State 801 west of Morehead. It has a well-stocked gift shop with books, music tapes, and other items. And it has handouts galore explaining all facets of the DBNF. Interpretive specialists are ready to answer questions and suggest places to go based on your interests. They tell me that fishing in Cave Run Lake is the most popular activity, with camping a close second.

Specialist Evelyn Morgan said, "They ask about whitewater rafting, too, which is shown in our introductory video but isn't available in our part of the forest. And they always ask, 'Where are the muskies?' We say: 'In the water!'"

Of course, she was referring to muskellunge, a popular game fish here. Pick up the brochure, "Fishing in Cave Run Lake," for tips on where and how to fish for muskies, black bass, rock bass, white bass, crappie, bluegill, and catfish. The Department of Fish and Wildlife Resources also publishes flyers detailing fishing waters, equipment, and methods. Or simply hang out at one of the bait shops that ring the shore-line for late-breaking fishing news.

Muskies and several other fish species are produced a few miles up the road at the Minor E. Clark Fish Hatchery. The hatchery has 111 rearing and brood ponds, outside raceways, and a display pool that holds live specimens of fish species from mid-April through mid-September. Visitors are wel-come to view the ponds at any time or go inside the hatchery from 7:00 A.M. to 3:00 P.M. on weekdays.

Around the lake are numerous picnic sites, 11 boat launch-ing ramps, campgrounds, viewing areas, and the only pioneer-weapons hunting area in Kentucky. The campgrounds open during the first week of April and close the end of October. The two major campgrounds, offering full facilities and pro-grammed recreation, are Twin Knobs and Zilpo. Both take advance reservations. Two marinas are in operation: Scott Creek Marina on State 801 just above the dam, and Longbow Marina at Beaver Creek on State 1274, five miles from French-burg. Both offer full services (pontoon boats, fishing boats, slips, offshore moorings, gas and oil, groceries, fishing sup-plies and accessories, and pump-out stations). Scott Creek additionally has a restaurant and houseboat rentals.

Twin Knobs Campground and Recreation Area has 216 campsites. Surrounded by mountains and the lake, it provides jogging and hiking trails, a 2,000-foot beach, boat ramps, scenic overlooks, an amphitheater, and outdoor recreation courts. Canada geese, songbirds, owls, and whippoorwills assure that things will not get too quiet. On the off-season, this can be a good place for cross-country skiing.

Zilpo is on a wooded peninsula with 172 campsites spread along three miles of shoreline. It offers the same amenities as Twin Knobs, plus a country store. Don't try to escape the wildlife: deer, squirrels, rabbits, foxes, wildfowl, owls, and bald eagles tend to make regular visits. Getting there takes you along the only National Forest Scenic Byway in Kentucky.

All Aboard for the Zilpo Scenic Byway!

Yes, pile a few friends in your vehicle for this trip. Some great places are meant to be shared, and this is one of them. On the auto tour, you'll eventually cruise along on a ridge top—but slowly, because on both sides are views you won't want to miss. The knobs have given way to sawtooth-topped hills, an indication of the rugged country that tugs at the heart of true wilderness buffs. If you are looking forward to an active day, the possibilities are endless.

From the dam, head west on U.S. Route 60 to the town of Salt Lick, then turn south on State 211. Ahead are places to access the White Sulphur Horse Camp, Clear Creek Iron Furnace and Recreation Area, Sheltowee Trace National Recreation Trail and other forest trails, the Pioneer Weapons Hunting Area (used also for its hiking trails), the prominent Tater Knob Tower, and—where the peninsula ends—Zilpo! The route is well marked with signs.

Along the 11-mile self-guided auto tour are signboards at places of special interest that explain what is going on in forest management for recreation, wildlife, timber, water, and cultural resources. For example, you'll learn how biologists place underwater attractors (substantially, brush) to provide shelter, shade, and feeding areas for the fish. At the next stop, we learn what a Kentucky iron furnace has to do with managing a national forest.

In any season, you will have plenty of opportunity to view wild-life along this route, especially if you look carefully about. For my taste, it's hard to beat a cool autumn day when falling leaves dance in little whirlwinds of motion while the air, marbled alternately by the warm sun and chilly breezes, swirls around like an invisible hot fudge sundae.

The Pioneer Weapons Hunting Area is unique in Kentucky. It contains 7,610 acres where the only kind of hunting allowed is with bow and arrow, crossbow, flintlock rifle, or percussion cap rifles. Excellent habitat has been provided here for deer, wild turkeys, and ruffed grouse. An intricate system of trails goes through, including ones for horses, bicycles, and mountain bikes. It is important to be aware of hunting seasons. Hikers should wear blaze orange then and keep horses off the trail.

Not all the knobs have given way. The Tater Knob fire tower is a distinguished landmark that was constructed in 1934. It's the only such tower left in the whole Daniel Boone area.

After Tater Knob, it's all downhill to Zilpo (but only literally!). The panorama of Cave Run Lake comes into view, with sailboats tacking into the wind, raptors soaring, fish jumping, and wildflow-ers covering the ground beside the road.

See what I mean?

Where: Best access from east and west is from U.S. Route 60 and State 801. From Interstate 64 going west, take exit 137 to Morehead, then go west on U.S. Route 60. From Interstate 64 eastbound, take exit 123 and follow U.S. Route 60 east. Go south on 801 to visitors center.

When: Visitors center, open daily 9:00 A.M. to 5:00 P.M. from Memorial Day through Labor Day (other months, five days,

8:00 A.M. to 4:30 P.M.). Campgrounds, open April 1 through October 30. Minor E. Clark Fish Hatchery, open weekdays from 7:00 A.M. to 3:00 P.M. (visit ponds and pool any time). *Admission:* Free. Fees for camping and some day-use areas.

Amenities: Visitors center; campgrounds; National Scenic Byway; boat-launching ramps; fish hatchery; marinas; hiking, horseback and mountain bike trails; picnic grounds; shooting range; pioneer weapons area; horse camp; stables; overlooks; lookout tower; historic furnace. U.S. Army Corps of Engineers has day-use recreation areas on lake near dam and at tailwaters, visitors center, parking area, nature trail, picnic area, and scenic overlook.

Activities: Fishing, camping, boating, sailing, parasailing, windsurfing, water skiing, hiking, backpacking, bicycling, mountain bike riding, horseback riding, cross-country skiing, photography, wildlife viewing, birding, nature study.

Special events: Summer programs in various locations. Check at the visitors center.

Other: Inquire about barrier-free areas.

For more information: District Ranger, Morehead, 2375 KY 801 South, PO Box 910, Morehead, KY 40351, 606-784-6428. (Quadrangle maps and local information, including Twin Knobs Recreation Area, Zilpo Recreation Area, cross-country skiing trails.)

For advance campsite reservations at Twin Knobs, 800-280-2267 or, for text telephone service, 800-879-4496. At Zilpo, 606-784-7788 (April through October).

For marina information and boat rentals, Cave Run Marinas, Inc., PO Box 174, Morehead, KY 40351, 606-784-9666.

Forest Supervisor, Daniel Boone National Forest, 100 Vaught Road, Winchester, KY 40391, 606-745-3100.

Kentucky Department of Fish and Wildlife Resources, Division of Fisheries, #1 Game Farm Road, Frankfort, KY

40601, 502-564-4336 (Pioneer Weapons Area, hunting, and fishing regulations). For guided tours of Minor E. Clark Fish Hatchery, call 606-784-6872.

Louisville District, U.S. Army Corps of Engineers, PO Box 59, Louisville, KY 40201, 502-582-5736 (Cave Run Lake outline maps). For lake information, call 606-783-7001 (twenty-four hours) or 606-784-9709 (7:00 A.M. to 4:00 P.M. daily).

Fall Color Advisories, 800-225-8747 (Kentucky Department of Travel Development).

Two addresses for topo maps: Kentucky Department of Economic Development, Maps & Publications, 133 Holmes Street, Frankfort, KY, 40601, 502-564-4715. Kentucky Geological Survey, Publications Sales, Room 104, Mining & Mineral Resources Building, University of Kentucky, Lexington, KY 40506-0107, 606-257-5863. (Quadrangle maps also available from Forest Service district offices.)

14

Along the I-75 Corridor

Interstate 75 is a well-traveled route that goes through Kentucky from Cincinnati to Knoxville, connecting with Lexington and cutting through the Daniel Boone National Forest between Mt. Vernon and London. A drive from Lexington to the Tennessee line is a travelogue in slow motion through a series of physiographic regions—from the rolling, pastoral Inner Bluegrass; through an area of round-topped knobs, ascending the Cumberland Escarpment; and finally enveloping the traveler on all sides with the rugged mountains of Appalachia.

In the national forest south of Livingston (which is just east of Interstate 75 from exit 59), beginning at State 80 and going southward to the DBNF Bee Rock Camping Area between London and Somerset on State 192, is the Wild River portion of the Rockcastle River, a challenging 17-mile, Class I to Class IV whitewater run. Above State 80, the river is much quieter, has good access, and is runnable generally from late fall to midsummer. Bob Sehlinger's book gives more details (see Reading Guide).

For more information: Wild Rivers Coordinator, Division of Water, Department for Environmental Protection, 14 Reilly Road, Fort Boone Plaza, Frankfort, KY 40601, 502-564-3410.

(Calendar of events available. River events dependent on weather.)

Rockcastle River Day (annual canoe float and tours showcasing wetland construction, solar energy, organic gardening, nature trails—June). Contact: Appalachia Science in the Public Interest (ASPI), Route 5, Box 423, Livingston, KY 40445-9506, 606-453-2105.

For USGS quadrangle maps for Rockcastle River, except Parrot and Sand Gap, District Ranger, London, U.S. Forest Service, PO Box 907, U.S. Highway 25 South, London, KY 40743, 606-864-4163. Obtain maps for Parrot and Sand Gap from Forest Supervisor, Daniel Boone National Forest, 100 Vaught Road, Winchester, KY 40391, 606-745-3100.

London/Laurel County Tourist Commission, 140 West Daniel Boone Parkway, London, KY 40741, 800-348-0095 or 606-878-6900. Full-service information center at Interstate 75, exit 41. Request list of current Rockcastle River outfitters.

Berea College Forest

Though Berea is well known for the historic Boone Tavern and for handweaving and other crafts, the Berea College Forest is less publicized and a little hard to find without specific directions. Its unique location where the Knobs, Mississippian Plateau, and Cumberland Escarpment converge gives a landscape unequalled in Kentucky. Elevations range from 900 to 1,500 feet, from steep-sloped hollows to escarpment-flanked ridge tops. One limestone/sandstone cliff is 100 feet high. Shale outcrops are common, and formations like Devil's Slide, Devil's Kitchen, and Fat Man's Misery give some clues as to what to expect. Five hundred acres and eight miles of trails in the Indian Fort Mountain area are open to the public. They are in interconnected sections that can be hiked in combinations of your choice.

The area has borne a lot of footprints: Hopewell Indians 2,000 years ago, trails blazed later by Daniel Boone, and pioneers who established homesteads. Your footprints can take you to some interesting lookout points. You do have an excellent set of choices with trail names like West Pinnacle, Davis Hollow, Dome Mountain, East Pinnacle, Indian Fort Lookout, and Eagles Nest. From West Pinnacle and Indian Fort Lookout are spectacular views of the Knobs and the Bluegrass to the west. From East Pinnacle, Eagles Nest, and Buzzards Roost the impressive Cumberland Mountains are seen to the east.

Some of the trails are fairly easy throughout most of their length, but others are strenuous. The access trail leads gradually upward before diverging. It's not too challenging at that point. I met a smiling senior jogger huffing uphill there, enjoying his daily morning outing.

Berea College was a pioneer in forestry education, offering its first program in 1898. It began acquiring land for forest development and now uses most of it as an outdoor laboratory in research and conservation education.

Below the 1,300-foot level are yellow poplar, oak, ash, hickory, sugar maple, walnut, and basswood. At 1,400 feet are some fine stands of yellow poplar. Higher up, pines, oaks, hickories, and poplars all thrive on the sandy soils above the sandstone caprock.

Forests are fragile, and even without man's intrusion they are subject to environmental impact. In nature, though, a devastating fire will open up the canopy, allowing successional growth to spring up and actually improve habitat. In 1987, 800 acres of Berea Forest were destroyed by fire. Subsequently, the newly sun-filled fields encouraged wildflowers and shrubby growth that attracted songbirds, deer, ruffed grouse, and small mammals. An ice storm in 1994 caused extensive damage, closing the trails while downed timber was harvested. Little by little, portions of the trail system have been restored. Openings left by the downed trees will ultimately lead again to a more diversified forest.

Meanwhile, there are plenty of mature tree specimens to appreciate and enjoy.

Where: East of Berea on U.S. Route 21E for two miles to Forest Service station on left. Go another mile and turn left into a large parking lot bounded by a brown rail fence. Take the paved walkway past an amphitheater to the gravel trailhead. A signboard shows a map and gives trail information.
When: Year-round, sunrise to sunset.
Admission: Free.
Amenities: Picnic area, eight miles of trails.
Activities: Hiking, picnicking, birding, photography, nature study, geological and archaeological study, wildlife viewing.
Other: Barrier free only at picnic area.
For more information: Berea College, Public Relations, CPO Box 2316, Berea, KY 40403, 606-986-9341. (Trail map and bird checklist available.)

District Ranger, Berea, U.S. Forest Service, 1835 Big Hill Road, Berea, KY 40403, 606-986-8434.

Berea Tourist and Convention Commission, PO Box 556, Berea, KY 40403, 800-598-5263 or 606-986-2540.

Cumberland Falls State Resort Park

Call it a moonbow or a lunar rainbow, but at Cumberland Falls the only such phenomenon in the Western Hemisphere

Cumberland Falls State Resort Park

rises from a wide waterfall called The Niagara of the South (125 feet wide and 65 feet high). With that distinction and with the lakes, mountains, wild rivers, natural and wilderness areas surrounding it, Cumberland Falls SRP is in a class by itself. Come and see if you agree with Daniel Boone (quoted at a high lookout point east of the park): "No populous city could afford so much pleasure to my mind as the beauties of nature I found here."

This park is on the Plattsville Escarpment, the very western edge of the Cumberland Plateau. The park's landscape is dominated by the Cumberland River Gorge and the falls, and most park facilities take advantage of this. Sections of trail follow the riverbank, and others are on high ground, providing sweeping views. DuPont Lodge is also high above the river. Park cottages are ultramodern but suited to the woodsy locale, with stone fireplaces and hearths. I enjoyed a stay in a bilevel cottage on a hillside with the gorge directly below.

The lodge and other accommodations are open year-round. Inside the lodge are the restaurant, gift shop, common room, and the Bob Blair Museum, where displays tell about the park, its history, and the life of settlers in the old days. They also include early Native American artifacts and exhibits relating to plants and animals in the park.

Who can resist making the falls their first stop here? Wooded hills rise above and a path leads between giant boulders to observation points below the falls. Looking upstream, you can see the spray rising from the thundering water. Lots of spray, blown by the wind, creates a misty effect like ghosts dancing. Swimming is forbidden, since the river is full of drop-offs and the current is swift. On a clear night when the moon is full, the white moonbow appears, best viewed from above the falls.

Here, a coffee shop (open April through October only) and a year-round gift shop are also popular places. The ice cream is among the best found anywhere. Maybe it just tastes better when mingled with the scent of pines?

"The Colonel" Says . . .

Park recreation supervisor/naturalist Mike Lynn is an honest-to-goodness Kentucky Colonel. Most recipients of this high honor are senior citizens, and young guy Mike didn't know how he got it. Under that title beats the heart of a true naturalist who says:

"We are a remote park, so this is one of the few places where you can wake up to birds singing and not go-carts. We have exceptional natural resources: 1,800 acres surrounded by the 300,000-acre Daniel Boone. Elevations range from 700 to 1,400 feet. We're also nestled in between Lake Cumberland and Laurel River Lake. So it's an outdoor enthusiast's dream.

"The Cumberland is a year-round river meandering from east to west, fed by three creeks coming together in Harlan, Kentucky. A 16-mile corridor is a wild river. That designation protects not only the river but the whole natural environment surrounding the river.

"Besides the commercial outfitters, individuals can bring their own equipment for canoeing or floating. There's enough water flow to run the river for about six miles below the falls from spring to fall. The river narrows below the falls, causing the water to go faster. Most whitewater rivers dry up in summer, but that's not the case here.

"As for common wildlife, we have migratory birds and small mammals, bobcats, and gray foxes. The largest mammal is the white-tailed deer, although occasionally black bears are reported in the area. They are coming out of the Appalachians, extending their range toward the west. The federally endangered red-cockaded woodpecker is here, and the river supports animals that were once endangered. I've seen river otters, and beavers are quite common. Great blue herons and wood ducks have been seen here, too, though these ducks have become quite scarce.

"If you really like the outdoors, you need to come and stay for a couple of weeks, take advantage of sightseeing, canoeing, backpacking, whitewater rafting, fishing, anything that goes on outdoors. Try one of the guided programs, like moonlight canoe trips, sponsored by the park. We offer programs that focus on geologic studies, the atmosphere, flora and fauna, and natural beauty."

In summer, the naturalist staff offers four to six activities each day, many geared to keeping kids entertained and busy. They include guided nature walks, arts and crafts, junior naturalist activities, campfire programs from a naturalist point of view, and special musical events. Also, square dancing at the park's outdoor pavilion is a long-standing tradition.

Special events are mostly in spring, fall, and winter. One is the very popular Moonbow Trail Trek in November hosted by the park, the DBNF, and local hiking clubs. It is a challenging 10⁸/₁₀-mile self-guided hike in a mixed mesophytic forest along the Cumberland River Gorge among waterfalls, cascading streams, towering cliffs, and monumental rock formations. A 4½-mile version is also offered.

More than two-thirds of the park, including the Cumberland River and trails west of the river and within the river corridor, is a State Nature Preserve. Among protected species (and all are protected in the refuge) are several rare mussels, the uncommon Eastern woodrat and green salamander, and plant species such as box huckleberry, brook saxifrage, riverweed, and Goat's-rue.

Trails in natural areas usually do not have barriers to keep people from falling off cliffs as they would in developed areas, so hikers need to be alert and cautious. This is one reason such trails are for day use only.

The park has 20 miles of trails ranging from 1 to 7 miles, plus short connectors that allow longer combinations. Some are quite easy, while others can be considered very challenging. One that almost anyone can negotiate is the ccc Memorial Trail, a self-guided interpretive trail that starts and ends at the lodge. It was built by the Civilian Conservation Corps during the Great Depression in the early 1930s. The ccc constructed trails, cabins, and the original lodge (which burned in 1940). Workers return to this place each year for a reunion.

The Eagle Falls Trail west of the river follows the cliff line for a mile on Trail 9, then descends for a view of a 44-foot-high waterfall where Eagle Creek plunges into the Cumberland. The lower portion can be underwater at times.

Trail 9 goes on, with a rugged climb across a ridge, to join Trail 10, a loop that provides an outstanding view of the gorge below the falls. The easier way to get there is to start at the second junction with Trail 9.

Speaking of views: the approach to the park from the east (on State 90) follows the top of a very high ridge for miles, with exceptional vistas on both sides, especially along a built-up section called the Dry Land Bridge. Expect to see a panoramic 180-degree scene of broad valleys and distant hills. A quick intake of breath is normal, so don't panic if it happens to you!

For nearby recreational opportunities outside the park, read on.

Where: Twenty miles southwest of Corbin. From Interstate 75, take exit 25 and go west on U.S. Route 25W, then split to the right at State 90 and follow it to the park.

When: Year-round, except park closes for several days during Christmas season. Lodge restaurant serves three meals daily. Campground and coffee shop, open April 1 through October 31 (coffee shop hours, 10:00 A.M. to 2:00 P.M. daily, until 7:00 P.M. on Saturdays). Gift shop in falls area, open 9:00 A.M. until 8:00 P.M. Rafting (weather dependent) from May through October. Stables, open Memorial Day through Labor Day. Five days each month are designated "moonbow dates."

Admission: Free. Fees for horseback riding, whitewater rafting, swimming (if not staying in lodge or cottage).

Amenities: Lodge, museum, restaurant, cottages, campground with store and laundry, gift shops, trading post, coffee shop, dance pavilion, nature trails, 1,294-acre nature preserve, 20 miles of hiking trails, tennis and other outdoor courts, swimming pool, stables, picnic grounds, and playgrounds, plus airport transportation from London and Williamsburg.

45 min. guide   10-5 $10   #83

Activities: Moonbow viewing, whitewater rafting, canoeing, scenic drives and views, camping, backpacking, hiking, swimming, fishing, horseback riding, nature study, wildlife viewing, birding, photography, tennis, square dancing, daily planned recreation in summer.

Special events: Square Dance Weekend (February), Kentucky Hills Weekend (March), Nature Photography Weekend (April), Spring Outdoor Adventure (May), Annual Photoscenic Weekend (October), Moonbow Trail Trek, Kentucky Clay Weekend (November). For Kentucky State Parks special events brochure, 800-255-7275.

Other: For barrier-free information, 800-255-7275. TDD equipped. Nature Preserve open for day use only. Watch for hazards. Copperheads and timber rattlesnakes are found here. Park trails go along high cliffs. River wading can be dangerous. Walking under the falls is prohibited.

For more information: Cumberland Falls State Resort Park, 7351 Highway 90, Corbin, KY 40701-8814, 606-528-4121. Reservations, 800-325-0063.

Sheltowee Trace Outfitters, PO Box 1060, Whitley City, KY 42653 (or in person, Holiday Motor Lodge Complex, Highway 90 at Cumberland Falls), 800-541-7238. Rafting and canoeing on the Cumberland, Rockcastle, and Big South Fork; backpacking and hiking, too.

Kentucky State Nature Preserves Commission, 801 Schenkel Lane, Frankfort, KY 40601-1403, 502-573-2886.

Laurel River Lake and Vicinity

The popular Laurel River Lake is just north of Cumberland Falls State Resort Park in the London District of Daniel Boone. Immediately to its west is the Somerset District, which manages a portion that includes the Natural Arch Scenic Area and the Beaver Creek Wilderness. Together, these districts provide all sorts of outdoor recreation. They can be your primary destination, especially if you enjoy camping, or you might stay nearby at Cumberland Falls or elsewhere.

Laurel River Lake, a deep lake with 5,600 surface acres and 192 miles of cliff-lined shore, is just west of Corbin. On a map, it looks like a giant jellyfish with tentacles reaching out everywhere. In reality, it is a beautiful lake with numerous bays and wooded islands, and it's known as a great fishing spot. It has two full-service marinas: Holly Bay, just north of the dam, and Grove, east of the dam on the south side of the lake. Detailed directions to each are given at the end of this section.

I stopped in at Holly Bay one September morning to get a report on fishing results. Stephen Smith was tending the store, where a sign said: "Coffee. Pour your own."

Hmmm—just like home.

"Walleyes are really biting right now," Steve offered. "We had a great guy who came down, a professional angler named Rick Marksberry who introduced us to walleye fishing. We didn't have a clue how to fish them until he showed us the Kentucky spinner rig. And smallmouth bass fishing is booming. We've had a lot of 6½- to 7-pound ones caught here. Trout fishing for rainbow is about the same—a lot of good-sized ones in the lake. Early in the year and late in the fall, they do a lot of trolling with AC-Shiners."

Laurel Lake is also fished for crappie, bluegill, channel catfish, and largemouth bass.

The Forest Service provides drive-in developed campgrounds at both marinas, boat-in campgrounds, a group campground for parties of 12 or more, and primitive camping at designated areas. Primitive camping is also allowed in undeveloped areas, but campsites must be at least 300 feet from roads, trails, streams, or the shoreline.

The U.S. Army Corps of Engineers manages 900 acres at the lake, including the dam, an overlook, a visitors center, the spillway swim area, and a picnic area. The rest of the lake falls under U.S. Forest Service management.

Laurel Lake is a wintering spot for a small number of American bald eagles. Some come down from the upper Great Lakes and lower Canada when lakes up there freeze over. This can be as early as the first of November, and these birds may stay until sometime in March. A few others migrate from Florida in spring and are seen on the lake in summer, then go south again in the fall. Since 90 percent of their diet is fish and they prefer a place where they can be undisturbed, Laurel Lake satisfies both needs.

The London Ranger District has 94 miles of hiking trails that are open to mountain bikes but that can present hazards as they wind around cliffs and rock ledges. All Forest Service roads (FSR) in the DBNF are open to mountain bikes unless posted otherwise. The district offices can provide details and help you choose a route.

One area that offers a seven-mile loop is the Rockcastle Recreation area west of the lake, following FSR 3497. On this route, you will see cliffs, cascades, Adirondack shelters, birds, and wildflowers, and will find places for fishing and camping. A longer trail allowing mountain bike use is in the Cumberland Falls area. It incorporates 10⁷/₁₀ miles of the Sheltowee Trace and 6⁷/₁₀ miles of Forest Service roads in a loop that leads to waterfalls, rapids, and Moonshiner's Arch. Another trail follows the lakeshore for several miles in the vicinity of Holly Bay.

Off-highway vehicles (OHVs or ORVs) may use many Forest Service roads. Check with the district offices for regulations and detailed maps.

Paddling opportunities on the Cumberland River include the Upper Cumberland from State 204 at Redbird Bridge to State 90 at Cumberland Falls SRP (Class I with Class II rapids), and the Lower Cumberland from Cumberland Falls to the mouth of Laurel River (Class III). Four stretches of the Rockcastle include the Upper Rockcastle from Livingston to the Interstate 75 Bridge (Class I+), from the Interstate 75 Bridge to State 1956 at Billows Bridge (Class I+), the Lower Rockcastle from State 1956 to State 192 at Bee Rock Campground (Class III and Class IV), and Bee Rock to State 3497 (on the backwaters of Lake Cumberland, rated for beginners).

Deep in the forest just beyond Bee Rock is a camp built for horse riders. Little Lick Campground is 8 miles south of State 192 on FSR 122 (this junction is 21 miles east of Somerset for those coming from the west). Horse provisions include a stock-watering pond, corral, and hitching rail. It has six single-family and two double-family camping units furnished with tent pads, fire grates, lantern holders, and picnic tables. The 16-mile horse trail offers beautiful scenery and has plenty of watering places along the way, including streams, ponds, and the lake.

Cross-country skiing is allowed in the forest, but this section has no prepared trails, so expect to encounter hazards.

A hike of special interest just north of Cumberland Falls SRP is the trail to Dog Slaughter Falls, a small waterfall in a scenic setting. From State 90 east of the park, go north on FSR 195 for 2⁷/₁₀ miles. Look for the trailhead on the left. Walk to the right after crossing a small footbridge and continue for 1½ miles to the falls.

The Beaver Creek Wilderness and WMA and the Three Forks of Beaver Overlook are in the Somerset District west of Laurel River Lake.

Access to the overlook is from U.S. Route 27 north of State 90. Look for a sign, Hammonds Camp, at FSR 50, a gravel road, where you turn right. Where the road forks left, continue straight to a parking area and walk to the overlook. If you do go into the wilderness, you'll need top woods skills to navigate the rugged 4,791 acres. The reward, though, is a pristine place to do both trail and compass hiking, primitive camping, horseback riding, and backpacking. Be aware of hunting seasons and dress accordingly in blaze orange. What if you get lost? Well, you'll be lost in paradise among sheer cliffs, cliff overhangs, waterfalls, mature trees, forest creatures, and more plant species than you may have ever seen.

On a junket to Three Forks of Beaver, another very scenic drive leads to the Natural Arch and the Great Gulf, which are also off U.S. Route 27. From State 90, turn south onto U.S. Route 27 for 4/10 mile, then right onto State 927 for 1 8/10 miles to the Natural Arch parking lot and picnic/playground area with shelter, water fountain, and rest rooms. You can take a short paved trail to an overlook and see the arch and other formations across a chasm. You can also walk to the arch, which is one of the largest in the state. Six trails begin here, from 3/10 of a mile to a 5 2/10-mile loop, all well marked with colors and numbers.

It would be a shame to miss more of this scenic road. Continue on for 1 2/10 miles to the Great Gulf parking area where additional trails begin, then to the Straight Creek overlook 2/10 of a mile farther. I found this to be the most spectacular view of all: a chasm and tree-topped cliffs and an interesting circular formation with a curved top and rocks fanning out at the base. Expect great splashes of color in fall in a landscape filled with oaks, maples, cedars, and pines.

For complete information about the extensive recreational opportunities throughout the DBNF (500 miles of hiking, backpacking, horse and mountain bike trails, plus rivers and other features), ask for maps and the 24-page publication, "Recreation on the Daniel Boone National Forest," available at any district ranger's office.

Where: Access the Laurel River Lake facilities from three main directions:

To north and west shores, from Interstate 75 take exit 38 and go west for 12²/₁₀ miles on State 192, then south on FSR 62 to Craigs Creek campground or continue on State 192 for 2 more miles to FSR 1193, then south 3 miles to Holly Bay Recreation Area. To reach Bee Rock campground, continue on State 192 for about a mile past 1193 (to where the Rockcastle River crosses the road).

To east shore facilities, exit Interstate 75 at Corbin (exit 29), and take State 770 west for 1 mile to State 312. To go to Laurel Bridge picnic area, turn left on State 312. To go to Flatwoods picnic area, turn right on State 312 for 1 mile, then west on State 363 for 1½ miles, then left on FSR 758 for 1½ miles.

To south shore facilities, exit Interstate 75 at Corbin (exit 25), and go west on U.S. Route 25W for five miles, then right on State 1193. Go north for two miles, then right on FSR 558 for three miles to Grove Recreation Area. (You can also reach Holly Bay on this route by continuing on State 1193.)

When: Year-round. Laurel River Dam Picnic Area, Laurel Bridge Day Use Area, and Craigs Creek Group Area, open April through October. Holly Bay Campground, open April 15 through October. Grove Recreation Area, open April 15 through September.

Admission: Free. Day-use fees in some locations.

Amenities: Visitors center (at dam), trails, campgrounds, picnic areas, marinas, boat-launching ramps, swimming beach, playgrounds, stables.

Activities (in area): Boating, sailing, fishing, hunting, camping, hiking, backpacking, kayaking, horseback riding, picnicking, rafting, canoeing, mountain bike and ORV riding, wildlife viewing, birding, nature walks, scenic auto touring, photography, cross-country skiing.

Other: Some areas barrier free.

For more information: Resource Manager, U.S. Army Corps of Engineers, Laurel River Lake, 1433 Laurel Lake Road, London, KY 40741, 606-864-6412. (Lake information and generation schedule, 606-878-9170.)

District Ranger, London, U.S. Forest Service, U.S. Highway 25 South, PO Box 907, London, KY 40743, 606-864-4163. (Quadrangle maps and information on eagle watching, mountain biking, off-highway vehicles, river floating, and other activities.)

District Ranger, Somerset, U.S. Forest Service, 156 Realty Lane, Somerset KY 42501, 606-679-2018 or 2010. (Quadrangle maps and local information.)

Forest Supervisor, Daniel Boone National Forest, 100 Vaught Road, Winchester, KY 40391, 606-745-3100.

Holly Bay Marina, PO Box 674, London, KY 40741, 606-864-6542.

Grove Marina, Inc., PO Box 1483, Corbin, KY 40702, 606-523-2323.

Corbin Tourist Commission, 101 North Lynn Avenue, Corbin, KY 40701, 800-528-7123.

Two addresses for topo maps: Kentucky Department of Economic Development, Maps & Publications, 133 Holmes Street, Frankfort, KY, 40601, 502-564-4715. Kentucky Geological Survey, Publications Sales, Room 104, Mining & Mineral Resources Building, University of Kentucky, Lexington, KY 40506-0107, 606-257-5863. (Also, free "Index to Topographic Maps for Kentucky.")

Big South Fork National River and Recreation Area

The train whistled in the distance, the high-pitched blasts sounding up the valley for miles to where I stood in a "ghost house" at the old Blue Heron mine site several miles from Stearns. I had driven earlier to an overlook, wishing in vain to see whitewater action in the river below (it was the wrong season), walked a rhododendron-lined trail, and then drove down the steep, twisting road to Blue Heron. What had been a mining and logging camp from 1901 to 1962 is alive now in a much different way, preserving voices and memories of the past.

The commanding feature in this historic community is the mine's tipple and its bridge. Trails lead to it and other structures, such as the shack, a former repair terminal for locomotives and tram cars. A trestle once connected it to the main tipple. Not far away, the boarded-up mine entrance conceals a tunnel going into the side of the mountain.

Blue Heron has a visitors center, a gift shop, and a fascinating depot museum with displays that tell the story of the mine, plus old photographs and even engineering drawings of the tipple. Nearby is a snack bar with an outdoor patio. And there are more trails, including the 6½-mile Blue Heron Loop that goes to an overlook near the campground.

What brings it to life, though, are the dozen ghost houses that replay the experiences of Blue Heron residents in the early part of the 20th century. Each is an open-sided structure with larger-than-life photographs of people who lived here, and each is decorated with authentic objects that represent a particular theme. Recorded narrations recall hardships and isolation but also meaningful friendships, the closeness of families, and the beauties of nature.

At the Trammell House, the subject was nature's bounty. The voices talked about fishing for bass, trout, and catfish in the river, about the whitewater rapids, and descriptions of the undergrowth where they hunted frogs, ginseng, mayapples, and muscadine grapes. Other hunts were for squirrels and minks. Their love of nature went a long way in making the hardships more bearable.

Another blast from the train, and it rolled up to the depot, caboose first. The bluegrass sound of a mountain ballad played by a local band filled the air as four carloads of people spilled from the train. Bandanna-wrapped lunches were waiting for them, the sun was shining, and at just that moment, the Blue Heron mining camp was undoubtedly the brightest spot on earth.

Stearns is the nearest town to the NRRA. It is the departure point of the Big South Fork Scenic Railway and the home of the Stearns Museum. The museum is in a 1907 building across the street from the old company store. A parking lot behind it makes access easy, and admission is a nominal fee. The display rooms re-create almost every aspect of local history through the 1940s. There are items and fixtures from an old country store and post office, kitchens, and a buggy room, plus articles relating to moonshine, music, mining, lumbering, and even wash day in rural McCreary County in the 1920s and 30s, when clothes were rubbed on a washboard, then boiled, and hung outside to dry. It's another perspective on Blue Heron and other Appalachian mining communities.

Blue Heron is a special place, but in the vast Big South Fork NRRA, it can demand only a share of the spotlight.

The Big South Fork of the Cumberland River and its main tributaries, Clear Fork, North White Oak, and New River are free-flowing streams that drain over 1,300 square miles of Tennessee and Kentucky. The NRRA was established in 1974, and in 1989, the National Park Service took over management of the 106,000 acres of mostly wilderness. A large portion is in Tennessee, but the Kentucky part (Area I), which lies within the Daniel Boone National Forest, has rugged and impressive areas suitable for high adventure sports like kayaking, rock climbing, or mountain bike riding. Mountain bikes are allowed on all horse trails and primitive and gravel roads, but dedicated hiking trails are off limits to these bikes and off-road vehicles.

People who are less active can enjoy the scenery by automobile and take short walks to easy-to-reach overlooks. Some sites that are wheelchair accessible include: the Blue Heron Campground, the Big South Fork Railway train to Blue Heron, the depot museum and some walkways at Blue Heron, and the Devils Jump Overlook.

The dramatic changes in elevation support a rich variety of diverse forest ecosystems and plant species. Wildflowers, which constantly appear from March through October along trails and by the roadside, are exceptional.

As to wildlife, this remote wilderness has been home to bison, elk, gray and red wolves, and panthers. Now it provides habitat for white-tailed deer, beavers, muskrats, coyotes, red and gray foxes, weasels, skunks, wild pigs, and river otters and for several species of small mammals like shrews, moles, bats, rabbits, squirrels, mice, and rats. Black bears were reintroduced in 1996.

The Kentucky portion of the Big South Fork NRRA has 53 miles of trails in addition to the Sheltowee Trace National Recreation Trail. Some of the most scenic waterfalls, arches, river overlooks, bluffs, and wildflowers are seen only by hikers.

The Blue Heron Campground, open mid-April through November, is 7 miles from Stearns off State 742. It has 45 sites, each with water, picnic tables, and grills. A bathhouse has electricity and a public telephone. A no-fee primitive campground is at Alum Ford on the river near Yahoo Falls, with no water or rest-room facilities provided. Backcountry camping is also allowed on this NRRA. Check at Blue Heron or the Stearns visitors center for trail information, maps, and backcountry regulations.

In the Daniel Boone NF to the west is the Bell Farm horse camp. It has five single-family units, a fire ring for campfires, and hitching rails. Water for horses is available in nearby Rock Creek, a wild river that is stocked in summer with rainbow trout. From Stearns, go west on State 92 for 6 miles, then south on State 1363 for 12 miles. At Bell Farm, turn east for half a mile across a bridge to the camp. Three miles south of Bell Farm on FSR 137 is the Hemlock Grove recreation area. Horseback riders can get on the Sheltowee Trace here and go south to Tennessee, then follow Rock Creek through a portion of the NRRA and into Tennessee's Pickett State Park. This is a very beautiful and pristine area of the forest.

Two miles south of Hemlock Grove on FSR 137 is the Great Meadow Campground, which is open year-round and has 20 sites for tent/trailer camping. It has water, sanitary facilities, and a large playing field. Access Rock Creek and the Sheltowee Trace from here, too.

Yahoo—a Waterfall, an Arch, a Universe

Danny Troxell, official Cherokee storyteller for the Big South Fork NRRA, was talking about Yahoo and arches.

"Yahoo is a Cherokee word that names, at 113 feet, the tallest waterfall in Kentucky. You can walk underneath and around in back of it. There is also a Yahoo Arch, which is very sacred to the Indians. At the arches, the Cherokee would light bonfires and then jump through the center of the universe.

"You see," he explained, "the natural arch is half a circle. The visible part is the upper half. Below the earth is the other half. So when you walk in the middle of the arch you walk through the center of the universe. You jump into another dimension."

I have to go there, I declared to myself.

Yahoo is about as far north as you can get in the Big South Fork, and it's a "well-trailed" area. Loop trails are everywhere, and the ubiquitous Sheltowee Trace comes right through here, too. A picnic area on top of the bluff has tables and primitive rest rooms. Several overlooks give views of Lake Cumberland, Yahoo Creek, and Yahoo Falls (which can be quite spectacular during the rainy season). The lower trail follows a portion of the trace. Though the trails are generally well marked, some places can be confusing. A good solution is the book *Hiking the Big South Fork*, by Brenda D. Coleman and Jo Anna Smith.

The nearby Alum Ford area has river access and the campground I mentioned. It seems that every worthwhile destination in the Big South Fork is down in the gorge, which means a steep descent. Tulip poplar leaves shimmered in the breeze as I breezed by, enjoying the roller-coaster ride.

By the way, this road goes right down to the river. If you haven't made a big splash recently, here's an opportunity!

Where: In the Daniel Boone National Forest west of U.S. Route 27 from the Tennessee line to a point west of Flat Rock. From U.S. Route 27, turn west on State 92 (toward Stearns) to the Big South Fork visitors center on the right. Farther north on the east side of U.S. Route 27 opposite State 1651 (north of Whitley City) is the U.S. Forest Service visitors information station. From Interstate 75, take exit 11 and go west on State 92 to Stearns.
When: Year-round. Stearns Museum open daily from 10:00 A.M. to 5:00 P.M. June through August and October (open Wednesday through Sunday mid-April through May 30 and during September). Big South Fork Scenic Railway operates from mid-April through October 30.
Admission: Free, except some fee use areas. Stearns Museum, modest fee. Scenic Railway, moderate fee; discounts for 12 and under, 3 and under free if with adult and not occupying a seat.

Amenities: Visitors centers, museums, scenic railroad, outdoor historical museum, campgrounds, horse camp, picnic grounds, recreation areas, scenic overlooks, trails, river access.

Activities: Camping (developed and primitive), wildlife viewing, birding, hiking, backpacking, nature walks, picnicking, scenic auto tours, horseback riding, trail-bike riding, fishing, hunting, swimming, canoeing, kayaking, whitewater rafting, rock climbing, photography.

Special events: Native American Culture programs throughout summer, mountain bike rallies, Blue Heron Run (footrace/walkers, call 606-376-3787—September). Special train excursions: Spring Fling (April and May), Coal Mining Days, Spring Fling Night Train (May), Old-Fashioned Homecoming (July), Gospel Music Celebration (August), Fall Fantasy Night Train (September), weekly October specials, Halloween Night Train (late October).

Other: Barrier-free access at Blue Heron Campground, Blue Heron information center, Blue Heron Scenic Train, and Devils Jump Overlook.

For more information: Superintendent, Big South Fork NRRA, Route 3, Box 401, Oneida, TN 37841, 423-569-9778. (Information, regulations, and list of licensed outfitters.)

Big South Fork Scenic Railway, PO Box 368, Stearns, KY 42647. Telephone, 800-462-5664.

District Ranger, Stearns, U.S. Forest Service, U.S. Highway 27 North, PO Box 429, Whitley City, KY 42653, 606-376-5323. (Quadrangle maps and local information.)

Stearns Museum, PO Box 452, Stearns, KY 42647, 606-376-5730.

For mountain bike events information, contact Richard Matthews, 4770 Squiresville Road, Owenton, KY 40359, 502-484-2998. E-mail, BikeButler@aol.com. Web page, http://members.aol.com/BikeButler.

Wild Rivers Coordinator, Division of Water, Department for Environmental Protection, 14 Reilly Road, Fort Boone Plaza, Frankfort, KY 40601, 502-564-3410. (Calendar of events available. River events are weather dependent.)

Two addresses for topo maps: Kentucky Department of Economic Development, Maps & Publications, 133 Holmes Street, Frankfort, KY 40601, 502-564-4715. Kentucky Geological Survey, Publications Sales, Room 104, Mining & Mineral Resources Building, University of Kentucky, Lexington, KY 40506-0107, 606-257-5863. (Free "Index to Topographic Maps for Kentucky.")

For additional information about the Tennessee side of the Big South Fork, see the companion book *Natural Wonders of Tennessee.*

15

Eastward Along State 80

From London, going east on the Daniel Boone Parkway through the Redbird District of the DBNF, you can connect with State 80 just west of Hazard. It is a straight four-lane road that gives you a fast, uncluttered route to Prestonsburg. Hollow after scenic hollow dips below the high road, etching the forested landscape on both sides.

The Redbird ranger station is at Big Creek, just off the parkway from exit 34 toward Peabody. Big Double Creek, an area for picnicking, fishing, and hiking, is 2 miles away. Here, you can access the challenging 65-mile Redbird Crest Trail, a loop that cuts a wide, meandering route through the forest and the Redbird WMA. The ranger station can provide all the information you need.

For more information: Redbird District Ranger, Daniel Boone National Forest, HC 68, Box 65, Big Creek, KY 40914, 606-598-2192.

Buckhorn Lake State Resort Park

An unspoiled area of the mountains just north of the Daniel Boone National Forest and west of Hazard made the perfect location for Buckhorn, a retreat where visitors can relax in comfort with no sacrifice of amenities. The Buckhorn Reservoir is an impoundment of the Middle Fork of the Kentucky River in the foothills of the Cumberland Plateau. It is a deep, clear lake created for flood control, water quality, and recreation.

The road to Buckhorn hints at what's ahead as it climbs, dips, and snakes through the mountains. The park is smaller in scale than some other resort parks, enhancing the hideaway feeling. It offers full amenities, with a 36-room lodge, 3 executive cottages, and a dining room that serves 3 meals daily and can seat over 200 people. Lake cruises, fishing, and social activities are emphasized here; and the roads in the nearby national forest extend the possibilities for wilderness appreciation. The lake has bass, crappie, bluegill, channel catfish, and muskie.

The park does have two trails: the short Leatherwood Trail, which is moderate to difficult, and the moderate 1½-mile self-guiding interpretive Moonshine Trail. Eighteen stations and a well-illustrated booklet guide you to special features and describe plants, animals, and geology along the trail. Look carefully—you may see white-tailed deer, opossums, skunks, raccoons, foxes, squirrels, rabbits, and woodchucks.

Buckhorn is a worthy destination for those who would like to stay in a truly beautiful and tranquil place.

Where: West of State 15. From Hazard, go north, then west on State 28 to State 1833 (follow signs). From Lexington, go east on the Mountain Parkway to Campton exit (43) and south on State 15 to State 28 and continue as above.
When: Year-round. Gift shop, open February 1 through December 31. Swimming pool, open 10:00 A.M. to 10:00 P.M. Memorial Day through Labor Day. Miniature golf, from April 1 through October 31.

Admission: Free. Fees for boat rentals and miniature golf.

Amenities: Lodge, cottages, restaurant, gift shop, meeting rooms, marina, rental pontoon and fishing boats, launching ramps, recreational courts, miniature golf, nature trails, swimming pool, playground, picnic shelters.

Activities: Fishing, boating, swimming, miniature golf, nature walks, birding, wildlife viewing, photography, shuffleboard, horseshoes, sand volleyball, tennis, basketball, indoor recreation, daily planned recreation in summer.

Special events: Mountain Showcase (March), Nature Photography Weekend (April), Spring Craft Fair (May), Muzzleloader Challenge (September and December), Fall Festival (October). For Kentucky State Parks special-events brochure, call 800-255-7275.

Other: For barrier-free information, 800-255-7275. TDD equipped.

For more information: Buckhorn Lake State Resort Park, HC 36, Box 1000, Buckhorn, KY 41721-9602, 606-398-7510. Reservations, 800-325-0058.

Jenny Wiley State Resort Park

Take the sky lift and catch the 60-mile view from Sugar Camp Mountain. Or catch some fish in a mountain lake— your choice of bass, bluegill, crappie, or catfish. Catch a Broadway-style musical in a 500-seat amphitheater, then catch your breath and join the boot-scootin' crowd for some country or square dancing. Are you ready now for a 163-mile backpacking sojourn to South Portsmouth on the Ohio River? Only at Jenny Wiley State Resort Park can you join in this particular mix of activities. You may not take in everything this park has to offer in one trip, but be alert to "come-back" fever. It's rampant here, and you're almost certain to catch *that*.

The park sprawls for miles along State 3 on the western shore of sparkling Dewey Lake at Prestonsburg, a mecca for year-round outdoor sports, indoor and outdoor recreation, and cultural events. Major access is from State 80 or from U.S. Route 23, a north-south route between Ashland and Elkhorn City. Like all Kentucky resort parks, it has modern, well-maintained facilities including lodge rooms, restaurant, cottages, and a full-featured campground.

An unusual building near the campground is the Josie D. Harkins School House, which was the last operating one-room schoolhouse in Kentucky and was located at Daniels Creek in Floyd County. It closed its doors in 1987 and was moved to the park. Now it is used for interdenominational church services during the summer.

The U.S. Army Corps of Engineers has a ranger station at Dewey Dam and provides recreation areas there (picnic grounds, shelters, rest rooms, boat access, ball fields, asphalt courts, playgrounds). The dam impounds Johns Creek, which flows into the Levisa Fork of the Big Sandy River.

The story of Jenny Wiley has several variations but is basically the true account of a pioneer woman who was captured by a raiding party of Shawnees and Cherokees in 1789 and held captive as the Indians moved westward and northward from camp to camp. She had many harrowing experiences but was able to escape the following year and was reunited with her husband.

The Jenny Wiley Trail, which starts at the park across from the marina near Cottage #132, is believed to follow much the same route as a portion of her historic journey. It is a challenging trail that sometimes goes through remote mountain areas and should not be hiked alone. Shelters and cistern water are provided approximately every 10 to 15 miles. Park visitors often hike a 3-mile segment that ends at the park campground. From there, a mile-long steep ascent goes to Tecumseh Overlook, then descends and follows an old trace that provides glorious views of Dewey Lake. The little community of Auxier is five miles from the trailhead. A mile farther north, the trail overlooks the spot where Jenny Wiley made her daring escape.

The park has another 5 miles of trails that are excellent for wildlife and wildflower viewing, nature appreciation, and birding. The Lakeshore Hiking Trail is 2½ miles but can be walked in shorter segments or combined with the 1³/₁₀-mile Moss Ridge Trail. It begins with a shoreline view of the lake among magnolias, hemlocks, tulip poplars, and carpets of ferns and wildflowers, then extends up Moss Ridge in a forest of pines, oaks, maples, and hickories. Moss covers the ridge top (as the name suggests), exposed sandstone rocks add dramatic visual elements, and white-tailed deer and small mammals may consider hikers intruders in their domain. The mile-long Steve Brackett Memorial Trail is accessible from either of the other two trails. The views are memorable and sometimes include wild turkeys in the landscape.

It would be reasonable to think that the Jenny Wiley Theatre in the Jenny Wiley Park at the end of the Jenny Wiley Trail would produce a historical drama about Jenny Wiley's adventures. Not so. It is in fact a professional summer stock company offering musicals (directed by Theodora "Teddy" Vaughn) that in one recent season included *Peter Pan*, *The Gin Game*, *Carnival*, and *A Funny Thing Happened on the Way to the Forum*. These productions are very popular and play to full houses, so early reservations are recommended.

This park has a really great mix of indoor and outdoor activities, as Ron Vanover explained. He directs both the interpretive and recreational activities.

"If you come in the summer, you'll find nature-oriented programs. There will be trail hikes, interpretive hikes, wild-flower walks, medicinal plant walks, owl prowls, and junior naturalist programs. On the flip side are activities that are purely recreation: pontoon boat rides on the lake, bicycle rodeos, musical events, and storytelling. We're right at the top of state parks that offer dance. I'm a western square dance caller, but we do mountain calling and country line dancing, too. Dance activities such as a western square dance weekend extend into other seasons."

In the fall, emphasis shifts to recreation for seniors. Activities range from bingo to boat tours and gospel music entertainment. The nine-hole golf course is open year-round when weather permits, and senior discounts are offered.

The recreation office had quite a few animal specimens on display. Two were fawns, and I asked Ron about them.

"All the animals are roadkills, since we would not kill anything deliberately," he explained.

He pointed out some other specimens, including two foxes, commenting about their vulnerability to predators.

"The red fox is swifter than the gray one you see behind it, but it usually will not burrow year-round, preferring to curl up in a ball—sometimes in the snow. With the coyote moving back into eastern Kentucky, a lot of us are really concerned about the fox population here."

For wildlife management, that's the eternal challenge: protecting species and maintaining a balance.

Where: East of Prestonsburg on State 3. Coming from the west on State 80, continue straight on State 3 where 80 turns sharply toward Pikeville. From the north on U.S. Route 23, after passing Paintsville take the second exit to State 3 where you see a "Jenny Wiley State Park" sign.

When: Year-round. Park closed Christmas Eve and Christmas Day. Campground, open April 1 through October 31. Pontoon boat rentals, from March through October (weather dependent). Theater performances, from late June through late August (curtain for evening performances is 8:15 P.M.). Sky lift, open daily May 15 through Labor Day and weekends September and October. Olympic-size community pool, open Memorial Day through mid-August. Historic Josie D. Harkins School House, open Memorial Day through Labor Day or by appointment.

Admission: Free. Fees for sky lift, theater tickets, boat rentals, golf, community swimming pool, and shelter rentals.

Amenities: Lodge, dining room, cottages, conference center, Pines Building for group rental, campground with all facilities and grocery, Jenny Wiley Theatre (summer stock), sky lift, marina, nine-hole golf course, two swimming pools, nature trails, picnic grounds, playgrounds.

Activities: Camping, boating, fishing, swimming, golf, hiking, picnicking, nature study, photography, birding, wildlife viewing, musical productions, and daily planned recreation in summer.

Special Events: Frontier Night (January), Big Sandy Senior Games (May), repertory theater productions and Kentucky Opry (late June through late August), Kentucky Highland Folk Festival (September), Jenny Wiley Festival (October), Western Square Dance Weekend (November). For Kentucky State Parks special events brochure, 800-255-7275.

Other: Transportation provided to and from local airport upon advance request. For barrier-free information (park), 800-255-7275. TDD equipped. Theater is wheelchair accessible and has hearing-impaired assisted devices.

For more information: Jenny Wiley State Resort Park, HC 66,

Box 200, Prestonsburg, KY 41653-9799, 606-886-2711. Accommodations, 800-325-0142. Shelter rentals, 606-886-6709. Sky lift information, 606-886-6303.

Jenny Wiley Theatre, PO Box 22, Prestonsburg, KY 41653, 606-886-9274.

Prestonsburg Tourism Commission, 130 North Lake Drive, Prestonsburg, KY 41653, 606-886-1341.

U.S. Army Corps of Engineers, PO Box 2127, Huntington, WV 25721 (Dewey Lake information). Shelter reservations, 606-789-4521.

Kentucky Department of Parks, 500 Mero Street, 10th Floor, Capital Plaza Tower, Frankfort, KY 40601-1974, 502-564-2172. (Jenny Wiley Trail guide and listing of topo maps.)

16

Pine Mountain to The Breaks

The dominant feature along Kentucky's southeastern border is Pine Mountain, a high ridge 125 miles long that extends from near Jellico, Tennessee, to Elkhorn City. The crest of Pine Mountain gains slowly in elevation from southwest to northeast and is highest in southern Letcher County where it attains 3,200 feet. It is actually the rim of a 25-mile-wide overthrust block of the earth's crust that was pushed intact for six miles to the northwest about 230 million years ago. It has a steep northwest face that overlooks the Cumberland Plateau and a much gentler back slope facing southeast. This sets the stage for some striking scenery full of cliffs, boulders, tumbling creeks, and wooded coves, and for some of the wildest places in Kentucky.

All of eastern Kentucky, from Pine Mountain to the Cumberland Escarpment, is within the Eastern Kentucky Coal Field region. On a map, this is basically the Daniel Boone National Forest and eastward. To travelers, this means being aware of the coal trucks that must use the roadways and allowing extra time to reach destinations. I found that the hours before 7:00 A.M. are the best for making good time on two-lane roads. At exactly 7:00 (or so it seems), coal trucks enter the roadways as if guided by the peremptory swish of a conductor's baton.

Pine Mountain State Resort Park

An excellent place to enjoy the view from the top of Pine Mountain and hike on rugged scenic trails in an old forest is at Pine Mountain State Resort Park. You can camp or stay in a modern lodge or cottage, and the access from Interstate 75 and U.S. Route 25E is easy. The park is one of the most pristine and protected areas in the state. It is adjacent to the 11,363-acre Kentucky Ridge State Forest, and the park includes two state nature preserves totaling 782 acres. It also has the distinction of being Kentucky's oldest state park.

Dean Henson, the park's interpretive naturalist, spoke about the park's other distinctive aspects.

"The natural integrity of our landscape is unparalleled," he declared. "Few localities in Kentucky have mature climax forest timber as is found in the Pine Mountain region. Most forests have been affected by flooding, geological upheaval, fire, or disturbance by man. Some of our forest has been allowed to mature for 350 to 400 years. This is as impressive as it gets in the East!"

Geologically, the Pine Mountain overthrust block underlying the region creates an unusual topography that sustains a variety of forest types. The north slope is very abrupt, with many sheer rock faces that rise from the valley floor over 1,000 feet below. Northern tree species are found on most north slopes and high ridges. The southern-facing slopes and their deep ravines get much more sun and are hospitable for southern tree species like the big-leaved magnolias. These trees have giant flowers and huge leaves that turn brown in fall and drop, their white undersides looking like crumpled newspaper pages on the ground. The Frazier magnolia, an uncommon variety in Kentucky, occurs only on Pine Mountain.

Two other uncommon plants found in this park are pale corydalis and showy gentian. The former, appearing on sandstone rock outcrops, has a yellow-tipped pink flower and bluish-green leaves; and the latter, seen on the upper slopes, is pale blue with faint vertical stripes.

Dean set the record straight on a couple of forest myths.

"The expression 'virgin timber' is not used much anymore when referring to indigenous North American forests, since it implies that the landscape and local habitat are altogether unaffected by the hand of man. 'Old growth' is a more accurate term that certainly applies to some stands of timber within the region. Our twin nature preserves showcase largely original forest cover and all the secondary components that go along with it, making for a very satisfying example of mixed mesophytic forests in the southern Appalachians.

"Some old-growth forest remnants are here for a couple of reasons. First, the landscape was nearly inaccessible in some areas, making timber harvesting difficult, often impractical. Also, mountainous areas were spared much of the early high-impact activities of the settlement era, since the flat tableland, desirable for raising crops and other farming activities, was settled first."

That brought up another subject: the American chestnut, which is often erroneously described as being extinct. It is true that in the eastern United States, these trees are always hit by the chestnut blight and never reach maturity.

According to several people I interviewed, it's not correct to call this species extinct, because old stumps still produce "pucker brush" (shoots or suckers) that may reach 12 to 15 feet before the blight kills them.

"These shoots are living American chestnuts with no hope of reaching maturity or nut production," Dean agreed, "but you can still get a leaf for your collection."

Research is being done around the country to produce a resistant strain or to blend the American chestnut with the genetic material of the Chinese chestnut. Other studies are looking at alternative ways to bring it back.

If you like the high places, Pine Mountain is definitely for you. The park has two entrances a mile apart. The Laurel Cove entrance quickly climbs to the top of Pine Mountain, where a right turn takes you along the crest to Lookout Point and a left turn follows near the crest to the campground, then descends more gently to the lodge, cottages, and nature center. A nine-hole golf course is near the main entrance, which is the more direct route to the lodge.

Park trails range from ½ mile to 1¾ miles, for a total of about 9 miles. Five of these start near the lodge, including the popular self-guided Hemlock Garden Trail within one of the nature preserves. It goes down into a ravine among centuries-old hemlocks, white oaks, and tulip poplars. It passes huge boulders along the cascading Bear Wallow Creek, and a ¼-mile spur trail leads to Inspiration Point which overlooks a natural rhododendron garden. Some other interesting plants along this trail are galax, partridgeberry, heartleaf, and American holly.

The Honeymoon Falls Trail is a 1½-mile loop that leads to a 25-foot waterfall. The Living Stairway Trail is an easy ½-mile loop that partly follows a sandstone outcrop from which the Log Mountains to the south can be seen. An extension of this trail is the Fern Garden Trail, a longer 1½-mile loop into forested ravines of hemlock and rhododendron and a very fine moist-plant community of ferns and sweet gum trees. Lost Trail descends for ½ mile into a beautiful ravine that may be difficult on the return ascent for some hikers.

Three other trails—Rock Hotel Trail, Chained Rock Trail, and Laurel Cove Trail—begin at the top of the mountain near Lookout Point. Rock Hotel Trail is a mile-long trail that leads to the largest sandstone rock shelter in the park near the main park road. The elevation change is 350 feet, which makes the return trip somewhat difficult. The Chained Rock Trail is a ½ mile long, descending 300 feet and leading to one of the best vantage points in the park, a spot where a boulder was chained to the cliff in 1933 as "protection" for the town below. Laurel Cove Trail is the longest and most strenuous trail in the park (1¾ miles long with a 1,100-foot elevation change). The good news is that you don't have to return if you arrange to be picked up at Laurel Cove where the trail ends near a natural amphitheater.

Also at Laurel Cove is the Azalea Trail, a short, easy trail (with a few stair steps at the start) that follows the base of a sandstone bluff and along streams.

Kentucky Ridge State Forest also offers hiking and backpacking opportunities on its 27 miles of trails. Get more information at the Kentucky Division of Forestry's Craft and Welcome Center on U.S. Route 25E just south of Pineville near the state park's Laurel Cove entrance.

Dean talked about the appeal of the different seasons.

"Spring is a lush time of rebirth in the rich, fertile woodland environment. Wildflowers bloom as trees unfurl new, yellow-green leaves, and the spring migration of warblers begins," he said.

"Summer, of course, is Kentucky's big tourist season. Pine Mountain provides daily naturalist-led activities which strike a balance between nature themes and outdoor recreation.

"Fall is an envious time. Because of the mountain topography and diverse geology, the colors are extraordinary—scarlet, gold, orange, and yellow leaves of deciduous trees providing a truly memorable spectacle."

The park is open in winter, too, providing both activities and a special kind of solitude. It's a good idea to keep an eye on the weather, though, since it controls in some degree what activities are possible.

Special event weekends begin in March with Astro-Observers Weekend, which offers lectures, audio-visual presentations and evening stargazing. The Kentucky Mountain Laurel Festival, a tradition here, is held in May and features a full week of festivities. Pine Mountain's "At the Top" 10K run offers a challenging footrace along the crest of the mountain. The Great American Dulcimer Convention in September draws some of the country's finest folk musicians and instrument makers, who play concerts and offer lessons. The Fall Photography Workshop in October features a slide competition and multimedia presentations by guest professionals.

As the saying goes, "Come early, come often." Out in nature, see flowering dogwood in mid-April, pink lady's slipper in late April, catawba rhododendron blooming in mid-May and mountain laurel in late May, red azaleas in mid-June, great rhododendrons in bloom and ripe blueberries in early July, and the peak of fall color the third week of October (well, usually!).

Where: From Interstate 75, take exit 29 and go east on U.S. Route 25E past Pineville, then right on State 190. Continue straight where State 190 turns left. The main park entrance is about 4½ miles after leaving 25E.

When: Year-round. Campground and miniature golf, open April 1 through October 31. Gift shop, open April through December. Swimming pool, open Memorial Day through Labor Day.

Admission: Free. Fee for golf.

Amenities: Lodge, dining room, gift shop, cottages, campground, convention center, nature center, trails, nine-hole golf course, miniature golf, swimming pool, outdoor recreation courts, picnic grounds and shelters, playgrounds.

Activities: Camping, swimming, hiking, wildlife viewing, birding, photography, nature appreciation, golf, miniature golf, picnicking, daily planned recreation in summer.

Special events: Astro-Observers Weekend (March), At the Top 10K Run, Kentucky Mountain Laurel Festival (May), Great American Dulcimer Convention (September), Fall Photography Workshop and Slide Competition (October). For Kentucky State Parks special-events brochure, 800-255-7275.

Other: Watch for copperheads and timber rattlesnakes on the trails. For barrier-free information, 800-255-7275. TDD equipped.

For more information: Pine Mountain State Resort Park, 1050 State Park Road, Pineville, KY 40977-0610, 606-337-3066. Reservations, 800-325-1712. Fax, 606-337-7250.

Kentucky State Nature Preserves Commission, 801 Schenkel Lane, Frankfort, KY 40601-1403, 502-573-2886.

District Forester, Box 130, Pineville, KY 40977, 606-337-3011. (Information about Kentucky Ridge State Forest.)

Pine Mountain Settlement School

The little-publicized Pine Mountain Settlement School 38 miles from Pine Mountain State Resort Park makes a nice day trip while staying at the park, though public access is limited. It began as a school that served the immediate community and today is an environmental education center for all of Kentucky. Its library has excellent resources about Appalachian culture, and it has some weeklong and weekend annual events open to the public on a limited registration basis. Close by are the Kentenia

State Forest, the Redbird District of the DBNF, and a segment of the famed Little Shepherd Trail.

First, go to Pineville on U.S. Route 25E and then east on State 66N (at the traffic light). Go 1½ miles, then exit to the right onto State 221E and continue for about 32 miles to where State 510 bears to the right. Turn onto 510, then immediately take another right and turn into the Settlement School entrance road.

The school was started in 1913 by William Creech, a self-taught country doctor who mandated that it be operated "for school purposes as long as the Constitution of the United States stands. . . ." It began as a boarding school that served the children of settlers in Pine Mountain Valley. In 1949, it affiliated with Berea College and continued as a traditional public school until 1972. That year, its campus on 632 acres of forested mountains, with clean water and prime wildlife habitat, was rechanneled as an environmental center. Since then, thousands of students from elementary school grades through college (and even adult study groups) come to this largely outdoor classroom each year and learn about nature, the environment, energy, resource conservation, and Appalachian cultural traditions.

Director Paul Hayes is a Settlement School graduate who returned in 1986 to take over the helm. As he escorted me over the grounds, a group of small children sitting around a picnic table under a tree were looking intently at some leaves. Were they finding out the difference between a beech leaf and a birch leaf? Expressing the difference between things is essential to learning, according to the school's philosophy.

"We have students from all over. Many are out of Louisville," Hayes said, "and all fifth-grade students in Kingsport, Tennessee, are required to spend a week here."

A requirement that must be easy to enforce in this peaceful atmosphere, I thought.

Two very popular three-day weekends are open to the public: a Spring Wildflower Weekend in April and a Fall Color Weekend usually around October 20.

"We provide meals, accommodations, instruction, and entertainment," Hayes explained. "We take people up on Pine Mountain, where in fall the color is absolutely gorgeous, to do a lot of hiking on our system of trails—four or five trails go to the top. We also transport people by van if they prefer. In the evenings, we have slide presentations, and on Friday and Saturday nights, we have a country dance.

"We can accommodate 78 people in one dorm and 12 each in two other dorms. People have been coming here for years and continue to come back, so reservations need to be made at least three months in advance.

"Another way we serve the public is with a weeklong Elderhostel four times a year. People can contact us to find out how to register."

The dining hall (Laurel House) and the dormitories had just been refurbished and had the aura of being well cared for and hospitable, as was true of the whole campus. I could see why people kept coming back.

Where: East of Pineville on State 510 at junction with State 221. Recommended route: from U.S. Route 25E in Pineville, go east on State 66N for 1½ miles, right onto 221E for about 32 miles, then right at State 510. Turn immediately right into the Settlement School entrance road.

When: Open to public during specific events.

Admission: Rates vary.

Amenities: Six-hundred-and-thirty-two-acre campus; dormitories; educational buildings; chapel; dining hall; trails; plant study center; Appalachian archives; exhibits of Native American artifacts, geology, coal, and fossils; library for environmental studies; spinning and weaving workrooms.

Activities: Nature appreciation and study, guided hikes, photography, wildlife and wildflower viewing, birding, evening slide programs, and dances.

Special events: Winter Botany Weekend (February), Wildflower Weekend (April), Big Black Mountain Wildflower Weekend (May), Elderhostel weeks (March, June, September, November), Edible Plants Weekend (June), Appalachian Family Week (July), Fall Color Weekend (mid-October).

Other: Events often sold out well in advance, so make reservations early.

For more information: Pine Mountain Settlement School, 500 Isaacs Creek Road, Bledsoe, KY 40810, 606-558-3571.

District Forester, Box 130, Pineville, KY 40977, 606-337-3011. (Information about Kentenia State Forest.)

Redbird District Ranger, Daniel Boone National Forest, HC 68, Box 65, Big Creek, KY 40914, 606-598-2192.

Cumberland Gap National Historical Park

I left Pine Mountain State Resort Park and turned south on U.S. Route 25E. Clouds were hanging low on top of Cumberland Mountain 10 miles away, and trees were just giving a hint of the fall color to come. It was barely October. Seeing the high mountains folding ahead in the distance, becoming smoky, ghostly images, is exhilarating—especially when you're going toward them.

Before 1750, Europeans knew of no way to cross the daunting Appalachians in the area of Kentucky. That year, explorer Thomas Walker discovered a route that Indians had been taking for generations to hunting grounds in Kentucky and were using as a warrior's path for raiding parties. This was the Cumberland Gap. In 1767, Daniel Boone crossed the gap to explore the West. He marked the trail that became the Wilderness Road (basically, the route of today's highway to Pine Mountain and beyond). Later, he settled in Kentucky. The gap was critically important in commerce until the 1820s, when railroads, canals, and steamboats began providing better transportation.

This 20,000-acre park is the second-largest national historical park in the United States. It straddles the Kentucky/Virginia and Kentucky/Tennessee lines on the spine of Cumberland Mountain, with roughly equal portions in the first two states, plus a smaller part in Tennessee. The park headquarters and visitors center is in Middlesboro, Kentucky, on the edge of town.

For the past several years, a project has been underway to route motorized traffic under the mountain through a pair of 4,600-foot tunnels, and eliminate the existing highway over the mountain between parking areas in Kentucky and Virginia. In its place, the original Wilderness Trail will be restored to a 15-foot-wide unpaved backwoods road for foot traffic. Finally, the tunnels are open. The new road on top of the mountain (not yet completed) will re-create the appearance and contours of the old road as it was between 1780 and 1810, with native canopy trees and grasses and understory plants, such as sassafras, redbud, and mountain laurel, as the dominant vegetation.

A display at the visitors center describes the project in detail. Other exhibits help visitors gain insight into the history and geology of the Gap and the cultural development of surrounding communities. First, though, I'd recommend watching the short introductory movie that shows nature's grandeur and emphasizes important historical events.

Back to the displays. Some tell about Native American tribes and trails, of Cherokee, Miami, Shawnee, Delaware, and Wyandot warriors who fought for control of the area. Others recall the early explorers and what they endured.

Cumberland Gap National Historical Park

Quotes from Dr. Thomas Walker's 1750 journal describe landmarks and give them names. What he called Gap Cave, for example, is today Cudjo Cave (named after a Civil War novel that depicted it as the hideout of a runaway slave named Cudjo).

Daniel Boone and other pioneers followed Walker. Once the Gap was known, traders, hunters, settlers, and speculators made their way into the new interior lands. The Gap was a critical artery during the Civil War, changing hands three times in hard-fought battles. In 1880, a tunnel through the mountain brought the railroad, and with the new, easier access, resort hotels sprang up.

The gift shop in the visitors center has a wide selection of books about nature and regional history to further enlighten readers.

On an earlier visit, I had gone up to the crest of the mountain on the Kentucky/Virginia line and enjoyed the breathtaking view from 2,440-foot-high Pinnacle Point. It was a steep, twisting drive to the top. Once there, a blacktop trail makes access easy even for the handicapped.

The park has more than 50 miles of trails that range from half a mile to 21 miles from point to point, with many combinations possible. They give the only access available to some places like Sand Cave and White Rocks. Major trailheads are at Pinnacle Point and Wilderness Road Campground, which has 160 campsites and is on the Virginia side along U.S. Route 58. It has no RV hookups but does have electricity, running water, modern rest rooms, picnic grounds, and an amphitheater. Trails from the campground lead to Skylight Cave and Gibson Gap.

Ridge Trail, the park's major trail, begins at the Pinnacle and goes east along the mountain's spine all the way to the edge of the park and down to Ewing, Virginia. Four primitive campsites are spaced along this trail, approximately five miles apart (a permit is required for overnight use). For details of all the trails, ask for free hiking guides at the visitors center.

Interpretive programs are given regularly during spring, summer, and fall at the Wilderness Road Campground's amphitheater and at the visitors center. Native American programs are performances of authentic stories, songs, drumming, and dances by Cherokees and Shawnees in period clothing.

The Hensley Settlement: Where Land Meets Sky

A park shuttle took us up Sugar Run Road, then east on State 217 past Hutch. Soon, we were craning our necks to see the top of imposing Brush Mountain on our right. We turned onto a gravel road, passed the falls of Shillalah Creek, and went onward and upward. We were going to the top of Brush Mountain, climbing from 1,100 to 3,400 feet in five miles on a journey that would end in a roller-coaster ride—down fast, around a sharp curve, and gunning the engine to make it up Dynamite Hill. The driver, interpretive specialist Bill Morris, knew exactly what he was doing and delivered us safely.

Suddenly, we realized that the shuttle had done more than bring us to a mountaintop—we had gone nearly 100 years back in time. Reading about pioneer settlements or watching popular TV shows that depict them—no matter how authentically done—is not at all like actually being in a whole community left just as it was shortly after the turn of the century, except that the people are gone.

Spread before us on the Hensley Flats were garden plots, fields surrounded by chestnut rail fences, an apple orchard, and the farm buildings that were required for self-sufficiency: houses, barns, granaries, smokehouses, henhouses, springhouses, woodsheds, hogpens, corncribs, and a blacksmith shop. The houses were of mud-chinked logs, with chestnut flooring and stone fireplaces. Inside were the furnishings and utensils used in bygone days.

Bill related the details of life in this harsh place. The making of lye soap and apple butter were typical activities. He pointed out little inventions such as a hole drilled in a beam where a man could place his pipe when he finished smoking. The remarkable story of the families who settled here for nearly 50 years in a remote outpost far from civilization is told in the book, *Hensley Settlement*, available at the park.

We inspected the Willie Gibbons Farm, then on to the cemetery and schoolhouse. Too soon, it was time to leave. As the wind swept by, bending tall grasses against a chestnut fence, I asked Bill what he hoped people would learn here.

"A better appreciation of the lifestyle, the struggles, and the teamwork," was his reply.

For our group of travelers, his stories had certainly accomplished that goal.

Where: U.S. Route 25E on Kentucky/Tennessee border between Middlesboro, Kentucky, and Towne of Cumberland Gap, Tennessee.

When: Year-round, daily. Park gates are open from 8:00 A.M. to dusk. Visitors center, 8:00 A.M. to 5:00 P.M. (closed Christmas Day).

Admission: Free. Fee for Hensley Settlement Tours (twice daily on weekends; one-week advance reservations required; discount for seniors and ages 8 to 15; under 8 free).

Amenities: Visitors center, auditorium, gift shop, 160-site campground (in VA), primitive campgrounds, hiking trails, caves (some accessible only by trails), Hensley Settlement, overlooks.

Activities: Scenic drives, wildlife viewing, hiking, camping, picnicking, interpretive programs, photography. Three-hour shuttle tours to Hensley Settlement (by reservation).

Special events: Cumberland Mountain Fall Festival (Middlesboro, October).

Other: Barrier-free access (some locations). Be cautious when in the wild, taking care not to fall, especially near cliffs, and watch for snakes and poison ivy. For safety's sake, never hike alone.

For more information: Superintendent, Cumberland Gap NHP, Box 1848, Middlesboro, KY 40965, 606-248-2817.

Bell County Tourism Commission, PO Box 788, Middlesboro, KY 40965, 606-248-1075.

The Wilderness Road Tours, 224 Greenwood Road, Middlesboro, KY 40965, 606-248-2626. (Guide service and publisher of *A Cumberland Gap Area Guidebook.*)

For more information about the Tennessee portion of Cumberland Gap NHP, please see *Natural Wonders of Tennessee*, published by Country Roads Press.

Kingdom Come State Park

The "Tri-Cities" area refers not to cities but to the towns of Cumberland, Benham, and Lynch along State 160, which crosses U.S. Route 119 just east of the Redbird District of the Daniel Boone National Forest. At Cumberland are Kingdom Come State Park (named after a Civil War novel, *Little Shepherd of Kingdom Come*, written by Kentuckian John Fox Jr.) and access to the Little Shepherd Trail, which goes through the park as it follows the crest of Pine Mountain for 38 miles between Harlan and Whitesburg.

From Pineville, go east on U.S. Route 119 (Kingdom Come Parkway), an excellent scenic road that frequently has extra lanes to allow passing. If you're tempted to sample some local cuisine along the way, look for a café sign that advertises "Fried Baloney." Around Harlan, the road descends into the valley of the Poor Fork of the Cumberland River and follows it for 24 miles to Cumberland. Here, turn left onto State 1254 at the Kingdom Come State Park sign.

The abrupt, steep climb to 2,700 feet is an immediate indoctrination into very rugged country. You are certainly in a different world from the valley below. From the mountain top, you can see Big Black Mountain looming 4,400 feet high a few miles to the south and Monopoly-board-sized houses below where Cumberland has suddenly become "Tiny Town." If you walk between the pines along a rocky trail at the top, you might even imagine that you are in the Rocky Mountains of the West.

The park encompasses more than 1,000 acres of wilderness. Nearly a fourth of its area is a state nature preserve that protects the north face of Pine Mountain and a large colony of federally endangered Indiana bats that hibernate in Line Fork Cave. Three other mammals are protected: the masked shrew, pygmy shrew, and the Kentucky red-backed vole.

The Indiana bats need protection only during hibernation, so cave visitation is allowed between May 1 and August 31 (by explicit permission, with arrangements made at the park).

Hiking is maybe the most popular use of this park, which has 14 hiking trails totaling 5 miles. They range from ⅛ to ⅞ of a mile in a configuration that has been compared to a spider web. Over half of the trails lead to Raven Rock in the center of the park, which has some of the best views of the surrounding area. At the base of Raven Rock is the Cave Amphitheater, electrically equipped for programs and meetings. Even though the trails are short, some can be quite strenuous or even dangerous. Remember that in wilderness areas the sheer rock faces do not have protective guardrails.

Besides the wildlife species found throughout Kentucky, this high country hosts an abundance of bobcats, ruffed grouse, and wild turkeys. It even has some black bears. Ravens can be spotted soaring in the higher elevations. These birds are similar in appearance to crows but larger. If in doubt, you can tell the two apart by their voice. We all recognize the "caw" of a crow, but the raven emits a strange-sounding "croak."

All is not wilderness here, though. The park has many picnic areas, some with playgrounds. Near the entrance is a three-acre lake edged with stonework. It is fished year-round for bass, bluegill, crappie, catfish, and trout. Trout are stocked in April, May, and October. Besides fishing, pedal boat rentals are available during the summer season. Imagine sharing this picturesque little lake with wild ducks and geese against a backdrop of pine trees. Overlooking the lake is a gift shop where you can pay for boat rentals or borrow recreation equipment. Miniature golf is another summer activity.

Primitive camping is allowed at the park's picnic sites but is prohibited along the hiking trails. Fees are charged, and campers must register with a park ranger.

The midpoint of the Little Shepherd Trail follows the crest of Pine Mountain through the park. This trail is of dirt and gravel construction, best navigated on foot or in a four-wheel-drive vehicle. It uses the blacktopped park road between the Bullock and Creech overlooks on the north face, so everyone can enjoy that part.

As I drove along the crest, the geology of the Pine Mountain overthrust created a peculiar phenomenon where air masses collided. Going eastward, the sheer north face was on my left. On the right (the south), a warm sun was shining in a perfectly clear sky. To the north, shaded by the mountain, clouds filled the air below, roiling upward (like sediment stirred by an unseen force) and spilling halfway across the road before rapidly dispersing under the sun's rays.

Where: At Cumberland, between Harlan and Whitesburg, off U.S. Route 119 and State 1254.

When: Year-round. Gift shop, miniature golf, public rest rooms, and picnic shelter rentals, open April through October; pedal boat rentals, May through October. Gift shop, open 11:15 A.M. to 6:45 P.M. April 15 through September 5, then closed on Wednesday and Thursday until October 31.

Admission: Free. Fees for camping, pedal boat rentals, and miniature golf.

Amenities: Visitors center, gift shop, trails, nature preserve, small lake, overlooks, miniature golf, picnic grounds and shelters, playgrounds, outdoor recreation courts, outdoor amphitheater.

Activities: Hiking, primitive camping, backpacking, caving (May 1 through August 31, by permission).

Special events: For Kentucky State Parks special events brochure, call 800-255-7275.

For more information: Kingdom Come State Park, Box M, Cumberland, KY 40823-0420, 606-589-2479.

Cumberland Tourism and Convention Commission, PO Box J, Cumberland, KY 40823, 606-589-5812.

Kentucky Coal Mining Museum

Coal mining defined the lifestyle for people of this region and for a long time was the primary staple income source, though times are changing and in the 1990s mining towns are increasingly becoming just memories. The museum in Benham is an interesting stop that will certainly add to the traveler's knowledge of coal-mining communities.

From Cumberland, go south on State 160 to Benham. The highway becomes Main Street. The museum is a three-story brick structure on the left between the fire department and the city hall. A parking area is across from it on your right.

Bobbie Gothard is the museum's director and was my tour guide.

"In 1979, the Tri-Cities Chamber of Commerce first started thinking about a coal-mining museum to preserve the history of the area," she said. "At first, they wanted to put it on top of Big Black Mountain where U.S. Steel's Mine number 32 had been worked out. That plan fell through, so in 1989, this building was acquired. It had been built in 1920 by International Harvester and was a company store or commissary until about 1960."

Museum personnel are always available to show visitors around and explain how the objects on display were used in mining or in the homes. Hearing anecdotes about the mines and miners adds so much interest to a visit.

On the museum's first floor are Indian relics from Cherokees and Shawnees who lived here in pioneer days; displays explaining how coal is formed in the ground; objects from early mining days (such as air onometers, used to detect air flow, and other safety features); modern objects shown for contrast; reminders of the importance of railroads in the mountains; details about the company hospital that served the community (during the heaviest mining activity, Lynch had 10,000 residents and Benham had 4,500, about 6 to 10 times today's population); old mining tools from the early 1900s and old photographs showing how they were used; explanations and exhibits of protection systems and protective clothing; a children's corner with a crawl-through mine; a home life corner furnished as in the 1920s; a commissary corner showing items that were sold; a gift shop that sells clothing and crafts, plus some authentic items such as soaps used at the U.S. Steel mine. On a wall are trophies—first aid and safety awards—given to International Harvester and U.S. Steel, beginning in 1913.

A viewing area offers two hour-long videos. They show the early days of U.S. Steel and International Harvester. Visitors can fast-forward over parts of lesser interest.

I found the canary cages an interesting highlight. We've probably all heard about how canaries were placed in mines as warning devices. When air flow became impaired, the birds would get woozy and go to sleep, alerting the miners to danger. Some local former miners have told Bobbie about using the bird cages and how they did indeed save lives.

An Oral History corner, with recorded voices of people who remember mining in the early days and with objects used in the mines, is an interesting part of the museum. It is a combination of life-size photo displays and the reminiscences that recall incidents miners and their families have experienced.

Bobbie pointed out a collection of lights. "You notice this little, flat black piece? It is from about the time the canary was being used. They put a tallow candle in it and set it in a niche of the tunnel. That was the light they had to work by before the carbide light came along in the 1800s. Then, around 1940 battery lights were introduced, which made the mines much safer."

One old light had a much bigger bracket. As Bobbie explained, it was the kind strapped onto the heads of the donkeys, mules, and goats that were used as draft animals in the mines.

Each mine had a bathhouse where every miner had two hangers, one for mining clothes and the other for clothes worn to and from the mine. As they came out of the mine, they showered and hung up their dirty clothes, boots, and hats. These were worn all week, then taken home to be washed.

On the museum's second floor are displays of farm equipment used during World War II in making victory gardens. Almost every family grew its own vegetables. Logging and carpenter tools recall the days when the town was built and logging was a major industry for acquiring the building materials.

"The town was well built. It had a theater, a clubhouse, school, and church. In those days, the company towns were segregated, with everything duplicated for the blacks and whites and everything of equal quality. Equal opportunity was practiced, with the same pay and same type jobs available to all," Bobbie explained.

A segregated society was never utopian, of course, but at least there seem to have been places where equality (even if separate) was a goal put into practice. In that sense, at the time, it was a step ahead.

Other second-floor displays are community-related, showing implements from a blacksmith shop and some old fire-fighting equipment, for example.

The third floor is dedicated to memorabilia from Kentucky's most famous coal miner's daughter, country singer Loretta Lynn.

Plans are to offer a guided deep-mine tour at Portal 31 in Lynch, two miles away, but today self-guided tours above ground at Portal 31 let you enjoy a walking tour of one of the world's largest coal-loading facilities. In the future, trolleys will run regularly from Cumberland to Benham and Lynch.

The town is getting face-lifts here and there. The Benham Garden Club is involved in a project to restore the historic Benham Theater. Meanwhile, the School House Inn has opened downtown in the old Benham schoolhouse that first opened its doors in 1928. It has been renovated to represent the period and has a restaurant, conference rooms, a banquet hall, and 30 guest rooms, including kings, doubles, and suites.

The museum in Benham plays a central role in all these plans. You can get the latest information there. In Cumberland, the Poor Fork Arts & Crafts Guild (address below) is another place to feel the pulse of the community, purchase authentic mountain crafts, and get information.

Where: Main Street in Benham, Kentucky, on State 160 just
south of Cumberland.

When: Year-round. Daily, April through October, 10:00 A.M.
to 5:00 P.M. Monday through Saturday and 1:00 to 4:00 P.M.
on Sunday. Closed Mondays and Tuesdays November through
March. Closed on national holidays.

Admission: Modest fee.

Amenities: Museum and gift shop, Loretta Lynn memorabilia,
children's play area, tours to mines.

Activities: Viewing displays and videos with focus on Appalachian culture and resource use.

Special community events: Spring Festival (Cumberland,
May), Benham Fall Festival (Benham, September).

Other: Barrier-free access.

For more information: Kentucky Coal Mining Museum, PO
Box A, Benham, KY 40807, 606-848-1530.

School House Inn, 100 Central Avenue, PO Box B, Benham, KY 40807, 606-848-3000.

Poor Fork Arts & Crafts Guild, 218 West Main Street,
Cumberland, KY 40823.

Benham Garden Club, PO Box 145, Benham, KY 40807,
606-848-5506.

Lilley Cornett Woods

It stands to reason that an area boasting the highest mountains
and most rugged terrain might also contain the largest rem-
nant of old-growth forest. In Letcher County, a few miles
north of Kingdom Come State Park, is a 554-acre tract of
forestland so well preserved that some of the oldest trees are
estimated to date back to the 1500s. Lilley Cornett Woods is
named for a man who, shortly after World War I, purchased

the first of five tracts that make up this forest. He and his heirs refused to let the timber be cut, even during the 1950s when most of the remaining old-growth forest in Kentucky was being harvested.

This prime property is now owned by the state and operated by Eastern Kentucky University as an Appalachian Ecological Education Station. It is a national natural landmark, a registered natural area, and a state wildlife refuge where no hunting is allowed. Coal companies have cooperated, too, ceding their surface-mining rights to the state and refusing to conduct mining operations on adjoining lands if Lilley Cornett Woods would be adversely affected in any way.

Most people get here from Hazard or Whitesburg, but I took the back way, a very scenic route from Cumberland. Go north on State 160, then left on State 1103, following the signs. The road takes a jog here and there, so use your instincts, too.

The visitors center has exhibits, posters, and photographs to help people understand the interrelatedness of living things and appreciate the diversity in nature. Some refer specifically to this property, telling, for example, what wildflowers are in bloom. A map shows where they may be found, and color photographs identify them. I decided to look for false foxglove, asters, Indian-pipe, Joe-Pye-weed, rattlesnake plantain, Queen Anne's lace, and jewelweed—all of which I should expect to find.

One display was a crosscut slice of a 400-year-old white oak that fell in 1979—it had died of old age. Others are not so lucky, due to the onslaught of Gypsy moths, which have caused great tree damage in the United States for more than a century. The moths were brought to Medford, Massachusetts, in 1869 by Leopold Trouzelot who wanted to cross them with an Oriental silk-

worm and start a silk industry in this country. When a windstorm tipped over the caterpillar cage, they escaped. They have since spread to the West and South, eating leaves off trees (oaks are their preferred diet) at the rate of 500,000 acres a year.

Lilley Cornett Woods has hollows, benches, steep slopes, and ridge crests, and elevation changes of 900 feet. Several forest types are represented. In cool, moist areas, American beech, eastern hemlock, yellow buckeye, white basswood, sugar maple, and tulip poplar are found. Streamside trees on Line Fork Creek are predominantly sycamores, with hackberry, slippery elm, and sweet gum growing alongside. The drier slopes host white oak, chestnut oak, red maple, sourwood, and hickory. There are even some snags of American chestnut, which still send up shoots and grow burrs. Robert Watts, the assistant superintendent, said the nuts inside the burrs grow to an inch or two but do not mature.

In an area of such diversity, 90 species of trees and shrubs and 500 different flowering plants are found. Wildflowers are prolific and include rare species such as red azalea, spotted mandarin, and sweet pinesap. The old-growth forest portion is estimated to play host to more than 700 breeding pairs of birds. Hooded warblers come in great numbers, attracted by rhododendrons in the deep ravines. Winged predators include the red-shouldered hawk, broad-winged hawk, and barred owl. Wild turkeys are plentiful. Small mammals are typical of those found in any mountain forest. The larger ones include white-tailed deer, bobcats, and red and gray foxes. Black bears are more often rumored than actually seen.

Visitors can choose a two-hour or a four-hour guided hike. The first covers about three miles, and the latter follows a loop trail to the top of a ridge, a sometimes strenuous climb that reaches a 1,900-foot elevation. Both pass through several ecological zones.

Where: On State 1103, accessed from the State 7 loop off State 15 between Hazard and Whitesburg (with "back door" access from Cumberland, described in the text). From Hazard, take State 15 toward Whitesburg for 6 miles, go right on State 7 for 13⁹/10 miles, then right on State 1103 for 7⁶/10 miles. Signs are posted at each intersection.

When: April 1 through October 31 (November through March by appointment only). Daily, 9:00 A.M. to 5:00 P.M. from May 15 through August 15. Weekends only, April 1 to May 15 and August 15 to October 31.

Admission: Free.

Amenities: Visitors center, trails.

Activities: Guided tours on designated trails, picnicking.

Other: Barrier-free access to visitors center. Restrictions apply to all uses. Camping is not permitted.

For more information: Superintendent, Lilley Cornett Woods, HC 63, Box 2710, Skyline, KY 41821, 606-633-5828.

Bad Branch State Nature Preserve

On an early morning I drove up to a fast-food restaurant in Whitesburg, looking for Morgan Jones's white Dodge Ramcharger. He was there, as planned. Thinking smart, I had hit the road at 5:00 A.M., allowing two hours before I would see the coal trucks. Tomorrow would be my last day on this trip to Kentucky, and I wanted to make the most of today, anticipating a hike to a waterfall on Bad Branch with Morgan as my guide.

From Whitesburg, we went south on State 119 on a steep and winding stretch that goes over Pine Mountain. After 7³/10 miles, we turned left (east) on State 832. The small dirt parking lot and Bad Branch trailhead were 1⁷/10 miles farther on the left, marked with a brown sign.

Morgan is Kentucky's Wild Rivers Program Coordinator for the Kentucky Division of Water, an agency that preserves some of the state's last free-flowing streams. Parts of nine streams are included, totaling 114 river miles. People who fish, hike, canoe, or kayak know exactly how important this program is. Morgan got that message in an unusual way.

"The TV show *Kentucky Afield* covers subjects for a broad audience, so they included a series on the wild rivers," he said. "One segment was about the Rockcastle River. For the filming, I paddled my kayak, and we talked about rivers and conservation. At the end, they gave our phone number. About 10:00 A.M. the next morning, I got an urgent call from our office receptionist. 'Leave the meeting and get back here' she said. 'We've already had 67 calls about wild rivers.' The phone rang like that all day. I found out later that *Kentucky Afield* is the most widely watched program on Kentucky Educational Television and one of the most popular state-produced programs in the country."

The entire Bad Branch watershed, from its headwaters on Pine Mountain to State 932, where it flows into the Poor Fork of the Cumberland River, is a designated Kentucky Wild River. This area includes the nature preserve. You might say it is triply protected: by The Nature Conservancy, the state Wild Rivers Program, and the State Nature Preserves Commission. Other wild rivers, by comparison, are only classified as wild rivers on certain segments.

At the trailhead is a brown box that holds maps and a sign-in sheet.

"Well, we have two options," Morgan announced. "We will go to the falls, but hikers can also go on up to the top of Pine Mountain. It's quite a view, but it's three or four hours of hard hiking."

That decision could come later. We were in the land of my dreams as we moved along the cool forest floor past huge thickets of rhododendrons, savoring the shade of hemlocks. This nature preserve encompasses 1,640 untamed acres and is said to have the state's largest concentration of rare and endangered species. They include an interesting mix of rare and endangered plants, an endangered long-tailed shrew, and the native arrow darter.

The Bad Branch Gorge is on the south slope of Pine Mountain facing what Morgan calls its mirror image—the north slope of Cumberland Mountain. They are a reverse contrast in topography, since Cumberland Mountain's steepest side is its south-facing slope.

"Pine Mountain is pretty famous for its rhododendron hells, as the locals call them," said Morgan.

I admit I'm often confused about whether I'm seeing mountain laurel or rhododendron.

"Mountain laurel has small leaves. Names change with the territory, though. In Leslie County and parts of Harlan County they call rhododendron 'laurel' and mountain laurel 'ivy.'"

"You can get lost in there."

"You sure can. There's one misconception here, though. People come here with the idea that Bad Branch is an undisturbed wilderness, but it was logged in the 1940s. The trees were so huge that it took years to get them all out. One local man remembered his daddy telling about welding together two two-man crosscut saws end to end in order to saw through some of the trees."

From the saws I've seen, that's about 14 feet of saw. Fortunately, some of the monster trees missed the crosscut blade and remain as reminders of what this forest will be again.

We had been climbing and had reached Bad Branch Cascade at the bottom of the falls. The cliffs were 100 feet higher, providing a fall that ended in a pile of boulders next to where we were standing.

"I've seen it with more water flow, where it shoots out 15 feet from the rock," Morgan said. "If you scramble down among these giant boulders and look up, you see a two-stage waterfall. There's a small drop above, then it goes down through a slot and then a 60-foot drop.

According to Morgan, the falls are spectacular in winter because of the ice that forms. He's seen it six or seven feet thick along the sides of the falls.

"The trail to the top goes practically straight up," he continued. "The only pair of ravens known to nest in Kentucky has been seen up on the cliffs. These birds are very sensitive to human disturbance, so a trail that used to follow below the cliffs has been relocated. As a nature preserve, the protection of all the plants and animals is paramount."

Keeping the Wild Rivers Wild

"At one time, there were proposals for dams on most of Kentucky's major rivers," Morgan Jones said. "That was the impetus for the Wild Rivers Act. The Federal Wild and Scenic Rivers Act had been passed four years earlier, in 1968, on the basis that the highest and best use of free-flowing streams is for the recreational, aesthetic, scientific, and natural qualities they possess.

"That was a pretty revolutionary concept at the time, but our legislation adopted the same stance.

"It does pose a sort of built-in miniconflict, though. The challenge of preserving a natural state and also providing recreational opportunity can be difficult, since usage almost guarantees some degradation.

"As for wild rivers, this designation can cause confusion in the minds of the public. The truth is, about half of the river segments go through private lands where there are no easements on the banks. In Kentucky, the landowner owns the bed of the stream. People can lawfully float in their boats, but the minute they step out to wade the stream, they could be trespassing. This is no problem where the wild rivers go through public lands, like the Daniel Boone National Forest or a state park."

I asked Morgan for his take on wild-river opportunities.

"I like the Cumberland River above the falls. It's a big river, pretty, enjoyable, and reasonably easy canoeing—as long as people know to get out when they see the bridge at Cumberland Falls.

"The Rockcastle is beautiful. For whitewater fans, you have to paddle a lot of flat water to get to the whitewater. Access is limited, but we're working at changing that.

"The Green River in Mammoth Cave National Park is a great family canoe float. It's very pleasant and doesn't get a lot of use. The river helped form the cave, but most people come to this area to see caves, not float rivers.

"The Big South Fork is very popular with whitewater enthusiasts, with most of the action beginning in Tennessee and ending at Blue Heron. There are several mandatory portages.

"I recommend to anybody who wants to get on the whitewater rivers to get a good guidebook and study it well. Don't ever go down these streams without a guide who is experienced in whitewater paddling and on that particular river. It's real important to scout areas and never run anything you haven't looked at first."

"Would you like to go up on Little Shepherd Trail?" asked Morgan.

He had read my mind.

We went back toward Whitesburg on State 119 to the crest of Pine Mountain and a historical marker where the "trail" (actually, a gravel road) begins.

"This was built as a fire-control access by the state but now has become a scenic drive. Of course, being dirt, it can become very slick after a rain. I've been riding my mountain bike on it for years, and I hope they don't pave it," Morgan said. "They are paving the other end down toward Harlan, and I've seen Cadillacs on it there."

No Cadillacs could negotiate this end today, I decided as the Ramcharger went easily over the rough spots. As we drove through a 100,000-acre Wildlife Management Area, a grouse ran ahead of us in the road. We followed slowly. Finally, it had had enough and flew away.

It was the time of year to see gentian on the ground or ravens soaring above. One hardly knew which direction to look, but almost any spot was good for long-distance viewing up here where the ridges are covered with an almost infinite variety of oaks and other hardy species.

"This is a mountain maple, *Acer pennsylvanicum*, named for Pennsylvania, my home state," Morgan announced.

It had a distinctive striped bark and glowing, fall-colored yellow leaves.

"You see them in the Smokies, but you have to be near the mountaintops in the South to find them."

We named some others. Chestnut oak, scarlet oak, northern red oak, red maple, and sourwood. It would be simply glorious up here at the peak of fall color. This was another place I knew I must visit again.

In a few miles, we had reached Kingdom Come State Park. According to the sign, the elevation was 2,560 feet.

Signs can only tell so much.

Where: South of Whitesburg. Go south on State 119 for 7³⁄₁₀ miles, then left (east) on State 832 for 1⁷⁄₁₀ miles to entrance on left.
When: Year-round.

Admission: Free.

Amenities: Trails.

Activities: Hiking, nature appreciation, birding, wildlife viewing.

Other: Not allowed: camping, picnicking, hunting, dogs, horses, and ORVs. Hikers should bring drinking water.

For more information: Kentucky State Nature Preserves Commission, 801 Schenkel Lane, Frankfort, KY 40601, 502-573-2886.

The Nature Conservancy, 642 West Main Street, Lexington, KY 40508, 606-259-9655.

Wild Rivers Coordinator, Division of Water, Department for Environmental Protection, 14 Reilly Road, Fort Boone Plaza, Frankfort, KY 40601, 502-564-3410. (Calendar of events available. River events are weather dependent.)

Breaks Interstate Park

The Breaks of the Big Sandy River must be the most dramatic gateway to any eastern state—or maybe any in the whole United States, for that matter. The forces of nature, though unwittingly to be sure, created a masterpiece as they pushed, shoved, and sculpted the land millions of years ago. They left a deep, rock-walled canyon rising high above the Russell Fork of the Sandy. The river carved a nearly perfect circular trench half a mile in diameter around a rock pyramid called The Towers. Now it churns around this curve, then straightens out in a run through the gorge, ending 350 feet lower after cascading and tumbling over massive boulders for five miles.

Naturally, such a location needs a park. Kentucky and Virginia cooperated by creating Breaks Interstate Park—popularly referred to as "The Breaks"—a jointly managed 4,600-

acre property. From Elkhorn City, Kentucky, go east on State 80 and, if you can keep your eyes off the gorge and the craggy landforms, just follow the signs.

The big draw here is nature, of course. Twelve miles of trails leading to overlooks, interesting rock formations, caves, ponds, rhododendron gardens, and prime birding spots are available year-round for hiking. Whitewater rafting in spring and fall is not for the beginner or faint-of-heart, because when a dam upstream releases water into the gorge, it becomes a Class IV to Class VI stream. Fishing and horseback riding are other popular activities. The river is stocked with trout; and the park's 12-acre Laurel Lake has bass and bluegill.

The Breaks is definitely in the resort class, with modern accommodations—a full-featured campground that can handle tents, trailer campers, and motor homes, an Olympic-size swimming pool, a lifestyle museum in the visitors center, and the Rhododendron Lodge restaurant with acclaimed gourmet cuisine.

Lovers of folklore will find this a fascinating place where legends abound. Tales of Pow Wow Cave where Indian raiding parties gathered, the Hatfield-McCoy feud, a hidden silver fortune, Daniel Boone's exploits, and logging operations mix history and drama—and who knows where truth ends and legend begins?

The museum sorts the truth from the fiction. We learn about geology and how The Breaks were formed, the mining industry and types of mines (and yes, there are legends), logging, mountain feuds, and the romance of a man and maiden from opposite warring Indian tribes. Artifacts of all these subjects are on display.

We also learn more about nature and forest communities through displays and interactive games. The exhibits teach how to recognize animals and their tracks, and trees and plants.

If you hear the word "sang," the reference is to ginseng. The "sang" hunters had a code of ethics: "Dig in spring only. Transplant to their own bed in the fall after the berries have ripened or have fallen. Plant the berries where they came from. Sell the bigger roots and move the smaller plants to a new place."

Outside the museum, an old moonshine still and farm implements are on display.

The small woodland animals are fearless here. I waited patiently in my car while two squirrels cavorted on the road in front of me. I was on my way to an overlook, one of the half dozen that show off the "Grand Canyon of the South" and the river 1,000 feet below.

Engrossed in the view, I faintly heard a little voice a few feet away. It was five-year-old Stephen Francis Burke from Pikeville, caught up in the spirit of adventure.

"I'm going to walk down to the river," he said tentatively, eyeing his mother, Cathy.

I asked if he had been having fun (he had) and what he liked best.

"The river."

"What did you see today?" Cathy prompted.

"I saw water. And do you know what I heard? I heard birds. And I smelled a berry."

Definitely a place for the senses. I walked on. A grin was tugging at my face.

Suddenly, a different voice spoke behind me. It had the ring of authority and the grit of an Olympic whitewater kayaker. It was all at once Kentucky's past, present, and future.

"Mom! I'm going down to the river—right now!"

Where: Thirty miles southeast of Pikeville and seven miles east of Elkhorn City on State 80 at the Kentucky/Virginia state line.

When: Year-round, daily. Park hours, 7:00 A.M. to 11:00 P.M. April through October; 8:00 A.M. to 6:00 P.M. November through March. Visitors center, open 8:00 A.M. to 4:00 P.M. Monday through Friday; 9:00 A.M. to 5:00 P.M. Saturday and Sunday. Lodge, open April through October. Swimming pool, open Memorial Day through Labor Day, 10:00 A.M. to 6:00 P.M. Monday through Friday and until 8:00 P.M. weekends. Boat dock, open Memorial Day through Labor Day, 10:00 A.M. to 6:00 P.M. Picnic shelters and playgrounds, available April through October, 9:00 A.M. through 11:00 P.M.

Admission: $1 per car parking fee from 9:00 A.M. to 7:00 P.M. daily from Memorial Day through Labor Day. Free rest of year. Fees for swimming pool, boat rental, horseback riding.

Amenities: Lodge, restaurant, gift shop, cottages, campground, amphitheater, visitors center, museum, scenic gorge, foot and horseback trails, Olympic-size pool, picnic area and playgrounds, shelters, fishing lake, boat dock.

Activities: Camping, hiking, backpacking, picnicking, guided trail rides, whitewater rafting, wildlife viewing, nature study, photography, birding, fishing, boating, square dancing.

Special events: Homemaking in the Mountains, Whitewater Rafting Weekends (October).

Other: Virginia fishing licenses sold at park headquarters daily, 8:00 A.M. to 4:00 P.M., April through October (Monday through Friday only, November through March). Kentucky state licenses are honored in Laurel Lake. Power boats and swimming not permitted in lake.

For more information: Breaks Interstate Park, PO Box 100, Breaks, VA 24607, 703-865-4413. Reservations, 800-982-5122. Mountain View Stables, 703-865-4295 or 5779.

Appalachian Expeditions, c/o Kenny J. Cox, 5 Keyser Heights, Pikeville, KY 41501, 606-437-6539.

Russell Fork Rafting, c/o Rusty Fork Cafe, Patty Loveless Drive, Elkhorn City, KY 41522, 800-444-7238.

Elkhorn City Festivals, PO Box 229, Elkhorn City, KY 41522, 606-754-7589.

Reading Guide
Author's Short List

H ere are some books that have been recommended by others or are my favorites.

Audubon Field Guides (Birds, Wildflowers, Butterflies, Insects & Spiders, Mammals, Mushrooms, Rocks & Minerals, Trees, Eastern Forests). I take these everywhere. So, who has room for luggage?

Backyard Naturalist, by Craig Tufts. National Wildlife Federation (1400 Sixteenth Street NW, Washington, DC 20036-2266), 1993. Paper. A great read that will get you digging and planting.

A Canoeing & Kayaking Guide to the Streams of Kentucky, by Bob Sehlinger. Menasha Ridge Press (3169 Cahaba Heights Road, Birmingham, AL 35243), 1994. Paper. All the facts you need for paddling Kentucky streams.

Caving Basics, Third Edition, edited by G. Thomas Rea. National Speleological Society (2813 Cave Avenue, Huntsville, AL 35810-4431, 205-852-1300), 1992. Paper. Before you start caving, read this, join a local grotto, and contact the NSS. Stay safe!

Columbus, Kentucky as the Nation's Capital: Legend or Near Reality?, by Allen Anthony. River Microstudies (PO Box 259, Fort Davis, TX 79734.), 1992. Paper. A compilation of historical accounts suggesting that Columbus, Kentucky, might indeed have become the seat of our nation's government.

A Cumberland Gap Area Guidebook, by Tom N. Shattuck. The Wilderness Road Tours (224 Greenwood Road, Middlesboro, KY 40965), Rev. 1993. Paper. Excellent guide to the Cumberland Gap area, including portions of the historic Wilderness Road.

The Geologic Story of Kentucky, by Preston McGrain. University of Kentucky Press, Special Publication 8 Series XI, 1983. Paper. Kentucky's varied topography explained and illustrated with maps and black and white photos.

Growing & Propagating Wildflowers, by Harry R. Phillips. University of North Carolina Press, 1985. Experts say, "Read this."

Guide to the Surface Trails of Mammoth Cave National Park, by Stanley D. Sides. Cave Books (756 Harvard Avenue, University City, MO 63130), 1991. More than 60 miles on 23 trails are mapped and described to aid the hiker.

Gurnee Guide to American Caves, by Russell and Jeanne Gurnee. R. H. Gurnee, Inc., 1992. Paper. A highly recommended, comprehensive guide to caves with public access.

Hiking the Big South Fork, Second Edition, by Brenda D. Coleman and Jo Anna Smith. University of Tennessee Press, 1993. Paper. A well-researched and valuable hiker's guide to this vast region.

Kentucky Wildlife Viewing Guide, by Carolyn Hughes Lynn. Falcon Press, 1994. Paper. A necessity if you're looking for wildlife, though some directions could be improved.

Kentucky's Land of the Arches, by Robert H. Ruchhoft. The Purelle Press (PO Box 19161, Cincinnati, Ohio 45219), Rev.

1986. Paper. Excellent trail guide to the Red River Gorge and Natural Bridge State Park, plus when to go and where to stay. Sections on geology and history of the area. Illustrated with diagrams, maps, and photographs.

Mammoth Cave, by John J. Wagoner and Lewis D. Cutliff. Interpretive Publications, Inc., (PO Box 1383, Flagstaff, AZ 86002-1383), 1985. Paper. With photography by Chip Clark, an excellent overview of the geology, history, animal life, and features of the cave.

Manual of the Grasses of the United States, by A. S. Hitchcock. Dover Publications, Inc., 1971 (reprint). Paper. When you really want to know, delve into this.

Old Growth in the East, by Mary Byrd Davis. Wild Earth, (PO Box 455, Richmond, VT 05477). By mail only, $20 postpaid. Facts you never even thought to ask about old-growth forests. Highly recommended by Milo Pyne, Tennessee's State Botanist.

Our Southern Highlanders, by Horace Kephart. University of Tennessee Press, 1976. The classic that describes Appalachian mountain people and their culture.

Sand County Almanac: And Sketches Here & There, by Aldo Leopold. Oxford University Press, 1949, 1987, 1989. Tops on everybody's list.

Wildflowers of the Central South, by Thomas E. Hemmerly. Vanderbilt University Press, 1990. Paper. Highly recommended by Frank Lyne.

Index

Falls of Rough, 92–94
  golf courses, 89
  hunting and fishing, 79, 89
  John James Audubon State Park
    and Nature Preserve, 83–87
  lodging, 90
  Museum of Science and History,
    76–78
  Panther Creek and Yellow Creek
    Parks, 79–82
  plant life, 80, 81, 88
  Rough River Dam State Resort
    Park, 87–92
  special events, 78, 87, 90–92
  swimming, 90
  trails, 79–82, 85–86
  wildlife, 80, 81, 84, 85, 88, 89
Owensboro Area Museum of
  Science and History, 79

Paducah area, 17–29
  hunting and fishing, 27
  lodging, 17
  Metropolis Lake State Nature
    Preserve, 21–25
  Museum of the American
    Quilter's Society, 18–21
  plant life, 23, 26–27, 28–29
  special events, 17, 21, 29
  trails, 22
  West Kentucky Wildlife
    Management Area,
    25–29
  wildlife, 22–24, 27, 28
Paducah Dogwood Trail
  Celebration, 18
Paige, Roger, 244
Paley, Mike, 89–90
Panther Creek Park, 79–81
Parade of Breeds, 240–41
Payne, Betty, 204–5
Pennyrile Forest State Resort Park,
  52–56
Pennyroyal Trail, 54

Peregrine falcons, 247–48
Perfect Harmony Weekend, 195
Pieces of the Past, 196
Pilot Knob State Nature Preserve,
  262–63
Pine Mountain region, 331–66
  Bad Branch State Nature
    Preserve, 356–62
  Breaks Interstate Park, 362–66
  Cumberland Gap National
    Historic Park, 337–40
  Kentucky Coal Mining Museum,
    349–53
  Kingdom Come State Park,
    346–49
  Lilley Cornett Woods, 353–56
  Pine Mountain State Resort
    Park, 332–37
  plant life, 333, 354–55
  Settlement School, Pine
    Mountain, 337–40
  special events, 336, 337, 340, 346,
    353, 365
  trails, 334–35, 343, 348
  wildlife, 347–48, 355
Pine Mountain Settlement School,
  337–40
Pine Mountain State Resort Park,
  332–37
Pioneer Museum, 216–17
Planetarium, 32
Plant life. *See also* Trees and
  forests
  Bowling Green area, 96, 99–100,
    102
  Eastern Cave Country Lakes
    area, 148, 151
  Frankfort and Lexington area,
    225, 230, 249–54, 257–58
  Great Bend of the Ohio, 211–12,
    214, 216
  Great River Road area, 10
  Interstate 75 corridor, 317
  Land Between the Lakes, 58